# SPCK INTERNATIONAL STUDY GUIDES

The SPCK International Study Guides incorporate the much loved and respected TEF series. Written by scholars with experience of the worldwide Church, they combine good scholarship with clarity, simplicity and non-technical language. Ecumenical in authorship and outlook, the Guides are ideal for first-year theology students, Bible study groups, multi-cultural classes, people for whom English is a second language, and anyone who needs a sound but accessible guide to the Bible and theology.

SPCK INTERNATIONAL STUDY GUIDE 37

# A GUIDE TO
# ST MATTHEW'S GOSPEL

### FRANCIS FOULKES

Published in Great Britain in 2001 by
Society for Promoting Christian Knowledge
Holy Trinity Church
Marylebone Road
London NW1 4DU

British Library Cataloguing-in-Publication Data

A catalogue record for this book is available from
the British Library

ISBN 0–281–05173–9

Typeset by WestKey Ltd., Falmouth, Cornwall.
Printed in Great Britain by The Bath Press.

# Contents

# *Using this Guide*

This Study Guide begins with a *General Introduction*, which discusses why Matthew's Gospel was written, and lists its four most important aspects. The General Introduction ends with an analysis of the Gospel and divides it into 11 parts. The Study Guide looks at each of these sections in turn.

Each of the 11 parts of *A Guide to St Matthew's Gospel* has a similar shape:

- Most have a brief *Introduction* which points to the main topic of the text we are going to discuss.
- We then break down the section of the Gospel into shorter passages, which we list in the *Analysis*.
- We then study each of the shorter passages, giving *Notes* on particular words or verses which seem to need explanation or discussion, and detailed interpretation of how we should understand the passage and apply it in our own lives as Christians.
- After each short passage there are *Study Suggestions*. If you are studying alone, these will help you to work more thoroughly, understand the message of Matthew more clearly and check your progress. The Study Suggestions are a real part of the commentary, and will help you to think about Matthew's message for yourself. People can also use them in the classroom or for group work.
- The best way to use these Study Suggestions is to
  - read the suggested Bible passages;
  - re-read the appropriate section of the commentary;
  - then put the Guide aside while you answer the question, either by writing it down or by discussing it in a group;
  - finally, check your answer with the Key to Study Suggestions on p. 275.

You cannot check your answers for all the Study Suggestions in the *Key to Study Suggestions*. Some of the questions ask you to relate what you have read to your own life and local circumstances (context); only you know the answer to these questions. Other questions ask you simply to find information for yourself from the Bible. For many of the questions, however, the Key suggests the points you should look for, either in the Guide or in the Bible.

## Additional Notes

At different places in the Guide you will find 13 *Additional Notes*. These provide longer notes on particular points, and word studies.

## Further Reading

The Bibliography lists some books which you may find useful for further study. It includes some useful older titles which may be out of print, but which you can probably find in a college library.

## Essays

At the end of this Guide you will find two *Essays*. The first essay discusses the parables of Jesus in more detail, with particular reference to the well-known and well-loved parables in Matthew. The aim of the other essay is to show you how Matthew's Gospel can be used in practical ways in preaching and teaching in different contexts.

## Index and Map

The Index includes only the more important names of people and places mentioned, and the subjects which occur in Matthew's Gospel. Page references in **bold type** show where particular subjects are treated in detail. The map on p. xvi shows most of the places mentioned in the Guide.

## Bible Version

*The Revised Standard Version* is a good and accurate translation for study purposes, and I have used it in most of the quotations in this book. Where it is important to have inclusive language (that is, not using 'man' where men and women are involved, and not using 'he' when both male and female are intended), I have quoted from *The New Revised Standard Version*.

# Further Reading

Some of these books are older, but you may be able to find them in a library. Others are quite new and you should be able to buy copies for yourself if you wish.

## Introductory Books and Background

R. T. France, *Matthew: Evangelist and Teacher*, The Paternoster Press, 1989.

John Riches, *Matthew* (New Testament Guides), Sheffield Academic Press, 1996.

Donald Senior, *What Are They Saying About Matthew?* Paulist Press, revised edition, 1996.

## Full-length Commentaries

R. T. France, *Matthew* (Tyndale New Testament Commentaries), Inter-Varsity Press/Eerdmans, 1985.

David Hill, *The Gospel of Matthew* (The New Century Bible Commentary), Marshall, Morgan & Scott/Eerdmans, 1972.

Donald Senior, *Matthew* (Abingdon Bible Series), Abingdon Press, 1998; ISBN: 0687057663 (you may need the ISBN number because there are two commentaries with similar titles).

# A Note on Translations of the Bible

The books of the Bible were originally written in Hebrew, Aramaic and Greek. The best way of understanding what the Bible says is to read it in the original languages. But most of us cannot read Hebrew, Aramaic and Greek. We have to rely on scholars to translate it into our own language. It is almost impossible to translate from one language to another with complete accuracy. Language reflects not just meaning, but the culture and society in which the language has developed. Another language, coming from another culture and society, may simply not have the words to express the original experience and understanding. So no translation of the Bible will be perfectly accurate.

For serious study of the Bible, we need a translation which is as close to the original as possible. For ease of studying, it is helpful if the translation also reads well in our own language. The English translation of the Bible which the editors of the International Study Guide series recommend for serious study is the *New Revised Standard Version* (NRSV). This translation is very accurate; when biblical scholars do not translate the text for themselves, most of them use the NRSV. It is written in clear English, but is not too modern. It aims to be 'as literal as possible, as free as necessary' and is essentially a literal translation which takes into account the latest textual discoveries such as the Dead Sea Scrolls.

You may already own another English translation of the Bible. The *Revised Standard Version* (RSV), the *New Jerusalem Bible* (NJB) and *New International Version* (NIV) are also suitable for serious study. The Standard edition of the NJB has excellent study aids, but is expensive. The *Good News Bible* reads well and is the basis for many recent translations by the United Bible Society. However, it is not very accurate. The *Revised English Bible* (REB) updates the New English Bible and combines accuracy with the modern English of daily speech. It is therefore excellent for public and private reading.

You will find it helpful to use a Bible which has cross-references (notes in the margin or at the bottom of the page which point you to other similar passages, or passages from the Old Testament which are quoted in the New Testament).

It is also helpful to have an edition of the Bible which includes the Apocrypha (books such as 1, 2, 3 and 4 Maccabees, Tobit and

Ecclesiasticus). Protestant Christians do not include these books with the rest of the Bible, because they do not accept them as having the same authority as the other books approved by the Church. The books of the Apocrypha are useful for private reading and study, because they provide important background material for under-standing the New Testament, but they are not generally used for public preaching in Protestant churches.

If English is not your home language, compare whatever English translation you use with the Bible translated into your own first lan-guage. You may find it helpful to read through each passage in your own language before you study the commentary on the English text.

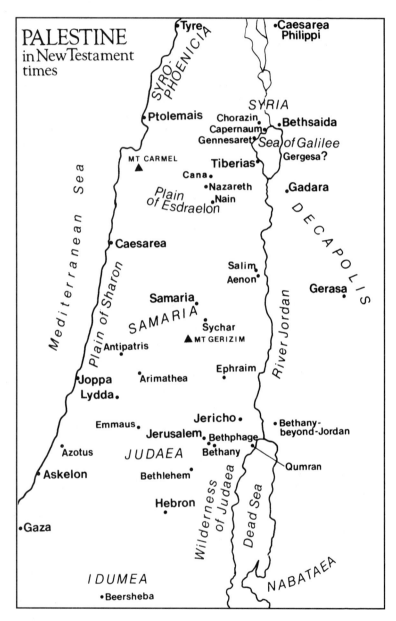

## PALESTINE
in New Testament
times

- •Tyre
- SYRO-PHOENICIA
- •Caesarea Philippi
- SYRIA
- •Ptolemais
- Chorazin
- •Bethsaida
- Capernaum•
- Gennesaret•
- *Sea of Galilee*
- MT CARMEL ▲
- •Tiberias
- Gergesa?
- Cana•
- •Nazareth
- •Gadara
- •Nain
- *Plain of Esdraelon*
- *Mediterranean Sea*
- •Caesarea
- DECAPOLIS
- Salim•
- Aenon•
- *Plain of Sharon*
- Samaria•
- Gerasa•
- SAMARIA
- Sychar•
- ▲MT GERIZIM
- •Antipatris
- *River Jordan*
- Ephraim•
- •Joppa
- •Arimathea
- Lydda•
- Emmaus•
- Jericho•
- •Bethany-beyond-Jordan
- Jerusalem•
- •Bethphage
- •Azotus
- JUDAEA
- Bethany•
- Qumran
- •Askelon
- Bethlehem•
- *Wilderness of Judaea*
- *Dead Sea*
- Hebron•
- IDUMEA
- NABATAEA
- •Gaza
- •Beersheba

Map taken from 'A Guide to St Mark's Gospel'

# General Introduction

## The Writing of Gospels

The Christian Church came into being following the ministry of Jesus, his life, death and resurrection and the experience of the Holy Spirit from the day of Pentecost. The first believers preached the gospel and established communities of Christians. The earliest of the writings that we have in our New Testament are letters, especially those of the apostle Paul, which come from a time almost certainly before any of our four Gospels. The Gospel writers compiled these four records of the life and teaching, death and resurrection of Jesus to meet the needs of the growing churches as they faced the challenge of the greatness of their task and the threat of persecution from both Jews and non-Jews (Gentiles).

## The Purposes of the Gospels

In order for us to understand more the purposes behind the writing of the Gospels, and of this Gospel in particular, it is helpful to try to think what it would have been like to have lived in the early days of the Christian Church before the writing of the New Testament books. If we think of the life of the first Christians like this, we can appreciate four reasons why those who served Jesus as Lord would have had a strong desire to have put into writing what they knew and so to pass it on to others:

1 They wanted to make a written record so that people who had not previously believed might come to believe through what they read. We can call this the *evangelistic motive* (as evangel = gospel). In the case of John's Gospel it says specifically of the 'signs' that the Gospel records, 'these are written that you may believe that Jesus is the Christ, the Son of God, and that believing you may have life in his name' (John 20.31). The first verse of Mark's Gospel explains the author's reason for writing it: 'The beginning of the gospel of Jesus Christ, the Son of God' – in other words, 'this is how the good news all began'. This kind of motive may have had some place in the writing of Matthew, but not a very important place.

2 They wanted to defend their faith when people attacked or misunderstood it. We can call this the *apologetic motive*, as the word 'apology' originally meant the defence of one's beliefs and convictions. Luke 1.1–4 says that the purpose of that Gospel was that,

relying on the testimony of 'those who from the beginning were eyewitnesses and servants of the word', the reader might 'know the truth concerning the things' that Christians taught. There were probably some misunderstandings that Matthew wanted to clear up, but again we must say that this was probably not a major motive in the writing of that Gospel.

3 The early Church also needed to have a record of what Jesus did and taught that Christians could read alongside the Hebrew Bible, our Old Testament, when they met for worship. We call this the *liturgical need*, as the word 'liturgy' means worship. We certainly know that when Christians gathered together for worship they might read an apostolic letter (see Colossians 4.16 and 1 Thessalonians 5.27). We also know that they read our Gospels in this way in the setting of worship, although we cannot be sure how early it happened. Jewish people had lectionaries to guide their reading of the Old Testament books, and so some who have studied Matthew closely feel that there are indications that the author planned it to provide readings for each week of the year. Others have not been convinced by the arguments in support of this.

4 Lastly, new Christians needed teaching, and the Church realized that it would be a great advantage to have a written record, instead of simply passing it on by word of mouth. We call this the *catechetical motive* (as catechesis = teaching, and a catechist is a teacher). We can be sure that this was a major reason for the writing of Matthew. The writer appears to have intended his Gospel especially for those within the life of the Church rather than for people who had not yet believed. He may have intended it particularly for its leaders and those who had the responsibility of teaching others. They needed to be clear about the great facts of the life, death and resurrection of Jesus. They needed to have a clear statement of the ethical teaching he gave, showing how Christians should live together in the fellowship of the community. They needed to see the mission which God had entrusted to them. They needed to be prepared to suffer. They needed to understand what their future hope should be. Some people have suggested that the Gospel writer may have written it for a kind of non-residential theological college or seminary, 'The School of St Matthew' a modern scholar has called it. That may not be right, but certainly the emphasis on teaching in the Gospel is very clear.

## Important Aspects of Matthew

We can say four important things to begin with about Matthew:

1 *It tells what Jesus taught.*
 When we compare this Gospel with Mark's Gospel we readily
 notice that it gives a great deal of space to the actual teaching of
 Jesus. When we look more closely, we find that similar words like,
 'When Jesus finished these sayings –' occur five times in the Gospel (in 7.28, 11.1, 13.53, 19.1 and 26.1). This helps us to realize
 that the author has deliberately arranged much of the teaching of
 Jesus in five main sections.
2 *It tells what Jesus did.*
 Between the teaching sections there are narrative sections with
 the emphasis on what Jesus did. For he is more than Teacher. He is
 shown in his ministry to have been 'mighty in deed and word'
 (Luke 24.19), and then his death and resurrection wonderfully
 completed his work and realized the purpose of God given to him
 to fulfil.
3 *It tells who Jesus is.*
 The Gospel tells what Jesus taught and what he did, but also makes
 clear what Christians believe about who Jesus really is. One of the
 particular ways in which we see this is in the names people give to
 Jesus. As in all the other Gospels, this one presents Jesus as the
 Christ, the Messiah (here in Matthew from the first verse). Chapter
 1 gives two other names: Emmanuel, meaning 'God with us', and
 Jesus, 'for he will save his people from their sins'. As in Mark and
 Luke, the name or title that is most on his own lips is 'Son of man',
 and we will need to study carefully the meaning of that as we go
 on. He is also 'King' (sometimes people speak of him as 'King of
 the Jews'), but more importantly we see that he speaks often about
 'the kingdom of heaven', God's kingdom or rule which should be
 the greatest reality in human lives. People also acknowledge him
 in the Gospel as 'Lord' and as 'Son of God'.
4 *It is a bridge from the Old Testament.*
 When Christians drew together all the writings of our New Testament, they put the Gospels first – not because they were written
 first, but because the ministry of Jesus came earlier in time than
 the life of the early Church. We can also see why they placed Matthew first of all, although it was probably not the first written
 Gospel. This Gospel is a kind of bridge between the Old Testament
 and the New because of the way that it stresses that the coming
 of Jesus fulfilled the hopes and prophecies and even the history
 of Israel. It begins with a genealogy which presents Jesus as
 descended from Abraham, the great ancestor of the Jewish people,
 and from the famous king David. We go on and we find that it
 often has words like those of 1.22, 'All this took place to fulfil what
 had been spoken by the Lord through the prophet –', and even
 where the Gospel does not use such words, it refers to or quotes
 the Old Testament more than a hundred times.

## Analysis of the Gospel

As we have noted (point 2, above) that teaching and narrative sections alternate in this Gospel, we will use this fact as a guide to indicate its main sections, and then in each section indicate later the
sub-sections into which we can divide it.

| | |
|---|---|
| 1.1—4.25 | Introduction – the coming of the Christ |
| 5.1—7.29 | Teaching – about the way of discipleship |
| 8.1—9.38 | Narrative – miracles of healing |
| 10.1–42 | Teaching – about the disciples' mission |
| 11.1—12.50 | Narrative – response to Jesus' ministry |
| 13.1–52 | Teaching – the parables of the kingdom |
| 13.53—17.27 | Narrative – leading to the confession of Jesus as the Messiah |
| 18.1–35 | Teaching – about fellowship in the community |
| 19.1—22.46 | Narrative – Jesus' journey to Jerusalem |
| 23.1—25.46 | Teaching – about the future kingdom and judgement |
| 26.1—28.20 | Narrative – the arrest, trial, death and resurrection of Jesus |

# PART 1: 1.1—4.25

## INTRODUCTION:
## THE COMING OF THE CHRIST

Each of the four Gospels begins in a quite different way from the others. Mark tells of nothing earlier than the preaching of John the Baptist. John begins with an introduction that speaks of Jesus as the eternal Word of God. Matthew and Luke are alike in the way that they both have a genealogy of Jesus, and they both tell of his birth, his home in Nazareth, and the beginning of his public work with his baptism, temptation and early ministry in Galilee. A difference of Matthew from Luke is in the strong stress that we have noticed on the fulfilment of the Old Testament Scriptures. We may subdivide these first four chapters as follows:

---

**Analysis**
1.1–17   The genealogy of Jesus
1.18–25 The conception and birth of Jesus
2.1–12   The worship of the wise men
2.13–23 The journey to Egypt and back to Nazareth
3.1–12   The ministry of John the Baptist
3.13–17 The baptism of Jesus
4.1–11   The temptations of Jesus
4.12–17 The beginning of the ministry of Jesus in Galilee
4.18–25 The nature of Jesus' ministry

# *1.1–17  The Genealogy of Jesus*

## *See also Luke 3.23–38*

### Introduction

To some people a long list of names may seem an unattractive way to begin a Gospel. To the Jews, as to many African, Asian and Pacific peoples, genealogies are important. Originally they were oral history, and as men and women passed them on by word of mouth, they gave a tribe or people its sense of identity. Genealogies provide the link with the ancestors who have gone before and whom people feel still to belong to their community. Christian people believe in 'the communion of saints'. That is, they see members of the body of Christ living on earth and those departed as members together of the 'people of God', the 'cloud of witnesses' of which Hebrews 12.1 speaks. There are many genealogies in the Old Testament.

### NOTES

The beginning and end of this genealogy present Jesus as Messiah (or Christ), the fulfilment of Israel's hopes. We may note six points about it:

1 It divides Israel's history into three periods, mentioning 14 generations in each period. They run from Abraham to David, David to the exile in Babylon, the exile to Jesus.
2 It starts with Abraham, because the Israelites always remembered the call of Abraham, the promises to him and the covenant with him as the beginning of the outworking of God's purpose for them.
3 Then David was equally important, not only as Israel's greatest king, but because God gave him promises that his house and his kingdom would be established after him (2 Samuel 7.10–16). Then in the prophets this promise became the hope of a great king who would rule in righteousness and bring peace and blessing to the people.
4 The line of kings in the genealogy went down to the people's

defeat by Babylon, and their exile. That was a turning-point in their history. The people came back, never to have kings like David, until at last there came 'Jesus the Christ, the son of David, the son of Abraham'.

5 The genealogy mentions several women. These include Tamar, who was abused by her father-in-law (Genesis 38); Rahab, who was a Canaanite and not a Jew (Joshua 2); and Ruth, another Gentile from Moab. The mention of the 'wife of Uriah' recalls the darkest deed of David's reign, his adultery and murder of Uriah (2 Samuel 11). In this way the beginning of the Gospel hints that grace triumphs over human sinfulness, and the promises to Abraham and David are not for Israel alone, but also for the Gentiles, and they concern women as well as men.

6 Although the rest of the chapter shows that Jesus was son of Mary but not of Joseph, the Jewish traditional way involved tracing the genealogy through Joseph, and it is not so much a strict succession from father to son all the way, but rather it gives the throne succession from David onwards.

---

### 📖  Study Suggestions

1 The opening words of verse 1 are literally 'book of beginning (genesis)'. In what way is this beginning of the Gospel like the beginning of the Old Testament in Genesis 1?

2 Verses 1, 17 and 18 speak of Jesus as 'the Christ' or 'the Messiah'. Both words, one from Greek and the other from Hebrew, mean 'anointed'. In Old Testament times it was the custom to anoint prophets and priests and kings (Exodus 28.41, 1 Samuel 16 and 1 Kings 19.16). So several Old Testament passages call the king of the house of David, whom people expected to come to bring justice and salvation, the Christ or the Messiah. Read 2 Samuel 7.1–16, Psalm 89.3–4, 132.11–18, Isaiah 9.6–7, Jeremiah 23.5–6 and 33.14–17.

3 Read the little book of Ruth in the Old Testament, noticing the genealogy at the end of chapter 4, that tells how Ruth came to have a place in the ancestry of Jesus.

4 In 1 Chronicles 1.34 and 2.1–15 we have genealogies such as would give the names for this one. Ruth 4.18–22 takes it down to David, and passages in 1 and 2 Kings name all the kings down to the time of the exile. The Old Testament does not provide us with the names in the last part of the genealogy.

5 What is the importance of genealogies among your own people? If they are important, why is this so? What can be learnt if you trace back and see who brought the gospel to your

people? How can you trace back their Christian ancestry, ultimately to the time of Jesus? Why do you think that it is important to go back from Jesus into the Old Testament?

# 1.18–25 The Conception and Birth of Jesus

## See also Luke 1.26–38

### NOTES

This section of the Gospel begins, 'Now the birth of Jesus Christ took place in this way.' We may note four very important things about this:

1 Very simply and without emphasizing how unique this event was, it says, 'Mary . . . was found to be with child of the Holy Spirit', and then an angel told Joseph, 'that which is conceived in her is of the Holy Spirit'. In this way this Gospel presents Jesus as truly human, born as a human child with Mary as his mother, and yet also of divine origin, rightly to be called 'Son of man' but also 'Son of God'.

2 While Luke's Gospel (1.26–38) tells how it was made known to Mary, and describes her amazement and her submission, this Gospel deals with Joseph's need to understand. In Jewish custom engagement was as firm a commitment as marriage itself. Jewish law required divorce if one partner was unfaithful to the commitment of engagement, even though the man had not yet taken his bride to his home in marriage. Because of Joseph's righteous character, it says that he would divorce the partner engaged to him, but do it quietly, so as not to 'put her to shame' in a public way. In a dream an angel reveals the true state of affairs to him, and thus Joseph, whom verse 20 calls 'a son of David', comes to be the protector of Mary and the child Jesus, and the

foster-father from whom therefore people could reckon the genealogy of Jesus.

3 In addition this section is important for the way that it gives two
names of Jesus, telling who he is and indicating the deepest purpose of his coming. The first one fulfils the words of Isaiah 7.14,
because the name Emmanuel applies uniquely to him, 'God with
us'. The old prophecy in the days of Isaiah, more than 700 years
before, no doubt had a fulfilment at that time. A young woman
gave birth to a child, able to be called Emmanuel because of the
sense of God's presence and blessing on the people then. The
Greek translation of the Hebrew of Isaiah used a word that could
only mean a 'virgin', one who had had no sexual relationships
with a man. So readers could understand a deep fulfilment, more
wonderful than that in the days of Isaiah. The whole story of the
Gospel that unfolds is of 'Emmanuel', 'God with us'.

4 We then read of the gift of the other name, a name also known in
the Old Testament, since the name Jesus is the same as Joshua or
Jehoshua, with the meaning 'the Lord saves'. Joseph gives this
name to the child of Mary, because 'he will save his people from
their sins'. (There may also be a deliberate use of the words of the
Old Testament in Psalm 130.8.) This Gospel will tell of Jesus as
Teacher, as Healer, as 'King of the Jews' (in the right meaning of
the words), but no words can describe the work he came to do
more fittingly than those that speak of him as saving his people
from their sins.

## ADDITIONAL NOTE A: THE VIRGINAL CONCEPTION OF JESUS

Some modern scholars interpret the records of the virginal conception of Jesus in Matthew and Luke as giving theological teaching rather than presenting historical fact. They compare the
Gospel accounts with ancient legends of divine births, but the
spirit of this narrative is very different from such legends. We
have nothing like the heightening of the miraculous as in the
later apocryphal Gospels that are not in the New Testament, and
nothing like the stories in some religions and cultures of the gods
having sexual intercourse with humans. Some scholars also suggest that the basis of the record here is the Old Testament passage
in Isaiah 7, seen to be fulfilled in Jesus, one who is greater than
David, truly the Christ, uniquely 'God with us' by the creative
working of the Spirit of God. It is certainly true that the virginal
conception of Jesus was not part of the basic preaching of the
early Church, though the apostle Paul's statement in Galatians
4.4, 'born of a woman' might be an allusion to it. It is also true

that the birth narratives of Matthew and Luke are very different, but they agree in their statement of the virginal conception, the gift of the name 'Jesus', the birth in Bethlehem and the childhood in Nazareth. There is also the deliberate statement in Luke 1.1–4 that that Gospel seeks to record 'events' vouched for 'by those who from the beginning were eyewitnesses and servants of the word'. We must respect the sincerely held opinion of those who see spiritual rather than literal truth in this narrative, but the Christian Church, from the second century in the Apostles' Creed and in the Nicene Creed from the fourth century, has confessed Jesus as 'conceived by the Holy Spirit, born of the Virgin Mary'.

 **Study Suggestions**

FOR GROUP DISCUSSION

1 Study Isaiah 7.1–17 and 8.5–8 and see the two uses of the name 'Immanuel'. How might you compare the experience of the coming of Jesus with the experience of the blessing of God's presence with the people in the days of Isaiah?
2 Make a careful comparison of this part of Matthew with Luke 1.26–56. In what ways are the two presentations of the virginal conception of Jesus the same and in what ways different?
3 Compare verse 21 with other similar statements in the New Testament that speak of the work of Jesus as bringing salvation. For example, see Luke 2.11, John 1.29, 3.16, 4.42, Acts 4.12, 5.31, 13.23, 39, 1 Timothy 1.15, Titus 2.14 and 1 John 4.14.
4 Do people in your society understand dreams as a way in which God often speaks to them? If so, how do you think you should recognize a dream that truly has a message from God and a dream that does not have such a message?
5 Does the way that people give names in your culture help you to appreciate the importance of Bible names and especially these names that Scripture gives to Jesus?

# 2.1–12 *The Worship of the Wise Men*

We have noticed, and will realize much more fully as we go on, that this Gospel is the most Jewish of all the Gospels. Yet surprisingly, while Luke tells us about the revelation of the birth of Jesus to the local Jewish shepherds, here Matthew tells us that it was to 'wise men from the East'. There are, in fact, a number of ways in which Matthew makes clear that (as the writer puts it in 8.11), 'many will come from east and west and sit at table with Abraham, Isaac, and Jacob in the kingdom of heaven', and the Gospel closes with Jesus telling those who followed him to 'go – and make disciples of all nations'.

A helpful way of studying this section is by looking at the people involved:

### The wise men

The proper name for these wise men is 'magi'. They were what today we would call 'astrologers'. Their own society recognized them as religious people who studied the movements of the stars to try to predict the future. Among such people there were sincere seekers after God, and history provides countless different examples of ways that God makes himself known to those who sincerely seek him. Scholars have offered a number of explanations for the star that the wise men saw and followed. One is that at that time the courses of two planets came close together and so observers saw the two as one very bright star. Another is that it was a comet such as we sometimes see in our skies. Another is that it was a visionary experience given to the wise men as a vision, and so it appeared to lead them right to the place where they could find Jesus. Some people have connected the star with Balaam's oracle in Numbers 24.17, but there the one the oracle expects to come is himself a star coming out of Jacob.

### Herod

The attitude of the wise men stands out in strong contrast to that of Herod and even that of the 'chief priests and scribes' whom Herod consulted. At the time of the birth of Jesus Palestine was a part of the Roman Empire, but Herod, partly Jewish and partly Edomite, was the local 'king' with some power allowed to him by Rome. He was very jealous of the power that he had, and historical records tell of the way that he tried to kill every possible rival to his rule. So he was 'troubled' when the wise men came and asked to know the birth-place of the new 'king of the Jews'. He gained all the information that he could from the wise men, so that – as he pretended – he might also 'come and worship him'. Happily the wise men received instructions in a dream not to return to Herod to help forward his murderous plans.

### The Jewish religious leaders

'The chief priests and scribes' were the people whom Herod con-sulted. There was strictly only one high priest at a time with supreme responsibility for the sacrificial worship that went on in the temple in Jerusalem. He was meant to be high priest for the whole of his life, but verse 4 can speak of 'chief priests' in the plural, either because the Romans often deposed one high priest and put another in his place, or because the high-priestly families might be called 'the chief priests'. The 'scribes' were those whom people recognized as the ones responsible for preserving and teaching the Jewish Law. Thus they regarded 'chief priests and scribes' as the experts in the Scriptures, and expected them to be able to tell from prophecy where the Mes-siah should be born. The chief priests and scribes quoted the words of Micah 5.2, speaking of Bethlehem, because the Messiah was to be of the house of David whose home was Bethlehem. The Gospel seems intentionally to indicate that while Herod wanted to know all he could and use it to kill the future 'King of the Jews', the Jewish religious leaders had the information they needed, and yet made no use of it. We have no word of their going to see if indeed their expected Messiah had been born in Bethlehem. Contrasting those religious leaders with the wise men, Bishop Stephen Neill puts it, 'It is a story of those who knew hardly anything and found everything, and of those who knew everything and found nothing.'

### The Child Jesus

The wise men 'rejoiced exceedingly with great joy' when they found the child Jesus, and 'they fell down and worshipped him'. They had three gifts, though the Gospel does not actually tell us that there were three 'wise men', nor that they were kings as pictures and Christmas carols have often described them. Gold was the richest of gifts they could bring. They used incense in worship and so it was an expression of the worship they offered. Myrrh was the sweetest fra-grance they could offer. We never read again of gold or incense being offered to Jesus, but the Gospels tell us twice more of myrrh. It was 'wine mingled with myrrh' that the soldiers offered Jesus to soothe

the pain of his crucifixion (Mark 15.23), and his followers used myrrh in the anointing of the dead body of Jesus at his burial (John 19.39).

---

📖 **Study Suggestions**

1 Follow out the use of the word that English versions translate as 'worship' or 'kneel before' in the Gospel in relation to Jesus. See 2.2, 8, 11; 8.2; 9.18; 14.33; 15.25; 20.20; 28.9 and 17.

2 From what we read of the 'wise men' in this passage, what marks of character and attitude do you think that they display? Do you think that we should understand these as qualities of those who seek after truth?

3 It may be right to connect this passage not only with Micah 5.2 in the Old Testament (quoted in verse 6), but also with passages which speak of the revelation of the glory of the Lord and people of other nations coming to worship. Read Isaiah 60.1–7, noting what it says about people bringing 'gold and frankincense' as gifts. See also Isaiah 49.7 and Psalm 72.10–11 which may have led people to think of the wise men as kings, though Matthew does not say this of them here.

4 Do you know of people who, without any direct contact with members of the Christian Church, and perhaps without any knowledge of the Bible, have come to faith in Christ? In what ways do you think that scientific knowledge today can help people to faith?

# 2.13–23 *The Journey to Egypt and Back to Nazareth*

There are two important things we can say about these verses:

1 Herod's attempt to murder the baby Jesus and his slaughter of the little children of Bethlehem fits in with what we know of Herod from other sources, especially the Jewish historian Josephus. Herod was determined to get rid of any possible rivals to his rule as 'king of the Jews'. This was a small thing in comparison with some of the massacres for which he was responsible. The Roman emperor Augustus said that 'it was safer to be Herod's pig than his son'. Sadly, history, ancient and modern, is full of the story of the cruelty of such tyrants, and the terrible bloodshed for which they have been responsible when they have felt that there have been others who threatened their absolute power and rule. When Herod died, the authorities divided his kingdom (with the permission of the Roman emperor Augustus) between his three sons. Archelaus was the one of these who inherited Judea and Samaria. He showed himself to have much the same brutal character that his father had. This explains what verse 22 says about Mary and Joseph taking Jesus to Nazareth in 'the district of Galilee' rather than staying in the area ruled over by Archelaus.

2 The Gospel sees these events as fulfilling the Old Testament, not just the Old Testament hopes and prophecies, but Old Testament history. What happened in the life of Jesus had parallels to the story of Israel in Old Testament times. We have three quotations in these verses:

   – The quotation from Hosea 11.1, 'Out of Egypt have I called my son.' Joseph and Mary took the baby Jesus into Egypt, and in the protection of Egypt they lived for a time as refugees. Centuries earlier, Joseph, son of Jacob, and then the other sons of Jacob had found protection in Egypt. Later the Hebrew people became slaves there, but were set free in the time of Moses and came up into the land of Palestine, to live as the Lord's people (as his 'son'), and to fulfil his purposes for them. Hosea presents it as the word of the Lord, 'When Israel was a child, I loved him, and out of Egypt I called my son.' So it happened now to the greatest Representative of Israel, the one Scripture says we can call God's 'Son'.

   – The quotation from Jeremiah 31.15, 'A voice was heard in Ramah, wailing and loud lamentation, Rachel weeping for her children; she refused to be consoled, because they were no more.' Jeremiah was a prophet in the closing years of the kingdom of Judah, and spoke of the time when the Babylonians would capture the people and take them off to Babylon. Rachel was the wife of Jacob and so the mother of the people of Israel. She was buried in Ramah not far from Bethlehem, and Jeremiah pictures her as weeping for her children as their captors carried them into exile. From the point of view of their life as citizens of the land, people could say, 'they are no more'. This was now the sad story of the children of Bethlehem. Ancestress Rachel must weep again for her children. It is important, however, to realize that the passage of Jeremiah, from which our quotation comes, also speaks of the Lord redeeming his people, and saying, 'I will turn their mourning into joy, I will comfort them, and give them gladness for sorrow' (Jeremiah 31.13). The sadness in Bethlehem would again be turned to joy. The One saved from that massacre would live – and die – to become the Saviour of the world, and that is the Gospel's story.

– When this Gospel records the return of Mary and Joseph with Jesus to Nazareth, it says that this is another fulfilment of the message of the prophets, and quotes the words, 'He shall be called a Nazarene.' Here, however, we have a problem, as this is not a quotation of anything that we have in the Old Testament. Scholars have made a number of suggestions to explain this, such as linking it with the Nazirites of whom we read in Numbers 6, or the Messianic prophecy of the 'branch' (Hebrew, *nezer*) from the root of Jesse (in Isaiah 11.1). We cannot really explain the words. It may be more important to see a link between the words in verse 20, 'those who sought the child's life are dead', and what God says to Moses when he tells him to return from Midian because 'all the men who were seeking your life are dead' (Exodus 4.19). Is there the suggestion that as Moses returned from Midian to Egypt to become the saviour of his people, now Jesus is returning from being a refugee in Egypt to do his work of saving his people?

---

## 📖 Study Suggestions

1 What answer can a Christian give to the problem of the suffering of innocent children such as we see here?
2 What advantages do you think there were in Jesus' family bringing him up in a place like Nazareth rather than Bethlehem, and in an area like Galilee rather than near Jerusalem?
3 What can we learn when we think of the context in Hosea

11.1–4 and Jeremiah 31.1–26 of the Old Testament quotations that we have in verses 15 and 18?
4 What can and should Christians do in the face of there being
so many millions of people in the world today who are political refugees? What comfort is there in our being able to say
that Jesus himself was a refugee?

# 3.1–12 The Ministry of John the Baptist

## See also Mark 1.2–11; Luke 3.1–22; John 1.6–8, 19–34

All the four Gospels speak of the ministry of John the Baptist and
link the beginning of Jesus' ministry with John's work. All of the
Gospels speak of him as preaching and baptizing people, and all
speak of him as preparing the way of Jesus and predicting the coming
of One much greater than himself. The first-century Jewish historian, Josephus, also writes of John the Baptist and of the way that
Herod imprisoned him and put him to death. In this Gospel there are
several things that the writer particularly emphasizes concerning
John the Baptist's ministry:

1 He called people to repent, just as the Old Testament prophets had
often done, but John made baptism in water a sign of that repentance. Verse 6 says he baptized people in the River Jordan 'confessing their sins'. Their repentance had to be genuine and had to
have 'fruit' in their lives. John apparently did not need to explain
the meaning of baptism. In early Jewish records we read how
Gentiles who became Jews had to undergo a baptism to wash off
from them the defilement of their Gentile world. We know also
that the Qumran community in the wilderness area near the Dead
Sea had washing rituals that both John and people generally
would have known.

2 He also said in his preaching, 'the kingdom of heaven is at hand.' This is the first of many times in the Gospel that we read about 'the kingdom of heaven' (the same as 'the kingdom of God', since 'heaven' was a reverential Jewish way of speaking of God). The 'kingdom of God' means God's rule. The Gospels show that the kingdom of God – God's rule – came uniquely into human life and history with the coming of Jesus. John's preaching ministry caused such excitement because he called people to prepare for this great event. (See the Additional Note C on the 'Kingdom of Heaven/Kingdom of God' on p. 29.)

3 As with so many things in this Gospel, the writer presents John's coming as the fulfilment of Scripture. Verse 3 quotes Isaiah 40.3 (just as later, 11.10 quotes Malachi 3.1 in relation to John). All that John wanted to say about himself (see John 1.19–23) was that he was like a 'voice of one crying in the wilderness', calling on people to prepare for the coming of the Lord.

4 John had a very simple lifestyle. Luke 1.80 says that he grew up in the wilderness, and it was to the wilderness that people came to see and hear John. When they came they found a man very simply dressed (verse 4 and compare 11.7–10), indeed dressed as an olden-times prophet (see 2 Kings 1.8 and Zechariah 13.4), and eating just the food that he could find in the wilderness.

5 We read here the special application of John's message to the Pharisees and Sadducees. We will see as we continue our study that Matthew is the most Jewish of the Gospels. It says more about these two Jewish groups than any of the other Gospels do.

– The Pharisees took over the ideals of the party called the Hasideans. These were people who, in times when the Jewish faith was under attack (200 years before this time of John's ministry), stood for faithful observance of the Law. There must have been many high-minded Pharisees (like Gamaliel of whom we read in Acts 5.33–39), but there were also many who, in insisting on countless detailed regulations, had lost the spirit and purpose of the Law. So they had become self-righteous, thinking that they were the only ones who were faithful to the Law. This explains the stern words of John – and later of Jesus – addressed to them, and the writer of the Gospel was conscious that this attitude could easily come into the lives of Christian leaders.

– The Sadducees are a group that we read of first about 150 BC and most of their membership was from the important priestly families. They held strongly to the Law, but they did not accept other Scriptures, and they felt that they should not accept beliefs about life after death and about angels because they were not in the Law (see 22.23–33 and Acts 4.1–3 and 23.6–10). They were concerned to hold on to their political power, and opposed any religious movement that might threaten their authority. John addressed the Pharisees and Sadducees as a 'brood of vipers', perhaps picturing them as wanting to escape judgement like snakes escaping from a grass fire. No doubt also John saw them as evil (the same words 'brood of vipers' appear in 12.34 and 23.33), because they had allowed pride and self-righteousness to exclude true righteousness and love from their lives. They might claim to be secure in God's covenant as children of Abraham, but someone needed to remind them that they could lose their privileges, which go to others instead.

6 John the Baptist not only said that the kingdom of heaven was at hand. He spoke of one who was to come, greater and more powerful than he, saying that he was not worthy even to carry his sandals (as his slave). These words of John are particularly interesting in that there was a saying among the Jewish rabbis that a disciple should do every form of service for his teacher except that of loosing the thong of his sandals. Few things therefore could more powerfully indicate John's sense of the greatness of the one whose way he came to prepare.

7 In particular John compared his water baptism (signifying washing from the filth of sin) with the baptism of the Coming One. That would be a baptism 'with the Holy Spirit and with fire'. The Old Testament prophets, and especially Joel (2.28–29), had spoken of a time when God would pour out the Holy Spirit. On the Day of Pentecost the signs of the Spirit's coming were wind and fire (Acts 2.2–4). Fire cleanses and gives warmth and light, but John's thought was more of the fire of judgement, as verse 12 shows. Later he was to realize that he had misunderstood the mercy and blessing that in the first place the coming of Jesus would mean (see 11.2–6). Verse 12 refers to the process in which the grain that was threshed was thrown up into the air by the 'winnowing fork', and all the straw would be blown away by the wind, and just the good grain would fall on to the threshing floor below. This provides, therefore, another picture of the judgement of God.

---

📖 **Study Suggestions**

1 As John called on people to have 'fruit' in their lives that showed the genuineness of their repentance, consider other ways in which the Bible speaks of the 'fruit' of repentance and faith or good deeds in people's lives. See Matthew 7.15–20; John 15.1–5, 8, 16; Galatians 5.22–26 and Ephesians 5.9–11.

2 Compare this record of the ministry of John the Baptist to the one that we have in Luke 3.3–20 and with the briefer one in Mark 1.2–8. What points are there in Matthew which are not

in the other Gospels? What do Mark and Luke have that we
do not have in this passage?

3 How far do you think that Christian preaching today should
be like the preaching of John the Baptist? What particular
sins in the life of your Church and your country today do you
think a person preaching like John would denounce?

4 From this passage, and also considering 11.7–19 and John
1.19–28 and 3.25–30, what do you think were the outstand-
ing qualities of the life and character of John the Baptist?

5 Think about the claim of the 'Pharisees and Sadducees' to be
right in their relationship with God because they were 'children of Abraham'. In what ways is it possible for Christians
today to have false confidence and so neglect the preaching
that calls them to repentance and to the whole-hearted
service of God?

## ADDITIONAL NOTE B: THE WRITING OF THE GOSPEL

### *(See also notes on pp. 32 and 82.)*

Scholars call the three Gospels, Matthew, Mark and Luke, Synoptic
Gospels, as the word 'synoptic' means seeing things from the same
point of view. When we read these Gospels carefully and compare
them one with another, we notice that in some things their
records are very closely similar but in other things they are different. The problem of explaining these similarities and differences is
known as 'the synoptic problem'. In particular it raises the question, as we study Matthew, of what written records the writer of
this Gospel had to draw on when he wrote, and also what information had come to him by word of mouth. When we compare this
passage we have been studying (3.1–12) with Luke 3.3–17 we find
some parts of it word for word the same. Other parts are different,
and there are things in Matthew that are not in Luke, and things
in Luke that are not in Matthew. We will find that this is often the
case where we have similar passages between Matthew and Luke
where there is not a close parallel in Mark. We will consider later
passages in Matthew that are closely similar to Mark. We might
explain these similarities and differences between Matthew and
Luke in one of the following ways:

1 They both received the 'oral tradition' (that is, what people
handed down by word of mouth rather than any written
record). This is possible, but when we consider that the earliest

oral tradition would have been in the Aramaic language which John and Jesus would have used normally, and there is such close similarity in the Greek of the Gospels, it would seem more likely that there is a literary connection and not just a connection in the oral tradition.

2 Matthew might have had Luke's Gospel to use, or Luke might have had Matthew's Gospel. Either of these is possible, but when we realize that in Matthew there are many important things that Luke does not have and in Luke there are many important things that Matthew does not have, it is hard to think that either had the full form of the other Gospel.

3 Both Matthew and Luke might both have had and used the same written source or sources. In particular Matthew and Luke both have a lot of the teaching of Jesus that is not in Mark. This is why some people have suggested that there was such a record of Jesus' teaching that both Gospels knew and used. Scholars have called this 'Q' (from 'quelle', the German word for 'source'). We must realize, however, that Matthew and Luke may have had not just one but several written sources that they both were able to use. Luke (in 1.1–4) actually says as much, that a number of sources were available to him, and those words with which he begins his Gospel indicate his use of both oral and written sources in the writing of his Gospel. The same may well have been true for Matthew.

# 3.13–17 The Baptism of Jesus

## See also Mark 1.9–11; Luke 3.21–22; John 1.31–34

All of the Synoptic Gospels record the baptism of Jesus by John (see Mark 1.9–11 and Luke 3.21–22). The silent years of the life of Jesus are over. His public work is about to begin, and it begins with his deliberately identifying himself with John in his ministry, his message and his baptism. There are two features of this record in

Matthew that are different from those of Mark and Luke, and two features that are similar:

1 Only this Gospel tells of the hesitation of John to baptize Jesus. This is understandable when we think of it alongside what this Gospel records of John's words about the greatness of the one whose way he came to prepare. The greater should baptize the lesser rather than the other way round. 'I need to be baptized by you, and do you come to me?'

2 Then we have the words of Jesus' reply to overcome John's hesitation, 'Let it be so now; for thus it is fitting for us to fulfil all righteousness.' We can explain the fulfilling of all righteousness in a number of different ways. It could mean simply to do what is right in God's sight, to do what fulfils God's purpose expressed in the Scriptures, to place oneself on the side of righteousness as those did who sincerely responded to John's call to repent and be baptized. People have also understood it to mean the fulfilling of the purpose of the righteous Servant of the Lord of whom Isaiah 40–55 speaks. He is the one who came to serve, even to suffer for others. In this way Jesus identified himself with sinful men and women who needed the baptism of repentance. At least it is true that he chose the way of accepting the will of the Father that in the end would lead to the cross.

3 This Gospel, like the other Gospels, speaks of the opening of the heavens and the Spirit coming on Jesus like a dove. The heavens are opened to bring blessing to humanity, the blessing of 'the kingdom of heaven'. Moreover, as prophets had said, this one sent from God is to be filled with the Spirit and so enabled to carry out his ministry. Isaiah 11.2 said of the one who would come as 'a shoot from the stump of Jesse' (that is, from the royal house of David, son of Jesse), 'The spirit of the Lord shall rest on him, the spirit of wisdom and understanding, the spirit of counsel and might, the spirit of knowledge and the fear of the Lord.' (See also Isaiah 42.1 and 61.1 and the quotation of the latter passage in Luke 4.18–22.) The One who is to baptize with the Spirit is first given the Spirit for his own life and work. People have often taken the dove as a symbol of gentleness (see 10.16) or of peace. It was also a symbol for Israel. In some way it symbolized the coming of the Spirit and what the ministry of Jesus in the gentle power of the Spirit was to be like.

4 The voice from heaven (in Mark and Luke addressed to Jesus, here declaring to the crowds, 'This is my Son'), speaks of Jesus as God's beloved Son, and the One with whom he is well pleased. Scholars have often understood the words as linking verse 7 of the royal Psalm 2 and the words of Isaiah 42.1, 'Behold my servant, whom I uphold, my chosen, in whom my soul delights; I have put my

Spirit upon him.' There is certainly good reason for thinking that Jesus went out from his baptism to his public ministry knowing his calling as Messiah. Yet different groups of Jewish people had different expectations of a Messiah. The Qumran community of whom we read in the Dead Sea Scrolls expected two Messiahs, a kingly one of the house of David and a priestly one. People like the Zealots looked for one who would be a military leader who would free their people from the power of the Roman empire. Others had different expectations. Jesus was not to be a Messiah of the kind that many Jews expected, but one who would serve and suffer (like the Suffering Servant pictured in Isaiah 40–55) to save his people from the wrong ways in which they had been living (see 1.21).

---

### 📖 Study Suggestions

1 'Righteousness' is a key word in this Gospel. See how the writer uses it in verse 15 here and in 5.6, 10, 20; 6.33 and 21.32.
2 What thought does the description of the heavens being opened to those on earth (3.16) convey? In the Old Testament see Genesis 28.10–17; Isaiah 64.1 and Psalm 144.5.
3 In what ways do you think that the baptism of Jesus was like that of others who came to be baptized by John, and in what ways do you think it was different?
4 What similarities are there between the baptism of Jesus and Christian baptism? How do you understand the link of the Holy Spirit with baptism in each case? Do you feel that the practice of baptism in your Church reflects well what the New Testament teaches about baptism?

---

# 4.1–11 The Temptations of Jesus

## See also Mark 1.12–13; Luke 4.1–13

In all three Synoptic Gospels the temptations of Jesus follow on directly from his baptism. Mark (1.12–13) simply states the fact that he was tempted, while Luke (4.1–11) gives the same temptations as Matthew does, though in a different order. We can understand Jesus' baptism as his dedication to his ministry, and after that came temptation. He was 'led up by the Spirit into the wilderness' for what would have been a preparation for public ministry. At the same time it was an experience of temptation 'by the devil'. Conscious of his Sonship he was tempted to question it. Twice he was challenged, 'If you are the Son of God'. Aware of the kind of tasks to which he was called, he was tempted to do something very different.

It is significant that the responses to Jesus' temptations are all in the words of Scripture, and all come from the book of Deuteronomy. This implies that similar temptations were experienced by Israel in their 40 years in the wilderness as by Jesus in his 40 days. (The writer may also have intended a parallel between the 40 days of Jesus and Moses' 40 days on the mountain in Deuteronomy 9.9 and the 40 days of Elijah in 1 Kings 19.8.)

## Israel's Temptations

1  As Deuteronomy 8.1–3 puts it, the wilderness experience for Israel meant that they had no human assurance of a supply of food as from crops in a fertile land. They had to face hunger so that they might 'understand that one does not live by bread alone, but by every word that comes from the mouth of the Lord'.
2  Israel faced temptations to put God to the test, expecting signs and miracles instead of trusting him. The reference of the words of Deuteronomy 6.16, quoted by Jesus, is to the incident at Massah recorded in Numbers 20. People recalled it generations later when Psalm 95.8–9 said, in the words of the Lord, that 'on the day at Massah in the wilderness . . . your ancestors tested me, and put me to the proof, though they had seen my work'.
3  Israel also faced the temptation to compromise. They saw themselves as Yahweh's people but they were tempted to give a place to the worship of other gods. So to them the words of Deuteronomy 6.13 were deeply relevant, 'Worship the Lord your God, and him only shall you serve.'

## Jesus' Temptations

In many respects there are parallels between the temptations of Israel and those that Jesus faced. We can appreciate, however, the special relevance of these temptations to Jesus as he set out on his ministry.

1  He was not only tempted at that particular time to use his powers and his vocation to meet his own physical needs, but he would be

tempted to be a bread-giving Messiah. As this Gospel is to show (14.13–21 and 15.32–39), Jesus would be concerned to provide bread to feed the hungry, but his greater ministry would be to feed people's spiritual hunger with the word of God.

2 He was tempted even by the words of Scripture, such as the devil could quote from Psalm 91.11–12, to put God to the test and to do the kind of signs that people would ask as proof of his claims (12.38 and 16.1). His signs, however, were to be the kind that showed the love and goodness of God and what it meant when the kingdom of heaven, the rule of God, came into human lives.

3 Jesus could well understand 'the kingdoms of the world and the glory of them'. He knew the degree to which they had fallen into the hands of the devil. They had to be won back to belong to the kingdom of God. He was tempted to use the devil's ways and the world's ways to win them back. Yet in his winning of the world there must never be a single moment of compromise with the evil one. He must not use wrong methods to do his work, or the ways in which people seek power and glory in the world. The only appropriate reply to the devil was in the uncompromising words of Deuteronomy 6.13 that Moses had taught Israel.

The purpose of this passage may not be literally to tell where the temptations of Jesus took place. There is not literally a mountain from which 'all the kingdoms of the world and the glory of them' can be seen. Yet we can realize that there are particular temptations that come when we are alone, others in the place of worship, others when we feel the attractions of the world around us.

What the writer says at the end of verse 11 about the ministry of the angels (in contrast to what the devil suggested might be their ministry in verse 6) indicates that God does provide in his own time and way for the needs of the one whose trust is in him and who seeks to do his will. When temptation is overcome, physical needs are met, deliverance is given, the kingdom is won – but in God's ways, and not in the ways of the world, the flesh and the devil.

---

### 📖 Study Suggestions

1 The word English versions often translate as 'tempted' in verse 1 they sometimes translate as 'tested'. See the following passages and consider the ways that they indicate that God allows us to be tested to strengthen our faith and obedience, but temptations to evil do not come from God: 1 Corinthians 10.13; Galatians 6.1; 1 Thessalonians 3.5; Hebrews 11.17 and James 1.12–15.

2 Study the contexts of the Deuteronomy passages referred to (6.10–19 and 8.1–6), and consider what was the true nature of

the temptations that the people of Israel faced. How far can we see Israel's experience as both testing from God and temptation to what was wrong in God's eyes?

3 Genesis 3.6 speaks of the temptation to take of the 'tree' that the woman saw to be 'good for food', 'a delight to the eyes', and 'to be desired to make one wise'. Do you think that there are parallels between that temptation and the temptations of Jesus? Consider this also with the words of 1 John 2.16 in the way that it speaks of 'the lust of the flesh and the lust of the eyes and the pride of life'.

4 How do you think that these temptations, if he had accepted them, would have affected the whole of the life and ministry of Jesus?

5 'Temptation often is the suggestion that we should try to get God to do what we want, rather than being willing to do what he wants and then trust him to provide for what we need.' Are there ways in which this is true of the temptations the Gospel records here?

6 In what ways can we see our temptations as being, in principle, like the temptations that Jesus faced – especially in terms of our physical desires, our desire to win support from other people, and the desire to have the possessions and power that the world offers?

7 What strength should Christian people find in the realization that Jesus faced temptations as we do, and what lessons are there for us in the way that he won the victory over them? See especially Hebrews 2.18 and 4.14–16.

8 What is the importance of each of these temptations being met with a quotation from the Scriptures? In what sense is it right to think of 'the word of God' as 'the sword of the Spirit' (Ephesians 6.17)? What is the right kind of way for us to use the Bible in temptations that we face? See Colossians 3.16.

# 4.12–17 The Beginning of the Ministry of Jesus in Galilee

## See also Mark 1.14–15; Luke 4.14–15

Mark and Luke tell of the beginning of Jesus' public ministry in Galilee as Matthew does, but again we should notice the particular things that this Gospel says about it:

1 Its beginning was when John's ministry was brought to a close by his arrest, which Luke (3.19–20) says was on account of his rebuking King Herod for taking his brother's wife. John had fulfilled faithfully his task of preparing the way of the Lord. The authorities had silenced the voice of John. The voice of Jesus would now be heard.

2 Jesus 'withdrew to Galilee'. He had associated himself with John the Baptist in his ministry in the south, where he baptized people in the River Jordan. John's Gospel tells more of those beginnings, but now Galilee is to be the place for a major stage in the work of Jesus. The Jewish historian Josephus tells how well-populated Galilee was at this time, with many towns and villages with thousands of people in them.

3 There was also a withdrawal from Nazareth where Jesus had grown up from childhood (2.22–23), and where Luke (4.16–30) tells of his preaching – and his rejection (see also Mark 6.1–6). Capernaum at the northern end of Lake Galilee became a base for much of Jesus' work in the whole area of Galilee.

4 In the way that we have seen is typical of this Gospel, the writer speaks of this move to Capernaum as a fulfilment of an Old Testament passage, Isaiah 9.1–2. That passage had a meaning in the time of the prophet Isaiah because Galilee (the tribal areas of Zebulun and Naphtali) had suffered at the hands of the Assyrians, but after dark times there was to be a new day for the people there. Those words, however, had a new and deeper meaning as the light of Jesus' ministry shone brightly there. Those in darkness now saw the light, and for those living under the 'shadow of death', a new day dawned. In the time of Jesus – as it had been even in the days of Isaiah – this part of the country was a semi-Jewish, semi-Gentile area, and there, surprisingly, Jesus was ministering. (Though in the time of Jesus the words 'across the Jordan' or 'beyond the Jordan',

as in verse 25, usually meant on the eastern side of the Jordan, in the time of the original prophecy in Isaiah, perhaps from the point of view of the Assyrians, it meant on the western side, where in fact Nazareth and Capernaum were.)

5 Jesus began with the very same message that had been on the lips of John the Baptist. There was the negative, 'Repent' – turn from evil. Then there was the positive promise, 'the kingdom of heaven is at hand' (see 3.2). The rule of God in human lives – with the blessings and the responsibilities that that involved – was to happen in a new way as the ministry of Jesus touched the lives of men and women, girls and boys.

---

### 📖 Study Suggestions

1 How does this Gospel use the words 'light' and 'darkness' to symbolize truth and love and life, over against ignorance, hatred and death? With verse 16 compare 5.14–16 and 6.22–23, and for Luke's and John's similar descriptions of what the ministry of Jesus would involve see Luke 1.78–79; 2.32; John 1.4–9; 3.19–21; 8.12; 12.35–36 and 46.

2 Jerusalem was the location of the temple and the centre of the religious activity of the Jewish people. Why then do you think that so much of the ministry of Jesus took place in an area like Galilee, which was partly Jewish with Jewish synagogues there, but people could appropriately call it 'Galilee of the Gentiles'?

3 When you compare what Matthew tells here of the beginning of the ministry of Jesus before the call of the disciples with what Luke 4.14–44 tells, what do you think of as the difference of point of view between the two Gospels?

4 In what ways do you think it would be true to say that the ministry of Jesus brought light into the darkness of people's lives, like the dawning of a new day? How does the good news of Jesus still do that?

## ADDITIONAL NOTE C: KINGDOM OF HEAVEN / KINGDOM OF GOD

We have seen that John preached, 'Repent, for the kingdom of heaven is at hand' (3.2), and then Jesus began his ministry with the same proclamation. We have observed (in 3.2) that 'the kingdom of heaven' and 'the kingdom of God' mean the same thing, as 'heaven' is used as a reverent way of speaking of God. Because these words are so often on the lips of Jesus, it is important that we try to understand more specifically what they mean.

The Old Testament speaks of God's kingdom, not meaning a land or area such as we might speak of as a kingdom today, but God's rule, or God's reign. In fact these might be better ways of translating 'the kingdom of God' in the Bible.

The Old Testament also had the hope of the anointed King of the house of David (the Messiah) who would come and bring in God's rule of righteousness and peace (see Isaiah 9.2–7 and 11.1–9; Jeremiah 23.5–6 and Ezekiel 34.23–24).

When, therefore, someone announced to Jewish people who knew the Old Testament teaching and hopes that, 'the kingdom of heaven is at hand', they would feel that they were about to see the fulfilment of the Old Testament. Several times in Matthew the writer makes reference to 'the gospel' or 'good news of the kingdom' (4.23; 9.35; 24.14) or the message as the 'word of the kingdom' (13.19).

Many of the parables of Jesus begin with the words 'the kingdom of heaven is like . . .', and so they indicate aspects of the rule of God, its blessings and responsibilities. We can see this especially in the parables in chapter 13. When Jesus says 'seek first his kingdom and his righteousness' (6.33), we can understand both the privileges and the responsibilities involved. Jesus' disciples are called to make God king whatever that may mean for their lives.

After the preaching in the beginning of Jesus' ministry, 'The kingdom of God is at hand', came the teaching and action that showed that the kingdom was actually present in his ministry. In 12.28 he says, 'if it is by the Spirit of God that I cast out demons, then the kingdom of God has come upon you.' Jesus speaks of entering the kingdom (5.20; 7.21; 18.3; 19.23–24; 21.31) and being members of the kingdom (5.19; 11.11 and 18.4), even inheriting the kingdom (5.3 and 25.34).

As, however, we read all that the Gospel says about the kingdom, we see that there is both a present realization of the rule of God and its blessings, and also a future hope. In 16.28, for example, the writer refers to 'the Son of man coming in his kingdom' at some future time.

# 4.18–25  The Nature of Jesus' Ministry

## See also Mark 1.16–20, 39; Luke 4.44, 5.1–11; John 1.35–42

This last part of the first main section of the Gospel gives us a glimpse of the main activities that the ministry of Jesus involved. Throughout this Gospel there is a great emphasis on discipleship, that is, what it means to be disciples (= learners) and so to be able to teach others. In fact right through the Gospel we see how Jesus relates to three groups of people: the crowds who came to him, the disciples who followed him, and the people who opposed him. The writer often directs our attention to people's 'faith' – or their unbelief. At the end of his life, his disciples forsook him, the crowds turned against him and his enemies seemed to triumph. But then the resurrection was the defeat of all his enemies, the restoration of the disciples, and their commission to go out to the nations of the world to teach them and make them disciples. Here we have the calling of four who were to be at the very centre of the group of disciples.

Then we see that Jesus' ministry from the beginning involved both teaching and preaching, and also healing and dealing with suffering people, so that the crowds came to find their needs met in him.

The record of the call of the first four disciples follows Mark 1.16–20 closely. Luke (5.1–11) tells in a different way the call of Peter. Mark (1.39 and 3.7–8) and Luke (4.14–15) have similar summaries of the early ministry of Jesus in Galilee to that which we have in verses 23–25.

This passage brings out five important things:

1  The call of Jesus to those who were to be at the heart of his band of disciples meant their leaving their work and their homes. 'They left their nets', 'they left the boat and their father' and 'followed him'. In a way it was how disciples might follow any Jewish rabbi. In another way it was different, and the meaning of following Jesus as a disciple becomes clearer as the Gospel goes on. Here Jesus said to those who had been fishermen, 'I will make you fish for people.' One of the essential tasks of Christian discipleship from the beginning has been to share with others the opportunity received of knowing and following Jesus.

2 The particular place of much of the teaching work of Jesus was the synagogue. The synagogue was the place in every town and village where Jewish people met to hear the reading and explanation of the Scriptures and to worship. We read many times in the Gospels and in the Acts of the Apostles of the Jewish synagogues which existed all over Palestine and in many other lands where Jewish people had gone. We know of synagogues dating from 300 years before this, but the origins of the synagogue may go back much further. When the temple at Jerusalem was destroyed in 586 BC and many of the people went into exile in Babylon, those concerned to hold to their faith would have met together to share it and to worship. When they returned from exile we read how the people gathered together under Ezra and heard the Law read and explained, and the people worshipped (see Nehemiah 8.1–8). This is what became a practice in the synagogues, which was also where the Jews educated children and controlled the life of their community.

3 As to the content of the teaching and preaching of Jesus, we have read that Jesus preached, as John the Baptist had preached, 'Repent for the kingdom of heaven is at hand' (verse 17). That was partly a warning message, but verse 23 makes clear that the message of Jesus was 'the gospel' (that is, good news) 'of the kingdom'. Where God rules, blessings abound in people's lives, as these verses show.

4 There was not just the comfort of the good news of the kingdom in the teaching and preaching of Jesus. We see also here the healing ministry of Jesus. These verses list the various ills of body and mind and spirit that people brought to Jesus, and tell us that 'he healed them'. Verses 23 and 24 here prepare us for the next two main sections of the Gospel, where we have the record of the teaching of the kingdom of God (chs 5–7), and the actions by which Jesus brought the blessings of the kingdom into human lives (chs 8–9).

5 These verses also describe the geographical scope of the impact of Jesus' ministry. Verse 24 says that 'his fame spread throughout all Syria', which may mean all the area to the north of Galilee. This would be of special interest if, as many people think, this Gospel was written in Syria. Verse 25 lists the places from which 'great crowds followed him', north and south, and east and west of the River Jordan (see map).

## 📖 Study Suggestions

1 This Gospel uses the word 'follow' 25 times. From this passage and from other references in Matthew what do you understand that it meant to 'follow' Jesus? See especially 8.19–22; 9.9; 10.38; 16.24–26; 19.21 and 27–28.
2 How does what we read in John 1.35–42 help us to see what may have led to the call of the four fishermen to discipleship as we read of it in verses 18–22?
3 How can and should the message of the kingdom of God involve both the preaching of repentance and also good news? What guidance does the Bible give us as to the way to relate the two?
4 At least four, and perhaps six, of the twelve disciples of Jesus were brothers (with verses 18–22 see also 10.3 and Mark 2.14). What does this say about the value of family links in the work of the kingdom of God? How should we see this alongside the warning that Jesus gives that sometimes loyalty to him involves division in a family (see 10.34–39)?
5 What do you think to be the significance of the fact that the first people whom Jesus called to be his disciples were fishermen?
6 In what ways are the call to discipleship and the work of disciples today similar to, and in what ways may they be different from, what we read here of the call of these four fishermen to follow Jesus?

## ADDITIONAL NOTE D: THE WRITING OF THE GOSPEL, CONTINUED

### *(see also notes on pages 20 and 82)*

When we compare verses 18–22 and Mark 1.16–20, we find that they are very closely similar, and we will find this to be true of many other passages where there are parallels between Matthew and Mark, and this is true also of parallels between Luke and Mark. Although not all who have studied the Gospels with care have agreed, most have come to the conclusion that Mark was written before Matthew and Luke, and that both those Gospels used Mark for their own writing. Some of the reasons for this conclusion are:

1 Where there are parallel passages between the three, or two of the three, Gospels, very often Mark has much more vivid detail and so it is more likely that Matthew and/or Luke has used Mark

and not included all Mark's details than the other way about. You see good examples of this if you compare Matthew 9.2–8; Mark 2.1–12 and Luke 5.17–26, or Matthew 8.28–34; Mark 5.1–20 and Luke 8.26–39.

2 Although the Gospels do not set out to describe the ministry of Jesus in detailed chronological order of events, the order in which Mark describes things is often the same as in both Matthew and Luke, and if it is not in one of the two it is in the other.

3 It is not likely that we can explain the similarities between the Gospels by Mark following Matthew or Luke, because then we would have the difficulty of explaining why Mark left out large and important sections of Matthew or of Luke. It is easier to think of Matthew and Luke using Mark and also having other sources of information, whether handed down by written or spoken word.

4 Where we have parallel passages and noticeable differences between one Gospel and another, it is often possible to see why Matthew and/or Luke may have changed Mark (rather than the other way round). Some of Jesus' criticisms of the disciples, for example, that we have in Mark, are toned down in Matthew, as we see when we compare Mark 4.10–13 with Matthew 13.10–13; Mark 4.40 with Matthew 8.26 and Luke 8.25.

# PART 2: 5.1—7.29
## TEACHING: THE WAY OF DISCIPLESHIP

We have noted in our Introduction (p. 3) that the teaching of Jesus in this Gospel is in five main sections, all ending in a similar way. In chapters 5–7 the conclusion is: 'And when Jesus finished these sayings . . .' (7.28). People have commonly called these chapters 'The Sermon on the Mount', and we can best understand them as setting out the lifestyle to which Jesus calls his disciples. A Jewish rabbi, Simeon the Just, said that 'by three things the world is sustained, by the Law, by the worship of the Temple, and by deeds of loving kindness'. We can say that after the description of the qualities of character that Jesus expects in disciples (in 5.3–16), we have Jesus' interpretation of the Law (in 5.17–48), of true worship (in 6.1–18), and of the way of reliance on God and single-minded service (in 6.19—7.27). Often in these chapters the writer contrasts the way of discipleship with the ways that others may follow, the way of the scribes and Pharisees (5.20), the way of those of former times (5.21, 27, 31, 33, 38, 43), the way of hypocrites (6.2, 5, 16), the way of Gentiles (6.7, 32). In the end it says that Jesus 'taught as one who had authority, and not as their scribes' (7.29), and we constantly hear that note of authority, 'You have heard that it was said . . . but I say to you . . .' 'Do not . . . but . . .' For this reason as we encounter the teaching of Jesus in these chapters we inevitably come face to face with the person of Jesus who calls men and women to be his disciples and to live accordingly. We may subdivide these chapters as follows:

## Analysis

5.1–2    Introduction
5.3–12   Qualities of character
5.13–16 Being like salt and light
5.17–20 Jesus' attitude to the Law
5.21–26 Murder
5.27–30 Adultery
5.31–32 Divorce
5.33–37 Oaths

5.38–42 A different way from 'an eye for an eye'
5.43–48 The law of love
6.1–4     Giving to those in need
6.5–15  Praying
6.16–18 Fasting
6.19–21 Treasure in heaven
6.22–23 The healthy eye
6.24     One master
6.25–34 Trusting God
7.1–5    Not judging others
7.6      Honouring what is holy
7.7–11   The potential of prayer
7.12     The golden rule
7.13–14 The two ways
7.15–20 The two kinds of fruit
7.21–23 Sincere and insincere allegiance
7.24–27 The two houses
7.28–29 The conclusion of the teaching

# 5.1–2  Introduction

## See also Luke 6.12, 20

In the way that Matthew presents this teaching, the crowds are in the background, and Jesus is teaching his disciples. Disciples are, in a way, always between Jesus and the crowds of the world. Jesus sat down to teach, as the Jewish rabbis did, and the Gospel says that it was on a mountain that he gave this teaching. A number of times in the Gospel already we have realized that the writer is making a comparison between Jesus and Moses, between Israel in the days in the wilderness and Jesus tempted in the wilderness. Moses received the Law on a mountain, Sinai (according to Exodus 19–20), and gave it to the people. Now on another mountain Jesus gave a new law, a better law, teaching that in fact was more than law.

# 5.3–12  Qualities of Character

## See also Luke 6.20–23

The sayings we have in these verses are often known as the Beatitudes, as *beatus* is the Latin word for 'blessed' with which each verse begins. Some translate the word as 'happy' or 'fortunate'. It is more than happiness in a normal human sense. Rather it has the idea of God blessing a person and giving them a true joy that the world can never give or take away. The form of this teaching, 'Blessed are those . . .' has its background in the Old Testament, in the Law (see Deuteronomy 28.3–6), in the Psalms (see 1.1; 32.1; 41.1), in Proverbs (see 8.32, 34), and the Prophets (see Jeremiah 17.7). It was a form of teaching that people could easily remember.

In Luke 6:20–26 we have a parallel to this, but there are important differences, as there are four 'Blesseds' and four 'Woes' instead of the nine 'Blesseds' here. Some have thought that Matthew changed Luke's form of the teaching, or Luke changed Matthew, or they both changed a common source. But we can also imagine that as Jesus moved from place to place in his teaching, at different times he may have given similar but slightly different forms of these Beatitudes. We can certainly understand both Matthew's and Luke's forms as equally well linked with what we know otherwise of priorities in Jesus' teaching about the life of discipleship. Both are revolutionary. Both are totally different from what the world would call 'blessed', or the way to find happiness through possessions, power and popularity.

The 'poor in spirit' are not simply those who are poor in terms of money. Far from being a blessing, economic poverty can in itself be degrading and make people miserable, although often 'the poor in the world' are 'rich in faith' (James 2.5), and great riches often do not bring people happiness. Jesus loved and cared for the poor (John 13.29), preached the gospel to them (Luke 4.18), and encouraged others to give to them and care for them (Matthew 25.31–46). Therefore this saying includes people who suffer from economic poverty, especially because such people often know the need for absolute trust in God. Furthermore, the Old Testament shows that God has a special concern and interest for the oppressed and poverty-stricken. Gaining the kingdom of God (the 'kingdom of heaven') includes the hope of eliminating the root causes of poverty. However, the 'poor in spirit' are people who know that they are spiritually poor and needy if they do not have the grace of God. In this sense, the beatitude is also meant for those who are rich in material things. The New English Bible translates here, 'How blest are those who know their need of God'. To say that 'theirs is the kingdom of heaven' is like Jesus' teaching that people must become like little children to enter the kingdom of heaven (18.3). We have to recognize our need if we are to receive God's forgiveness and help, God's wisdom and strength, and if we are to live as members of God's kingdom.

'Those who mourn' are next in order among the blessed. What a contradiction of the world's search for happiness! In reality, we do not find happiness by seeking it. It comes to us as a result of a life that truly and deeply satisfies. The picture here is of a person who cares deeply, is sad about his or her own failures, comes close in sympathy and help to those who are broken and hurting in their lives, and grieves for the injustice and oppression there is in the world. Such people find comfort in God's forgiveness of their own wrongs, find joy when someone comforts the sad and discouraged, and in what God is doing to change unjust situations and evil people. The world's pleasures offer no joy and comfort that we can compare with that satisfaction. Psalm 126.5–6 speaks of the kind of sorrow and joy that this beatitude refers to, and the early Christians showed the same spirit when they said it was a privilege to suffer for Christ's sake and with him (Acts 5.41 and 1 Peter 4.13–14). There is comfort now, but the apostle Paul gives us the further picture when he says, 'I consider that the sufferings of this present time are not worth comparing with the glory that is to be revealed to us' (Romans 8.18).

'The meek' are not the weak. The writer uses the same word of Jesus himself (in 11.29 and 21.5). The Old Testament describes Moses as 'meek' (Numbers 12.3) when he refused to stand up for his own rights. It is the opposite of self-centred. Those who are always striving to get their own way or to win their own rights have no time and strength to enjoy the rich inheritance of the earth that God offers to us all (the words here are a quotation of Psalm 37.11). Those who live as God's children and as disciples of Jesus may not have title-deeds of great properties like the rich and powerful in the world, but they enjoy to the full what they have, and are thankful to God for it. They know the truth of Paul's words 'all things are yours, . . . and you are Christ's, and Christ is God's' (1 Corinthians 3.22–23).

'Hunger and thirst for righteousness' comes next. Hunger and thirst are among the strongest human desires. To want righteousness as much as a hungry person wants food and a thirsty person longs for water, is blessed. Righteousness is first a matter of our being put right with God by forgiveness. Then it means our wanting to keep going in the right way in relation to God and to other people. To long for righteousness is to want to see justice in the world, but even more than justice, to see people going on in the right way. If we were to pray with all our hearts, 'your name be hallowed, your kingdom come, your will be done on earth as it is in heaven', that would be expressing a hunger and thirst for righteousness, and there would be no satisfaction or joy greater than seeing God answer that prayer.

Being 'merciful' means both being forgiving and showing kindness to others. The link between forgiving and being forgiven is also in the Lord's Prayer which challenges us to pray, 'Forgive us . . . as we forgive . . .'. God is 'rich in mercy' (Ephesians 2.4), both in his willingness to forgive us, and also in his kindness and patience in dealing with us. When we see ourselves as people in need of forgiveness and often in need of help, we will be more inclined to forgive and help others.

Jesus called his disciples to be 'pure in heart'. The person who is concerned for what others think may try to keep pure in outward actions and in words. The Bible stresses that God looks on the heart (1 Samuel 16.7), and so we must have the ideal of inner purity, single-mindedness of life, and freedom from hypocrisy. People who have this ideal 'will see God'. Beyond this life they will see God in a way that we cannot imagine now, but even in this life they will come to understand more and more what God is like, in greatness, majesty, holiness, love, wisdom and strength.

Next come 'the peacemakers'. One contemporary political leader in the Middle East, who had pursued a policy of military confrontation for many years, turned round to try and make peace, and he said, 'It's much more costly to make peace than to make war.' Sometimes we cannot have peace in this life without denying principles or denying our Lord himself. Jesus knew that, and showed that we must not seek that kind of peace (see 10.34). But most frequently struggles arise through human selfishness and desire for power. Then the disciple of Christ will try to be a peacemaker. And between individuals, groups of people, or nations, true peace must be peace with justice. Such peace is hard to make. But the world desperately needs peacemakers. And we can rightly call peacemakers 'children of God', people who have that measure of God-likeness, because God is a 'God of peace' (Philippians 4.9).

The last is perhaps the most surprising of all the beatitudes. Can it ever be a blessing to be 'persecuted' or to be 'reviled'? To have people 'utter all kinds of evil against you falsely'? It depends on the company. If the company is the faithful prophets and Jesus himself, it soon becomes clear that it is better to face persecution in such company, than to be a persecutor along with a Herod or a powerful king, emperor or president. It is also better to face persecution in such company than to be part of the spectator crowd who lack the courage to stand with either side. It becomes clear too whose is the kingdom of heaven. 'Rejoice and be glad' if you are on that side, Jesus says, and 1 Peter 4.13–14 echoes the words.

# 5.13–16  Being like Salt and Light

## See also Mark 4.21, 9.50; Luke 11.33, 14.34–35

Disciples are to be like salt, and the prime purpose of salt is to give taste to the food we eat. The great Indian Christian Sadhu Sundar Singh explained how salt has to dissolve in the pot of rice if it is to impart flavour to it. 'If it dissolves, its savour spreads through the thousand grains of rice in the pot. Though hidden from sight, we know its presence by the taste. We likewise can serve others only by losing ourselves.' We may well ask how the salt that we use day by day loses its taste. The answer may be that people sometimes added things to salt before they sold it, or that they sometimes washed out much of the genuine salt from the rock salt with its impurities before they sold it. Whatever we may think of this interpretation, it is sadly possible for disciples of Christ to lose the influence that they should have in the world around them. Then as disciples they are 'no longer good for anything'.

This Gospel has already spoken (in 4.16) of the coming of Jesus as the coming of light into the darkness of the world. He could say, 'I am the light of the world' (John 8.12). Then he called his disciples to be as 'the light of the world'. As the purpose of salt is to give taste, the purpose of light is to shine out. At night-time people can see a city on a hill-top and the shining of the lights in its houses and streets can lead them to it. Inside a house it is foolish to have a lamp and put it under a barrel. There it helps no one to see the way or to do anything.

Dietrich Bonhoeffer, who died for his faith in Nazi Germany just before the end of World War II, said, 'A community of Jesus which seeks to hide itself has ceased to follow him.' Someone else put it, 'There can be no such thing as secret discipleship, for either the secrecy destroys the discipleship, or the discipleship destroys the secrecy.' The light shines through the 'good works' of disciples, especially through what they do for others, but Christians must do these works not to glorify themselves, but to bring glory to the Lord whom they serve.

---

## 📖 Study Suggestions

1 What thoughts come to your mind when you think of the word 'pure'? Do you have different thoughts when you add 'in heart' to the thought of purity? See 23.25–26 and Luke 11.37–41 for the warning about outward purity without inner purity. See also how Psalms 24.4; 51.10 and 73.1 emphasize being 'pure in heart'.

2 In what ways do you see Luke 6.20–26 as different from verses 3–12 here, in their meaning, and in the way they would apply both in the time of Jesus and now?

3 Do you think that the blessings Jesus promises in verses 3–10 apply to the present, or to a future life?

4 Which of the 'beatitudes' would you say the parables of Jesus in Luke 10.29–37; 18.9–14 and Matthew 18.23–35 illustrate?

5 How do the words of the Epistles, like 2 Corinthians 4.4–6; Philippians 2.14–15; 1 Peter 2.9 and 1 John 2.7–11 add to what Matthew says here about what it means for Christians to be as light in the world?

6 From your own use of salt what do you think is specially meaningful about this Gospel calling Jesus' disciples 'salt of the earth'? What can we learn also from what Mark 9.50 and Luke 14.34–35 say about salt?

7 Think of all the purposes that light on a dark night serves (for example, to guide, to cheer, to enable us to do what we need to do). In view of this, what should it mean for Christians to be 'the light of the world'?

# 5.17–20 Jesus' Attitude to the Law

## See also Luke 16.17

The whole of the rest of chapter 5 shows us the attitude of Jesus to the Law. First, we have, in this paragraph, three principles, and then we have six examples which illustrate them. It is important to interpret these verses 17–20 by the examples, or we might think Matthew is presenting Jesus as very legalistic, and we might understand the teaching of Jesus in a very different way from the understanding that we have from the other Gospels and from Paul. Here are the three principles:

1 He came 'not to abolish but to fulfil'. People accused Jesus of trying to abolish the Law, especially because of the things that he did on the sabbath. But he came to 'fulfil', and that meant giving the Law its fullest meaning, realizing the purpose that God intended for it.

2 Everything in the Law was important. It is easy for people to be very strict about keeping some parts of the Law but to neglect other parts. It is easy also to be very legalistic about details of the

Law and at the same time to neglect what it really means. We will see how the words of Jesus about oaths in verses 33–37 illustrate this, as does his teaching about the fifth commandment in 15.3–6. Jesus did not honour those who taught others to break the Law, or to find ways of not having to keep it. Rather he honoured those who truly obeyed it and taught others to do so.

3 His standard of righteousness was very different from that of the scribes and Pharisees. He was concerned with the spirit and purpose of the Law and not just the letter of it. To Jesus penitent sinners are the ones who find true righteousness, not those who think they have earned a place in the right with God by what they have done (see Luke 18.9–14).

# 5.21–26 Murder

## See also Luke 12.58–59

The sixth commandment forbade murder (Exodus 20.13 and Deuteronomy 5.17). To Jesus it was not only the act of murder that was wrong in God's sight. He said that the murderous thought also breaks the Law, and so do words that can destroy a person's reputation or self-esteem. It may not be right for us to press the details of the angry or insulting or abusive words, or the particular judgements linked with each. The spirit of the passage is like that of 1 John 3.15, 'All who hate a brother or sister are murderers, and you know that murderers do not have eternal life abiding in them.' There is a practical way to deal with bitter anger and the murderous word, the way of seeking forgiveness and reconciliation; and no gifts are acceptable to God where there is not that reconciliation and forgiveness. These verses tell us to treat the need for reconciliation with the kind of urgency of someone who would seek to deal with a wrong done against another person before it comes to court.

# 5.27–30 *Adultery*

The seventh commandment forbade adultery (Exodus 20.14 and Deuteronomy 5.18). God made us male and female, and sexual relationships are part of God's beautiful creation. But the place for those relationships is in the shared life of a man and a woman with a life-long commitment to each other. Someone commits adultery when they seek sexual relationships with a person already committed in marriage. The act is wrong. The desire for it is also wrong. If someone allows the desire to remain in their heart, it can easily lead to the action. Verses 29–30, though Jesus does not intend his hearers to take them literally, call for radical action in dealing with temptation. There is a repeat of the same demand in 18.8–9 (and see Mark 9.43–48).

# 5.31–32 *Divorce*

## *See also Mark 10.11–12; Luke 16.18*

The Old Testament Law provided for divorce (see Deuteronomy 24.1–4), as any state laws must do, but the teaching of Jesus always presents the highest standard and the highest purpose of God for those who would be his disciples. It had become all too easy in Jesus' time, as in many countries of the world today, for people to get a 'certificate of divorce'. When (in 19.3–9) the Pharisees asked Jesus what were appropriate grounds for divorce, his answer was, 'For your hardness of heart Moses allowed you to divorce your wives, but from the beginning it was not so'. God's highest purpose was a life-long marriage union. Verse 32 says that Jesus believed that the only reason for divorce was 'unchastity'. We have to face two difficulties here:

1  What is the meaning of 'unchastity'? It at least includes unfaithfulness to the marriage relationship, because this is destructive of the partnership that marriage involves. But it can also refer to any

kind of unlawful sexual relationship, that is, sexual relationships outside the bond of marriage.

2 Although Matthew also gives this exception in 19.9, there is no exception in the similar teaching in Mark 10.11–12 and Luke 16.18. Did Jesus give his teaching with no exception, and then did the Church in Matthew's time come to allow this exception? Or did Jesus allow the exception and Mark present a stronger view? The answer may be 'No' to both questions. It is possible to argue that in Jewish law 'unchastity' did not just allow divorce but required divorce to take place, and the wording in Mark may understand this, while Matthew actually states it.

# 5.33–37 Oaths

The word that was spoken to those 'of old' here is what we have in passages like Numbers 30.2 and Deuteronomy 23.21 about keeping true to oaths, vows and promises (see also Psalms 15.4 and 24.4). Leviticus 19.12 gave as the word of the Lord to the people, 'you shall not swear by my name falsely, and so profane the name of your God.' People, however, had come to say that some oaths were more binding than others. If a person said, 'I swear by God . . .', that was more binding than 'I swear by heaven', or 'by earth', or 'by Jerusalem' (see Matthew 23.16–22). This made two different standards of truth. Jesus insisted that truth was truth. Heaven and earth and Jerusalem were all part of God's creation. Jesus' disciples must have only one standard of truth. If people are trustworthy their word should be enough and they should not need to add any oath.

Christians have sometimes taken this to mean that they should not take an oath when the state requires it, as in a court of law. That is not the point. People can do that if the law requires it, but in our ordinary relationships we do not need to make any oaths. A simple statement of the truth is enough. (See how James 5.12 repeats this teaching.)

# 5.38–42 *A Different Way from 'an Eye for an Eye'*

## See also Luke 6.29–30

The Old Testament had the law that said literally 'an eye for an eye' and 'a tooth for a tooth' (see Exodus 21.22–25; Leviticus 24.19–20 and Deuteronomy 19.21). It was a law which, like the earlier law code of Hammurabi, required justice and prevented people from taking revenge and inflicting much greater damage for a wrong done. Laws in our countries today may not require 'an eye for an eye and a tooth for a tooth', but there are just penalties for assault and other crimes. What Jesus is speaking about here is the way of life that his disciples should follow. They will refuse to take revenge in any way. They will think more of giving than getting. Even when people treat them unjustly they will act with good will and not just try to get their own back (see an application of this in 1 Corinthians 6.1–8). As with so much of Jesus' teaching, we must follow the spirit of it rather than give a literal sense that he did not intend. If we took verse 42 absolutely literally it could mean that all Christians would finish up with no possessions at all! At the same time, we must face the challenge of the spirit of this demanding teaching.

# 5.43–48 *The Law of Love*

## See also Luke 6.27–28, 32–36

The Old Testament Law certainly said people should love their neighbours (Leviticus 19.18). There was no command to hate one's enemies, though people sometimes spoke of hating those who did evil or who worked against the purposes of God. The way of Christ is, above everything else, the way of love. We are to love enemies and pray for persecutors, even as Jesus prayed for those who nailed him to the cross (Luke 23.34). This is a way that is totally different from the world's way. People, whoever they are, Jesus said, have no special difficulty in loving those who love them and greeting as friends those who greet them. It is a harder way to which Jesus calls his disciples, but it is a God-like way, since God 'makes his sun rise on the evil and on the good, and sends rain on the just and on the unjust'. To respond to the call to 'be perfect' as God is, means neither more nor less than having for ourselves the highest standards, however much we may fail again and again to keep to them.

---

## 📖 Study Suggestions

1 The words Jesus quotes in verse 22, different in different English translations, are words of insult and abuse. How do people think of evil words in your situation, and what words in particular could they understand as doing harm to a person?

2 The word English versions translate as 'perfect' in verse 48 also appears in 19.21; 1 Corinthians 14.20 and Philippians 3.15. What do you think it means to try to be 'perfect'? The parallel to this verse in Luke 6.36 uses the word 'merciful'; how does that link with 'perfect'?

3 In the terms of verse 17, and in other ways, how do you think that the law and the prophets are 'fulfilled' in Jesus?

4 How does the teaching of 19.3–9, and especially the use of Genesis 1.27 and 2.24, throw light on what Jesus says about marriage and about adultery?

5 Compare what this passage says about oaths with 23.16–22. Are there double standards of truth in your culture according to the ways in which people say things?

6 In what ways does 1 John develop the teaching about love and hatred in these verses? See especially 1 John 2.7–11; 3.10–18 and 4.16–21.

7 Look up the parallel to the teaching of verses 39–48 in Luke 6.27–36. In what ways are Matthew and Luke similar and in what ways different?

8 Do you think that what Paul says in 1 Corinthians 6.1–8 about Christians not having lawsuits against each other is a fair application of the principles of verses 38–42?

9 How should Christians in your society seek to uphold and teach Christian standards of marriage, and yet act with compassion towards those who have not had those standards, or whose marriages have broken down?

10 In what ways is it necessary that the laws of any nation should
be different from the principles that guide the lifestyle of
Christians? Should there be any difference in the ways that
Christians act as citizens of a country and in normal social life,
and the way that they act towards their fellow-Christians?

## ADDITIONAL NOTE E: IS MATTHEW ANTI-JEWISH?

Verse 20 has spoken of the way that the righteousness of Jesus' disciples must 'exceed that of the scribes and Pharisees'. As we go
through this Gospel we will find much more that is critical of the
scribes and the Sadducees and Pharisees. This has led some to say
that Matthew is the most anti-Jewish of the Gospels. So there is a
fear that people could use it to strengthen anti-Jewish feelings
today. Sadly, over the centuries, Christians have sometimes used
the Gospel to justify anti-Jewish attitudes and actions. This is
wrong. It was not what the Gospel intended and it misinterprets
the context of the Gospel. The author of Matthew's Gospel was
almost certainly a Jew and he wrote it mainly for Jewish Christians. Although Mark explains Jewish terms and customs, Matthew does not do so (as chapters 15 and 23 specially show). Was it
then that the Gospel dates from a time when there was conflict
between the Church and the Synagogue, between Christians and
the Jews who had not become Christians? Some have thought that
this was the case. About the year 85 the Jewish religious authorities finally excluded Christians from synagogue worship and
added a curse on 'Nazirites and heretics' (that is, Christians) to the
synagogue liturgy. Yet the issues of those times were not the same
as those of the time of Jesus' own ministry. Jesus was concerned
about people observing the sabbath according to the spirit of the
law rather than the letter, and in other ways he opposed legalism.
We read also his criticisms of the Sadducees, but they were no
longer a party with any importance after the fall of Jerusalem in
the year 70. It seems more likely that we have a true indication of
the differences between Jesus and the Jewish religious leaders in
the time of his ministry, and the Gospel records them, not with
anti-Jewish feeling, but for their warning to Christians, and especially Christian leaders, not to follow the way of the scribes, the
Pharisees and Sadducees, in the particular respects that the Gospel
mentions.

# 6.1–4 Giving to Those in Need

We have seen that while 5.17–48 shows the attitude of Jesus to the Law, 6.1–18 shows his attitude to those practices which were the outward expression of life lived in the service of God. Some English translations use the word 'piety' in verse 1. The Good News Bible has 'your religious duties'. It is really the same word 'righteousness' which we find in relation to the Law in 5.20. This part of chapter 6 speaks of three duties: giving to the poor, praying, and fasting. The three sections (verses 2–4, 5–6 and 16–18) are parallel, as they begin, 'When you give alms . . .'; 'When you pray . . .'; 'When you fast . . .'. The teaching each time is the same. We are not to do it, as 'hypocrites' do it, in order for other people to see us and praise us, but for God to see us. Worship means the offering of what we do to God. When the person who gives or prays or fasts is the centre of attention rather than God, it is no longer worship. We cannot seek the glory of God and our own glory at the same time.

Sometimes it is not possible completely to avoid the attention of others when we give to the poor or to the life of the Church, but the principle is clear. We are not to do it so as to gain attention. In verse 2, as again in verses 5 and 16, the writer uses a word in the Greek that people put on receipts that they gave for payments made, 'received', 'they have received their reward'. The idea is that if we carry out our giving or praying or fasting so that other people can see us, their praise will be our full reward or payment. We, as it were, have our receipt for it. There will be no approval from God who sees and knows all that we do, and knows perfectly the motives for our actions.

# 6.5–15  *Praying*

## *See also Mark 11.25–26; Luke 11.2–4*

This section first says the same things about our praying as verses 2–4 have said about giving. We are not to do it to 'be seen by others'. Personal prayer should be in private, addressed to God alone, and never done to make other people think that we are very religious. Of course, there is prayer that we do with others, whether with our families or in church. Others will see that, but the principle is that we are not to pray or go to church in order for other people to see us and think well of us. Where Christians face persecution for their faith and for meeting together as Christians, this is hardly a problem!

The second part of the teaching here on prayer is that it is not to be a matter of 'heaping up empty phrases' and using 'many words'. That means that the test of a true prayer is not its length, or the number of times we say it. Prayers do not work in any magical way. Prayer is bringing to God our lives and the lives of others, things to thank him for, things that are needed. Our heavenly Father, who knows the hearts and situations of all, knows what we need, but by our prayer we show that we depend on him and look to him to meet our needs.

Then we have what we speak of as 'the Lord's Prayer'. It is also in Luke 11.2–4 in words slightly different from those here in Matthew. There are small variations also in different early manuscripts of the New Testament, probably because people used the prayer in slightly different forms in the early Church just as they do in the life of the Church today. In Luke 11.1 it says that Jesus gave it when the disciples came to him and said, 'Lord, teach us to pray'. Jewish people used many of the parts of the prayer, but they did not draw them together and put them in the order that we have in the Lord's Prayer. We can imagine that Jesus may often have taught the disciples the way to pray in terms like these, and there are certainly tremendous lessons about prayer in the few sentences of this wonderful prayer.

1  It addresses God as 'Father', because we come to him as children would come to an earthly parent, bringing their needs or requests. We have a relationship with God because of his acceptance of us (see John 1.12 and Romans 8.14–17), and on the basis of that we come. It is not just an individual relationship. God is 'our' Father. We come with our sisters and brothers in mind and their needs and not just our own.

2  Then before we talk about our own needs, the prayer teaches us to

think of God's name, God's kingdom, and God's will. God's name means all that Scripture reveals about who God is, and so when we pray for his name to be hallowed, we are praying that we and others will honour him for who he is. That is like having a reminder at the beginning of our praying of what Jesus, like the Old Testament, said was the first and greatest commandment, to love God with heart and soul and mind and strength (22.37). Then the prayer for the coming of God's kingdom is the prayer that he will rule in our lives and the lives of others. In practice this means doing God's will. God has his will and purpose for every human life, and nothing could be better than that for any of us (see Romans 12.1–2). We can never ask anything better than that God's will might be done in our lives and in the lives of others, and as perfectly as it is done in heaven.

3 The first human need to be brought to God then in prayer is for our 'daily bread'. For people in Palestine in the time of Jesus bread was literally the staple diet. Ours may be different, but in this prayer we ask God for our immediate physical needs. It is a prayer that rich and poor people alike can pray. We are not to pray for luxuries or expect them from God. And we are not to pray for what may be our needs far ahead in the future, but what we need for today. There is more later in the chapter about our trusting God like that to provide for us what he sees that we need.

4 Then we have spiritual needs, and the first of these is forgiveness. The Bible constantly shows that sin is the one great barrier between us and God. If we are to know and to keep a right relationship with God, it can only be by our asking forgiveness for every sin that we commit. But we, when we say this prayer sincerely, make our request for forgiveness only on the basis of our forgiving others. In fact, the words put on our lips are, 'as we also have forgiven'. Verses 14 and 15 at the end of this section make this teaching abundantly plain, as does Jesus' parable of the two debtors in 18.23–35 (see also Mark 11.25).

5 People have been puzzled by the words of the next clause, 'lead us not into temptation', or as other translations put it, 'do not bring us to the time of trial'. Does God tempt us? It is certainly true that God never tries to persuade us to sin (see James 1.13–15), but he does allow us to face the tests and trials of life in order to strengthen our faith and purify our Christian lives (see 1 Peter 1.67). What we are asking is that nothing will bring us into temptation too strong for us, but that God will strengthen us and 'deliver us from evil' (or we could take it as rescue us from 'the evil one'). This was Jesus' own prayer for his disciples, as in John 17.15 he said, 'My prayer is not that you take them out of the world but that you protect them from the evil one' (New International Version).

6 Our Bible translations differ as to whether or not they have at the end of the prayer, 'For thine is the kingdom and the power and the glory for ever'. This is because some early manuscripts have these words and some do not. It was common for Jewish prayers to have that kind of doxology, and even if it were not written in the prayer, it might be said. Such praise of God is always appropriate, as it is always right to confess his great glory, the fact that all power belongs to him, and he is King and Lord over all.

# 6.16–18 Fasting

The Jewish people had a special annual fast on the Day of Atonement (Leviticus 16.29–31), and they kept other fast days too. Many Jews fasted every Monday and Thursday. Jesus was not against fasting, although when some people criticized his disciples for not fasting like the disciples of John and the Pharisees, he gave a good reason why they should not fast at that time (see 9.14–17). The self-denial of fasting should lead people to a humbler dependence on God. But people go further away from God rather than closer to him when they perform their religious practices so that others can see them.

## 📖 Study Suggestions

1 What do you understand by the word 'hypocrite'? How do these verses and 7.1–5, 15.7–9 and 23.13–36 illustrate what it means? In what ways are Christian people today in danger of hypocrisy?
2 How does the Old Testament background, speaking of the 'name' of God, help us to appreciate the meaning of praying, 'hallowed be your name'? Consider especially Psalms 5.11; 7.17; 9.10; 20.1; 22.22; 44.20; 74.10; 116.4; 148.13 and Proverbs 18.10.
3 What does it mean in the Lord's Prayer when it speaks of sins to be forgiven as 'debts'?
4 If we understand that God knows what we need before we pray, what reasons are there for prayer, and, in particular, for telling God of our needs?

5 Is there a right place in the Christian life for thinking of rewards and expecting rewards from God? As well as these verses see 5.12, 10.41 and the parables in 25.14–30 and 31–46.

6 What do we learn about what may be the place of fasting in the Christian life from such New Testament passages as Acts 13.1–3 and 14.23?

7 How does Mark 12.41–44 add to or illustrate the teaching of Jesus here about giving?

8 In your church situation are there practices in relation to giving to the poor or to the Church which need to face the challenge of the teaching of this passage? How should people act so as to avoid publicity in giving?

9 What motives do you think people have for giving to the poor or giving to good causes in the community? Which of these are worthy motives?

10 How do 1 Kings 18.26 and Acts 19.34 illustrate verse 7? Are there ways of Christian or non-Christian praying in your community that involve just 'empty phrases' and 'many words'?

# 6.19–21  Treasure in Heaven

## See also Luke 12.33–34

Following the parts of the Sermon dealing with the Law (5.17–48) and worship (6.1–18), the rest of the Sermon deals with single-minded service and trust in God. Many of the sections present the two ways from which all people must choose. Much of the teaching in these sections is in the form of poetry, like the Psalms, the Proverbs and much of the teaching of the Prophets. In this poetic form there are often two statements that say the same thing in slightly different words, or present two opposite ways, as in these verses. There is the choice between two sets of values, between earthly possessions and heavenly possessions. Earthly possessions may be clothes that moths can eat, or things that rust or corrode, or jewellery or other treasures that thieves can steal. On the other hand, there are things that moths cannot eat, things that cannot rust or corrode, and that thieves can never steal. They are the spiritual qualities of life, spiritual gifts, the gift of life itself in relationship with God. Nothing in life or even in death can take these away.

The human heart is always set on one kind of treasure or the other, and the mind-set or the heart-set will always determine the way a person lives. Jesus made this same teaching very vivid in his parable of the rich man in Luke 12.13–21, and James 5.1–5 takes up some of the words of Jesus that we have here.

# 6.22–23 The Healthy Eye

## See also Luke 11.34–36

Jesus in his teaching often spoke about light. Luke's parallel (11.34–36) to the teaching here is linked with what Matthew 5.15 has about the lamp being put on a lampstand. The eye is the lamp of the body in the sense that the way that we see things makes all the difference to the way we speak or act. The eye has to be 'sound' or 'healthy', or 'single' as more literal translations put it. It thus speaks of the single-mindedness which the Sermon on the Mount emphasized constantly. Linking it with the last section, we can say that if we are always looking at things from the point of view of their value as earthly possessions, we will not be thinking of loving God or of loving other people. We will not be generous with what we have, but want to keep it to ourselves. 1 John 2.11 says that when we do not love others we are in fact going about in the darkness, or we are like blind people. Without love we never see other people as they really are. If we have love for God and love for other people, then that is like light filling our whole lives. When we shut out that light which comes from God, 'how great is the darkness!'

# 6.24 One Master

*See also Luke 16.13*

It is hard to be employed by two people and have two jobs to do. In New Testament times with the institution of slavery, people who were slaves belonged to their masters with all their time and everything that they had. So it was not only hard, but quite impossible, to serve two masters. The uncompromising teaching of Jesus says that it is equally impossible really to serve God and at the same time to have wealth as our master. The word 'mammon' that is kept in most translations is simply the word for money in the Aramaic language, which was the language that Jesus spoke. If money is most important in people's lives, then things will become more important than people, and any desire to serve God will be lost. As 1 Timothy 6.10 puts it, 'the love of money is a root of all kinds of evil. Some people, eager for money, have wandered from the faith and pierced themselves with many griefs' (New International Version).

# 6.25–34 Trusting God

*See also Luke 12.22–31*

As we read these verses (paralleled in Luke 12.22–31), it is valuable to remember that probably they were first addressed to people with a very simple lifestyle, probably many of them quite poor – not to people with a home, a car, a well-paid job and money in the bank. Yet what Jesus said about trusting God and not being anxious can be applied to all. Notice seven things in the teaching here:

1 There is a clear command, 'do not worry', not even about food and drink nor clothes to wear, the basic essentials of life.

2 Life is more important than food and the body than the clothes it wears. This may seem a hard thing to say to those who don't know whether they have enough to feed and clothe their families. But it is not saying, 'Just think about spiritual things and not material things.' It is saying, 'Your life matters to God.'

3 God cares for the birds. God cares for the flowers. 'Are you not of more value than they?' You are people God has made in his image and for a higher purpose than the birds and the flowers, beautiful though they are and important to God.

4 Worrying never helps. The New Revised Standard Version takes verse 27 as, 'can any of you by worrying add a single hour to your span of life?' Otherwise it could mean that you cannot add to your height by worrying. How does worrying ever help us in anything?

5 It is the way of the world to worry and strive. Verse 32 speaks of the 'Gentiles', meaning those who do not know themselves as God's people. Those who realize that they are children of God, and that God is always with them, should not worry. They realize that they have a heavenly Father who knows all their needs and cares for them.

6 One thing matters most for those who are disciples of Jesus: to seek first for the kingdom of God and God's righteousness. These words in verse 33 are like the teaching on prayer in the Lord's Prayer – put first God's name, God's kingdom, God's will. Then we can trust God with everything else.

7 One day at a time is enough to think about. Jesus does not promise an easy life. Every day brings its difficulties and problems, but we should not try and face tomorrow's difficulties and problems today. 'Let the day's own trouble be sufficient for the day.'

> I have today – yes, just today
> to work and pray;
> tomorrow is a dream unborn
> and yesterday
> is gone for ever from my hand.
> I have today.
>
> (Joan Suisted)

---

## 📖 Study Suggestions

1 What sort of activity does the word 'seek' bring to your mind?

2 How does this relate to verse 33, and also to what 7.7–8; 13.45 and 18.12 say?

3 In Matthew it is always disciples who are called 'little-faith' people. In what ways do 6.30; 8.26; 14.31 and 16.8 suggest that disciples should have more faith?

4 Follow out what other parts of the New Testament say about
the worth of earthly riches compared with the worth of spiritual riches. See Matthew 13.44–46; Luke 12.21 (which comes
just before a close parallel with the teaching of Matthew
6.25–34), Luke 18.18–30; 1 Timothy 6.6–19 and Hebrews
11.23–26.

5 How does the New Testament teach that either to worry about
tomorrow or to boast about tomorrow are wrong attitudes to
the future ? With verse 34 see Philippians 4.4–7; 1 Peter 5.7 and
James 4.13–16.

6 In what different ways do you think the words of verses 22–23
apply to the way we see things in life, or to what catches our
eye and our attention most from day to day?

7 What does this whole section (verses 19–34) indicate about
what it means to know God both as heavenly Master and as
heavenly Father?

8 How should we understand 'treasures in heaven' (verse 20)?

9 In ministering to others how should we deal with anxiety in
the poor, and in the rich?

10 How do we rightly relate the teaching of this section to the fact
that there are millions of people in the world who are starving,
and to the fact that many who have trusted in God have been
allowed to suffer and die for their faith?

# 7.1–5  Not Judging Others

## See also Luke 6.37–38, 41–42

Judging others means looking for faults in other people and condemning them for them. When we spend time and energy seeking
and drawing attention to the faults of others we are usually blind to
our own faults. There are four aspects in this teaching of Jesus:

1 The direct command, 'Do not judge'.
2 The warning that inasmuch as we judge others we will be judged.
It works out often in life that what we give we get, the treatment
we give to others will come back on ourselves. Ultimately in the

justice of God that will be so. In 6.14–15 this has been applied to forgiving or refusing to forgive others.

3 When we judge others we are – to use Jesus' humorous description – like a person with a log in his or her eye trying to take a speck of dust out of someone else's eye. In other words, we don't think of our own big faults but give all our attention to other people's smaller faults.

4 There is a place for helping other people with their faults and weaknesses, but only when we are aware of our own. The spirit of this is expressed in the words of the apostle Paul in Galatians 6.1, 'if someone is caught in a sin, you who are spiritual should restore such a one in a spirit of gentleness. But watch yourself, lest you also be tempted.'

# 7.6 *Honouring what is Holy*

The teaching for disciples was that they are not to judge others in the sense of fault-finding and condemning, but there is need of discernment of people, as the words of this verse show. If people just laugh at what we value as heavenly treasures (6.20), we are not to give them opportunity to trample on those things and take advantage of us. An example of what is meant is the kind of situation where the enemies of Christians have come into their services or gatherings and used what they have heard without any spiritual understanding to mock and even persecute them.

Sometimes this will happen whatever Christians try to do, but where they can avoid it happening they should do so.

# *7.7–11  The Potential of Prayer*

## *See also Luke 11.9–13*

This section speaks of prayer in the three ways of asking, seeking, knocking:

1 Many times Scripture encourages us to ask from God the things that we need. When we ask we show that we know that we rely on God to meet our needs.
2 Prayer is also seeking, or searching. When we think of discoveries in science or in the world around us, we realize that those discoveries have been made by those who have been willing to give time and trouble to search. In the spiritual life there is also a place for searching to know God better, to know the will of God and the purpose of God, and to know what he wishes to do in those concerns in life that we bring to him.
3 When we meet a closed door, it may not mean that we are not intended to go in. It may invite us to knock and have it opened to us. In dealing with people Jesus sometimes encouraged them to be persistent, and in this way their faith grew (see 15.21–28 and Luke 18.1–8).

Jesus pictures a child asking its father for bread or fish (the most common things of Galilean people's diet), and it would be a terrible father who would give a stone instead of bread and a snake instead of fish. Those of us who are parents are not always such good parents as we ought to be. We are all evil in our different ways. Some people have had such an unhappy experience of fatherhood that they might find it difficult to think of God as Father. But God is truly wise and good and loving, as well as all-powerful, the perfect example of fatherhood. So we can always come to him knowing that he will always 'give good things to those who ask him'. In fact often he will give far better than we ask because we are not always wise in our asking.

# 7.12 The Golden Rule

## See also Luke 6.31

In many parts of the world people know the negative form of this rule: 'Don't do to others what you wouldn't like them to do to you.' The Jewish rabbi Hillel said, 'What is hateful to you, don't do to your fellow.' The positive is more powerful than the negative, and calls for generosity and genuine love. Think of any situation where you might need the help of others. What you would like them to do for you in that situation is a guide to the way that you should act to help others.

---

### Study Suggestions

1 What situations in life do the words 'ask', 'search' and 'knock' bring to your mind? How do these situations help in thinking about prayer and about Christian living generally?
2 In what ways do you think that the 'golden rule' in verse 12 is the teaching of 'the law and the prophets'?
3 The teaching that we have here in 7.1–12 is also in Luke 6.37–42 and 11.5–13. What can we learn from the way that Luke presents it and the settings of it there?
4 Compare the teaching here about not judging others with that in Paul's and James's letters, especially Romans 2.1–11; 14.1–13; 1 Corinthians 4.1–7 and James 4.11–12.
5 In what situations known to you do you see an application of what verse 6 says?
6 Which do you find easier, to criticize others or to accept their criticism? Note the teaching of the Book of Proverbs (6.23; 10.17; 12.1; 13.18 and 15.31–33) in the Old Testament about the wisdom of accepting the reproof or criticism of others.

---

# *7.13–14 The Two Ways*

## *See also Luke 13.23–24*

Each of the remaining sections of the Sermon presents the choice between two ways. There is a strong Old Testament background for this. The Law, especially the Book of Deuteronomy, did this. It spoke of the 'blessing' of obedience and the 'curse' of disregarding the Law, and the two ways were expressed dramatically in a ceremony on Mount Gerizim and Mount Ebal (Deuteronomy 27—30). The Psalms often speak of the two ways, most clearly of all the very first Psalm. The Book of Proverbs often contrasts the way of the 'fool' and the way of the 'wise'. The prophets did the same, and like Deuteronomy, Jeremiah puts it in the word of the Lord, 'I set before you the way of life and the way of death' (Jeremiah 21.8 and see Jeremiah 17.5–8).

In these words of Jesus there are four differences in the two ways:

1 The entrance to one is 'narrow', to the other is 'wide'. It is easier to go on in one's self-chosen, self-centred ways than to determine to deny self and follow Jesus.
2 One road is itself 'easy' – or perhaps we should translate it 'spacious', having plenty of room for all – and the other is 'hard'. The way of discipleship is often difficult, with trials and sorrows that Jesus made clear to his disciples that they must face.
3 The goals are different – the goal of the one road is 'life' in the full meaning that the Gospels give to the word; at the end of the other road life is lost.
4 There is a difference between the numbers on the road, the 'many' and the 'few'. It is clear in the teaching of Jesus, however, especially from such a passage as Luke 13.23–24 that we are not to speculate on the numbers or to judge who are the 'saved'. To the question, 'Lord, will those who are saved be few?' Jesus gives an answer that emphasizes the questioner's own responsibility, 'Strive to enter by the narrow door.' In other words, you are to give attention to what you do, not to judge what others are doing.

# 7.15–20  The Two Kinds of Fruit

## *See also Luke 6.43–45*

This section begins with a warning about those who wrongly profess to be messengers of God's word. In the Old Testament there were true prophets and false prophets, and there was a need for guidance to enable people to see the difference between them (see Deuteronomy 13.1–5; 18.15–22; and Jeremiah 23.9–40). In the days of the early Church believers needed the warning about false prophets (see Matthew 24.4–5, 11 and 23–24). The disciples of Jesus have always needed the warning. They are not to judge in the way of being deliberately critical of others (verses 1–5), but they are to be discerning. The shepherd of the flock may wear a sheepskin, but some who do this actually seek to harm the flock of God like wolves. The test is, 'You will know them by their fruits.' In other words their lifestyle, character and actions will show the difference. Again a simple parable illustrates the meaning. You get fruit from a tree according to what the tree is in its very nature. There is a difference also between a tree that is essentially good and will surely produce good fruit, and a tree that is bad and diseased, and such a tree will not be able to produce good fruit at all (compare 12.33).

# 7.21–23  Sincere and Insincere Allegiance

## *See also Luke 6.46, 13.26–27*

At times in his ministry many people honoured Jesus and were prepared to address him as 'Lord, Lord' and say that they wanted to be his disciples, but not all who did so really followed him. The next chapter tells of one who said, 'Teacher, I will follow you wherever you go', and in response Jesus had to question whether he was truly willing and able to do that (8.19–20). It is the true follower who enters the kingdom of heaven. It is interesting also to link the words here with those of the Lord's Prayer that Jesus taught in this Sermon (6.9–13). There the prayer for the coming of God's kingdom is followed by asking for the will of God to be done. So here Jesus makes it clear that belonging to the kingdom is a matter of doing God's will.

Some will claim to have been prophets, exorcists and miracle workers. Some will claim to have said much and done many things in his name, but Jesus will not acknowledge them as the Lord's own, when in reality they have been 'evildoers' rather than doers of the will of God.

# 7.24–27 The Two Houses

## See also Luke 6.47–49

The teaching of the Sermon – and especially the last few sections on the two ways – ends with this simple but powerful parable about the building of two houses. Both had to face all the storms that came. One stood firm and the other fell. The difference was in the foundations. Jesus compares the difference between the two builders to that between two people. Both hear the words of Jesus, but one hears 'and does them', while the other hears and 'does not do them'. The parallel in Luke 6.47–49 follows what in Luke is the equivalent to Matthew's verse 21: 'Why do you call me "Lord, Lord" and not do what I tell you?' In the Epistle of James, which has many links with the Sermon on the Mount, there is the counsel, 'be doers of the word, and not hearers only, deceiving yourselves' (James 1.22).

# 7.28–29 *The Conclusion of the Teaching*

We have seen already that the conclusion here is like that at the end of all the sections of teaching in the Gospel (see 11.1, 13.53, 19.1 and 26.1), 'when Jesus finished these sayings . . .' Then the record says that people 'were astonished at his teaching, for he taught them as one who had authority, and not as their scribes'. (This is what we read also in Mark 1.22, and now as we go on to chapters 8 and 9 we are to find close parallels to Mark.) Between Jewish rabbis and Jesus there was a great difference, both in teaching style and above all in the authority they assumed. We can read the Jewish rabbinic teaching collected in the Mishnah and the Talmud. They are later than the time of Jesus, but include the teaching of rabbis of many earlier generations. They constantly quote the authority of other rabbis. They rarely speak with the essential authority that we have seen right through this Sermon, the authority of absolute statements of principle, the authority of 'I say to you', the call to hear 'my words' and do them.

---

 **Study Suggestions**

1 The word English versions translate 'Lord' in verses 21 and 22 is a proper one for addressing God, but sometimes it is just a polite way of addressing a person, like 'Sir' in English, and there are all the stages of meaning in between. Which do you think is closer to the meaning the Gospel writer intends in 8.2, 6, 21, 25; 9.28; 11.25; 13.27; 14.30; 17.4 and 25.37?

2 We find the word English versions translate 'astonished' in verse 28 also in Matthew 13.54; 19.25 and 22.33. What are the feelings this word describes, and what were the causes of such feelings in these four places?

3 The Bible says a great deal about the difference between the 'fool' or 'foolish person' (as in verse 26) and the 'wise'. What does it say are the characteristics of the fool, and by contrast, the wise? See Psalm 14.1; Proverbs 1.5; 14.3, 8 and 16; Luke 12.16–20; Romans 1.21–23.

4 In what different ways does this Sermon in chapters 5–7 show the authority of the teaching of Jesus?

5 Follow through the references given in the discussion of 7.1–5

to 'false prophets'. See in the different situations in what ways these people were false prophets, and see also what kinds of false prophets the New Testament speaks about in Acts 13.6; 2 Peter 2.1–3 and 1 John 4.1. In what ways do Christian people today need to be aware of the danger of 'false prophets'?

6 What are things which people today might claim to be doing 'in the name' of Christ (as in verse 22), and at the same time be living a life contrary to the will of God?

# PART 3: 8.1—9.38
# NARRATIVE: MIRACLES
# OF HEALING

All the Gospels show Jesus as 'mighty in deed and word' (Luke 24.19). In Matthew chapters 5—7 we have seen the grace and the authority of Jesus in his 'word', as the record has displayed his teaching. Now we see grace and authority in 'deed', in his actions (see how these chapters speak of 'authority' in 8.9 and 9.6 and 8). In chapters 8 and 9 we have three sets of three incidents where people saw the power of Jesus in action, and frequently faith is the right response to what Jesus was doing. Then between the first and second set and between the second and third set we have teaching about what it means to 'follow' Jesus (we have the word for 'follow' in 8.1, 10, 19, 22, 23; 9.9, 19 and 27). Most of the incidents that Matthew records here are also in Mark, but there are two kinds of differences. Sometimes there is a difference in order, as Matthew has his own plan for drawing things together, as we have seen in chapters 5—7. Also Matthew's narratives are usually shorter than Mark's, often leaving out Mark's vivid descriptions, and concentrating on the words and actions of Jesus.

We may subdivide this section as follows:

## Analysis

8.1–4    The healing of a leper
8.5–13   The healing of a centurion's servant
8.14–17  Healings at Capernaum (with a summary of Jesus' healing ministry)
8.18–22  The cost of following Jesus
8.23–27  The calming of the storm
8.28–34  Exorcisms in Gadara
9.1–8    Forgiving and healing a paralysed man
9.9–13   The call of Matthew, and Jesus eating with tax collectors
9.14–17  Jesus' response to a question about fasting
9.18–26  Raising a young girl to life and healing a woman

9.27–31 Restoring the sight of two blind men
9.32–34 Another exorcism – a dumb man
9.35–38 The greatness of the harvest, the fewness of the labourers
(leading on to chapter 10)

# *8.1–4 The Healing of a Leper*

## *See also Mark 1.40–45; Luke 5.12–16*

Mark and Luke also record this incident. Matthew's account is briefer. He links it with the end of 'the Sermon on the Mount' ('when he came down from the mountain') and says it took place in the presence of great crowds of people.

It is not certain whether everything that the Bible calls leprosy is the same as what we know as leprosy today (Hansen's disease). People who have leprosy today can be completely cured with medical treatment, and there is no need to keep those with the disease far away from other people.

Some things, however, are very clear about what it meant for a person in Old Testament times or in the time of Jesus to have leprosy:

1 The person had to live apart from other people, and even when other people approached had to shout 'Unclean' to warn them not to come near (Leviticus 13.45–46).
2 It was not just a most unpleasant disease, but it made a person unclean from the point of view of not being able to take part in normal social and religious life.
3 If a person was healed of leprosy he or she had to go to the priests (as health officers) to get them to declare him or her clean (Leviticus 14).

This man came very humbly to Jesus, but also with faith. His hesitation was whether such a person as he was had any claim on Jesus or right even to ask him to help. So he said, 'if you will, you can make me clean.'

Jesus must have startled the crowds by his response, a response in word and action. 'I will', he said, but he also 'stretched out his hand, and touched' the unclean leper. Mark says that it was because Jesus was 'moved with pity' that he acted as he did. Then, not wanting the people to proclaim him far and wide as a miracle-worker, Jesus said that the man should not tell others what had happened. He had to do just what the law required, to show himself to the priest. The New Revised Standard Version translates the words at the end of verse 4, 'as a testimony to them'. This may have meant a proof that the man was certainly healed, or showed that Jesus respected the Old Testament law, or perhaps the testimony was to the work of the kingdom of God that Jesus was doing.

📖 **Study Suggestions**

1 How do you understand the wider use of the word 'witness', especially of the witness that should be borne by those who find life and healing in Christ (10.18, 24.14 and Acts 1.8)?
2 Why do you think that Jesus told the man whom he cleansed of leprosy to 'say nothing to anyone' about it? How does this link with similar instructions in 9.30; 12.16; 16.20 and 17.9?
3 How do you compare the attitude to Jesus of the person who said, 'If you choose, you can help me' (8.2) and that of the person who said, 'If you are able to do anything, have pity on us and help us' (Mark 9.22)?
4 How do people in your area react to a disease, like leprosy or AIDS, that they greatly fear? What is the right Christian attitude?

# 8.5–13  The Healing of a Centurion's Servant

## See also Luke 7.1–10

Of special significance in the last section was the fact that Jesus was willing to touch and heal one who had leprosy whom other people would not go near. Here what Jesus does is done for a Gentile. The man was a 'centurion', a junior officer in the army (literally one who commanded 100 soldiers). He may not have been a Roman, but perhaps was in the local army that the Roman authorities allowed Herod Antipas to keep. He certainly was a Gentile, as verses 10–12 make clear, and Luke's record of this incident says that Jewish elders came to Jesus on the centurion's behalf.

This passage says three noteworthy things about this centurion:

1 He had a great concern for his slave. In a society in which slavery was an institution many masters and mistresses had little care for their slaves. If one died they could get another. This centurion

cared deeply that his slave was 'paralysed' and 'in terrible distress'. Forgetful of himself and his own position, he sought a way to find healing for him and so came to Jesus.

2  He showed remarkable faith. He thought of his own situation and his ability to tell his soldiers and his slave what to do and they would do it. Because he was himself 'under authority', he was able to act with the authority of the ruler whose agent he was. Jesus, he thought, must be like that. He is able to heal because he has the authority of God behind him. He sensed a truth that few others had come to appreciate.

3  He came very humbly. The world might see him as an important and powerful person as an army officer. He said, 'I am not worthy to have you come under my roof.' He perhaps specially thought of the way Jewish people regarded Gentiles.

The attitude and words of Jesus bring out things that find special emphasis in Matthew: the unbelief of so many in Israel, and the opening of the door of the kingdom to Gentiles. Jesus could say of this centurion, 'not even in Israel have I found such faith'. The man was thus a forerunner of those who would inherit the kingdom that God promised first to Abraham and Isaac and Jacob, a forerunner of those who would believe when Jesus' followers went out to east and west to make disciples of all nations (28.18–20). Those who should have been 'heirs of the kingdom' would lose the blessings that had been within their grasp. (Compare the words of Jesus in Luke 13.28–29.) The Gospel speaks of their judgement in the traditional terms of 'outer darkness', 'weeping and gnashing of teeth' (compare 22.13; 24.51; 25.30 and see Psalm 112.10).

---

### 📖 Study Suggestions

1  For our own attitudes to other people, what can we learn from the centurion's attitude to his servant and from Jesus' attitude to the centurion as a Gentile?

2  In the light of verse 11 how does the Bible indicate the purpose of God in bringing non-Jewish (Gentile) people to share the blessings of Israel? See Genesis 12.1–3; Isaiah 2.2–4; 42.6; 49.6; 60.1–3 and Zechariah 8.20–23, and in Matthew, 2.1–12; 15.21–28; 24.14; 26.12 and 28.18.

3  Have you had the experience of seeing the faith of someone who comes to Christ from right outside the Church which seems to be greater than the faith of very many people who have been in the Church for a long time? What do you think is the reason for this?

# 8.14–17 Healings at Capernaum (with a Summary of Jesus' Healing Ministry)

## See also Mark 1.29–34; Luke 4.38–41

In Mark (1.29–34) and Luke (4.38–41) where we have this same story, it follows on from an incident in the synagogue in Capernaum, in which Jesus frees a man from demonic possession.

Here it is simply a chosen example of the healing power of Jesus. Matthew says the same things as Mark and Luke, though more briefly. The scene is Peter's home. His mother-in-law is sick with fever. Jesus touches her and heals her. She gets up and immediately goes back to looking after him as a guest in her home.

The other Gospels explain what Matthew leaves unexplained, when he tells of the crowds that came for healing and for exorcism in the evening. It had been the sabbath. They had come from the synagogue to Peter's home. Only after sunset would people be free to come and bring their sick to Jesus. Matthew's characteristic addition to what is in the other Gospels is the quotation of Scripture, as fulfilled in Jesus. Here it is Isaiah 53.4, 'He took our infirmities and bore our diseases'. We have seen how the words of 3.17 and the meaning of the temptations of Jesus indicate that the role of the Servant of the Lord in Isaiah 40–55 was to find fulfilment in the ministry of Jesus. The Suffering Servant role that Isaiah 53 especially shows was to find fulfilment supremely in the redemptive sufferings of his death (see 20.28). But all his ministry involved his identification with the 'infirmities' and 'diseases' of suffering people. He bore them and bore them away.

# 8.18–22 The Cost of Following Jesus

## See also Luke 9.57–60

As we have seen, Matthew in these chapters 8 and 9 links together examples of the miracles of Jesus with teaching about discipleship. 'Great crowds' come to him, but they must see that his purpose is not just to do striking miracles, but to make disciples. The two illustrations here of the meaning of discipleship are about one who was too ready to offer to be a disciple without thinking of the cost, and one who was not ready to take it seriously.

The first one was a 'scribe' who perhaps had been a disciple of one of the Jewish rabbis. He was attracted to Jesus and wanted now to be his disciple. 'I will follow you wherever you go,' he said in his enthusiasm. But he had to learn that just as the teaching of Jesus was very different in style from the teaching of the rabbis (7.29), so to be his disciple meant a very different lifestyle from that of being a disciple of a rabbi. It meant being prepared to have a lifestyle like that of Jesus. And Jesus' words reveal a great deal about his lifestyle. There were those who ministered to him and his close followers as they went about their work (Luke 8.1–3). There were those, like Peter, who opened their homes to him, but he had no home of his own in the years of his public ministry, and less of a fixed lodging-place than the birds or the foxes.

What the second man said was in effect, 'I will follow, but not yet.' It was something of great importance for a son to be faithful in carrying out the funeral arrangements for his father, and in that situation in Palestine burial usually took place within 24 hours of death. So it is almost certain that the man's father had not yet died, and he was really saying, 'Wait till my father dies, and then I will be your disciple.' But if a person's commitment to discipleship is serious, the kingdom of God must have a higher priority than that (see 10.37 and Luke 14.26–27). Jesus honoured family life and family relationships, but they were not to be put above duty to God and the call to discipleship.

### 📖 Study Suggestions

1 What do 2 Corinthians 8.9 and Philippians 2.6–8, along with verse 20 here, say about the simplicity and humility of the life that Jesus lived?

2 In what ways do you feel that responses to the challenge to discipleship today are like those of the two people in 8.18–22? What place in our lives as Christians should our concern for our parents have? What place should we give to the desire for comfort for ourselves and our families?

## ADDITIONAL NOTE F: THE NAMES AND TITLES OF JESUS

In this last section we have had for the first time two of the titles that people applied to Jesus, 'Teacher' and 'Son of man'. It is helpful to consider the main titles or names that Matthew uses for Jesus in the Gospel.

### *Christ or Messiah*

'Christ' is the Greek form and 'Messiah' the Hebrew form of the word meaning 'anointed', and its use implies the fulfilment of a great Old Testament hope. That was the hope of one to come, who would be specially anointed by God and rule in righteousness and peace. The hope goes back to the promises to David in 2 Samuel 7.12–16. Then a number of the prophets spoke of the king who would come as a descendant of David (Isaiah 9.6–7; 11.1–5; Jeremiah 23.5–6; Ezekiel 34.23–24 and Micah 5.2–4). Matthew's first verse speaks of 'Jesus Christ, the son of David' and the genealogy that follows shows him to be descended from David. This Gospel uses the title 14 times, and when it calls Jesus 'Son of David' (as in 9.27; 15.22, and especially 21.9 and 15) it intends reference to his Messiahship. We should link with this also reference to Jesus as 'King' or 'King of the Jews'. Although the Gospel unmistakably claims that Jesus is Messiah and Peter's confession of Jesus as Messiah is seen as a climax in the ministry of Jesus and a turning-point in the Gospel (16.16), Jesus himself does not make use of the title, but rather after Peter's confession 'charged the disciples to tell no one that he was the Christ'. Undoubtedly the reason for this was that there were many different hopes that the Jewish people had for their Messiah, some of a strongly political and military leader, far from what Jesus intended to be.

## Son of man

This is the expression that Jesus uses more than any other in speaking of himself (30 times in Matthew), but others do not normally use it of him. In fact in the New Testament as a whole, the title 'Son of man' is used only twice other than as spoken by Jesus (Acts 7.56 and Revelation 1.13), and so it is not likely to have been a title in regular use in the life of the early Church. Whereas people could use the title 'Christ' with different understandings, 'Son of man' was an expression that might be used with little meaning or have a great deal of meaning. It could just be equal to 'man' or 'human being' as in Psalm 8.4. On the other hand 24.30 and 26.64 clearly link it with the references in the Book of Daniel (7.13–14) to one 'like a son of man' coming 'with the clouds of heaven'. 'And he came to the Ancient of Days and was presented before him. And to him was given dominion and glory and kingdom . . .' When we study the places in which (like the other Gospels) Matthew uses 'Son of man', we see its use in three kinds of setting:

- in places which speak of his humiliation, suffering and death (as in 17.22 and 20.18 and 28; 26.2, 24 and 45),
- in places that speak of his future glory (as 24.30; 25.31 and 26.64),
- in places where it seems just the equivalent of 'I', as in 8.20, and compare 16.13 with Mark 8.27.

## Son of God

Nine times in Matthew Jesus is spoken of as 'Son of God', by the devil (4.3 and 6), by demons (8.29), by disciples (14.33 and in Peter's confession in 16.16), at the crucifixion by those who mocked him (27.40 and 43) and by the Roman centurion (27.54). When the high priest asked Jesus whether he was indeed 'the Christ, the Son of God' (26.63–64), he could not or would not deny it. From the Old Testament 'son of God' could be understood in many ways. The Old Testament uses it of Israel (Exodus 4.22 and Hosea 11.1) and of Israel's king (Psalm 2.7). Yet, although Matthew does not speak of Jesus using 'Son of God' of himself except at his trial, he indicates that Jesus was indeed of the divine nature. 'Emmanuel', 'God with us' (1.23) was his name, and he spoke of having a unique relationship with God the Father (11.25–27). He taught with authority greater than the Law and the Prophets (as 5.17–48 shows). He claimed authority to forgive sins (9.2–8) and he called disciples to give him a place in their lives and a loyalty such as is due only to God (16.24). The Gospel, moreover, closes with the instruction to baptize people 'in the name of the Father and of the Son and of the Holy Spirit', and – corresponding to the

'Emmanuel' at the beginning of the Gospel – with the promise of Jesus, 'I am with you always' (28.19–20).

### Teacher

People address Jesus as 'teacher' several times in the Gospel. He clearly set out to teach, and by the arrangement and by the content of the Gospel, Matthew certainly shows Jesus as teacher. Yet he was more than teacher, and it is significant that in Matthew the people who call him Teacher were those who were quite limited in their understanding or their willingness to believe in him (as in 8.19; 9.11; 12.38; 17.24; 19.16; 22.16, 24 and 36).

### Lord

English translations of the Gospel differ in the way that they translate the Greek word *kurios* because it could mean quite different things in different contexts. As we have noted already, it could be just a polite way of address, as 'Sir' in English, but it was also the word the Old Testament uses for God as 'Lord'. On the lips of those who use the word in 8.2, 6, 8, 21, 25, and 9.28 and 38, we may understand anything between those two extremes of meaning. There are places, however, where we must take it in its fullest meaning (as in 22.43–45 and 24.42) in the way of the distinctive Christian confession 'Jesus is Lord' (1 Corinthians 12.3 and Romans 10.9).

# 8.23–27  The Calming of the Storm

## See also Mark 4.35–41; Luke 8.22–25

Three more miracles of Jesus follow the section about discipleship. Mark, after the teaching of Jesus in parables (Mark 4.1–34), gives four miracles, showing the power of Jesus over the storm, over the demons, over incurable disease and over death (Mark 4.35—5.43). Matthew has two of them here and two later. He introduces the first by saying that Jesus 'got into the boat' to cross Lake Galilee and 'his disciples followed him'. Matthew thus seems to make a connection between this episode of the storm on the lake and what has gone before. Their following Jesus led them into trouble, a storm so great that their faith would be sorely tested, as 'the boat was being swamped by the waves', and Jesus 'was asleep'.

As so often, the parallel account in Mark (4.35–41) is more detailed (see also Luke 8.22–25), but we have the four essentials that give this incident its importance:

1 The disciples' distress and urgent rousing of Jesus, 'We are perishing!' In Mark the words are harsher, 'Teacher, do you not care if we perish?'
2 Jesus' rebuke of them as unnecessarily 'afraid' and 'of little faith', when so much that Jesus said and did was intended to encourage faith in those who followed him.
3 The action of Jesus stilling the storm, recalling what the Old Testament speaks of as the work of God, 'he made the storm be still, and the waves of the sea were hushed' (Psalm 107.29 and see also Psalms 65.7 and 89.9 and Job 38.8–11).
4 The amazement of the disciples, not only at what happened but at the person of Jesus, 'What sort of man is this, that even winds and sea obey him?'

# 8.28–34 Exorcisms in Gadara

## See also Mark 5.1–20; Luke 8.26–39

Even more than in the case of the last section, we see here that Mark's and Luke's records of this incident have many vivid details that Matthew does not mention. In all three Gospels this incident follows the stilling of the storm, as if to show that the one who had power over the forces of nature had power over the forces of evil that no human being dared to confront (verse 28). Matthew speaks of two demoniacs while Mark and Luke have just one. There are also different place names in different early manuscripts of each of the Gospels, but perhaps Gadara was the original reading. Although the town of Gadara was a little distance from the lake, some of the Gadarenes' land might have gone down to the water.

In our modern 'scientific' age people, especially in Western societies, find difficulty with the records of 'demon possession' in the Gospels, and sometimes say that in biblical times all sickness was thought to be the result of demonic influence. Yet in a number of passages in the Gospels (as in 4.24 and 8.16) a distinction is made between sicknesses of body and mind and demon-possession. Significantly also it is a feature of the Gospel records that when they describe Jesus, as here, as confronting demoniacs, the demons acknowledge him as 'Son of God' or 'the Holy One of God' (with verse 29 compare Mark 1.24; 3.11; Luke 4.34).

What about the fate of the herd of pigs? To Jewish people that part of the story may have read like a joke, as pigs were unclean animals and the herdsman should not have kept them for meat. In the setting of the narrative perhaps it was important that people saw that the demons had gone from the men whom they had possessed. To some modern critics, there is a moral problem, though they may think nothing of the slaughter of countless pigs for them to have bacon and pork to eat (!). The records of Jesus indicate his respect for all creation, and yet that he had a regard for humanity and human health of body, mind and spirit, higher than his regard for other living creatures (see 6.26 and John 2.15). The attitude of those who kept the pigs, and seemingly the other people in the town appears, by contrast, to have been that pigs mattered more than people. At least it is a sad ending to Jesus' visit and work among them that 'they begged him to leave their neighbourhood'.

---

## 📖 Study Suggestions

1 What do you think that the narrative in verses 23–27 might have meant to those for whom Matthew wrote his Gospel as they faced the storms of life and even of persecution in their following of Jesus?

2 What biblical parallels can you suggest to the way that Jesus did not press to stay among the Gadarenes when 'they begged him to leave their neighbourhood'? Is there a similar implication in Revelation 3.20?

3 What beliefs are there in your area about demon possession and about exorcism? How do these relate to things that you find in the Bible? What do you think should be the place of exorcism in the life of the Church today? If exorcism is a true Christian

ministry, how should Christians identify the presence of the demonic?

4 What situations do you know of where recognizing the power or truth of Jesus leads people not to want anything more to do with him? What situations do you know of where there is the opposite effect, the healing or liberating power of Christ drawing others to him?

# 9.1–8 Forgiving and Healing a Paralysed Man

## See also Mark 2.1–12; Luke 5.17–26

Again we have here the record of a healing miracle which Mark and Luke describe in much more vivid detail. Matthew has the bare essentials needed to bring out the ongoing importance of the incident.

1 The description of those who came to Jesus bringing a paralytic, and 'their faith' which Jesus recognized.
2 The words of Jesus, telling the man before anything else to 'take heart', and know that his sins were forgiven.
3 Although the rabbis taught that people could not be healed unless their sins were forgiven, 'some of the scribes' present took it as blasphemy that Jesus should declare forgiven the sins of the paralysed man.
4 To this Jesus responded in three ways:
   – He asked them the question, which was easier, to speak of forgiveness being given that no one could prove or disprove, or to say 'Rise and walk', a command that would immediately be put to the test.
   – The claim that 'the Son of man' had authority on earth to forgive sins (for 'the Son of man' see notes on p. 75).
   – The fact that the man was empowered to obey the order given to him, 'Rise, take up your bed and go home.'

5 We then have a description of the reaction of the people in three
   key statements:
   - As the New International Version puts it, 'They were filled with
     awe.'
   - 'They praised God.'
   - They recognized the 'authority' behind the words and actions of
     Jesus. In that verse 8 speaks of such authority being given to 'hu-
     man beings' (in the plural), there may be the suggestion that,
     stemming from Jesus, his Church has authority to pronounce
     the forgiveness of sins of all who come to God in repentance and
     faith (compare John 20.23).

# 9.9–13  The Call of Matthew, and Jesus Eating with Tax Collectors

## See also Mark 2.13–17; Luke 5.27–32

As in Mark and Luke, the incident of the healing of the paralysed
man, leading to the criticism of Jesus for claiming to have authority
to forgive sins, is followed by the story of the call of Matthew, the tax
collector (Levi in Mark and Luke). That led to another criticism of
Jesus, for sitting and eating with 'tax collectors and sinners'. None of
the three records tells us anything about the background of this call
that came to Matthew. Had he come to know about Jesus through his
earlier disciples? Had he for some time had the opportunity of hearing Jesus' teaching and seeing the things he did? We can imagine
that he had.

Matthew's work was probably to collect taxes from the caravans
that carried goods for sale across the frontier into the area of Herod
Antipas. No collectors of taxes are ever popular, but the system of tax
collecting in those days was such that a tax collector could become
rich by taking as much money as he could from people and then
handing on only what he had to. No doubt Matthew, like the other
tax collector of whom we read in Luke 19.1–10, was prepared to turn

from dishonest ways in following Jesus, but here it is Jesus, not the tax collector, who faces criticism.

Matthew implies a link between the call of Matthew and the coming of 'many tax collectors and sinners' to the house where Jesus was sitting with his disciples. Luke (5.29) says that it was the person whom Jesus called who 'made him a great feast in his house'. What matters most for the record in this Gospel is the criticism by the Pharisees and the response of Jesus to it. In that response there are three statements:

1 The statement that it is the sick who need a doctor, implying that it is the sinner who needs a Saviour.
2 The quotation of Hosea 6.6. True religion is not a matter of being able to boast about the sacrifices we have offered, but showing mercy to others (compare 5.7).
3 The whole purpose of the 'coming' of Jesus was to 'call sinners' and offer them forgiveness and new life, not 'the righteous' or those who thought themselves righteous.

---

## 📖 Study Suggestions

1 In the strict Jewish sense, 'blasphemy' was speaking against the name or character of God. Notice, however, its use in Matthew in 9.3; 26.65 and 27.39 (which English versions sometimes translate 'derided' or 'reviled'), and also in Mark 3.28–29 and Acts 13.45; 18.6; 19.37.
2 In what kinds of situation do you think it is right to link forgiveness of sin closely with a person's need of healing? When would it be wrong to do so? See John 9.1–3.
3 Who did Jesus' critics think of when they spoke about 'sinners'? What is the difference between using the word of other people, and of ourselves? See Luke 18.13.
4 Compare with verses 11–13 the way that Jesus in Luke 15 met the criticism, 'This man receives sinners and eats with them'. See also Luke 7.36–50.
5 In your church situation who are the people that you are most likely to regard as 'sinners' and beyond hope of being any different?

## ADDITIONAL NOTE G: WHO WROTE THE GOSPEL, WHEN AND WHERE?

### *(see also notes on pp. 20 and 32)*

Of any book that we read we may want to ask the three questions, Who wrote it? When? Where? We can read this Gospel from beginning to end and find no clear answer to these questions. We can go on to ask, however, whether there are any indirect indications of an answer to any of the questions in the content of the Gospel, or whether later Christian writers help us to find an answer to our questions.

When we ask who wrote the Gospel, it is important to emphasize the fact that this Gospel, as is also true of Mark and Luke, does not say a word that tells us who the writer was. All of the Gospel writers were more concerned to tell of Jesus than to say anything about themselves. People added the title 'The Gospel according to Matthew' later. In 9.9 we have all that the New Testament tells us about Matthew other than his name in the lists of the twelve apostles. (The parallel passages in Mark 2.14 and Luke 5.27 speak of the tax collector as called 'Levi' rather than Matthew, though it was by no means uncommon for two names to be used for the one person, as Simon/Peter, John/Mark, Saul/Paul.) From the end of the second century Christians have accepted this Gospel as Matthew's Gospel. As early as AD 130 the Christian writer Papias said that Matthew composed in the Hebrew language what he called the *logia*, and everyone translated them as they were able. But were the *logia* the Gospel? And was the Gospel composed in Hebrew (Aramaic)? There is doubt about both of these things. Did Papias mean this Gospel when he spoke of the *logia*? Possibly, but those who have studied the Gospel very carefully do not think that it was first composed in Hebrew (or the Palestinian vernacular Aramaic) and then translated into Greek. The New Testament uses the word *logia* in Hebrews 5.12 and 1 Peter 4.11 in the sense of teaching, and in Acts 7.38 and Romans 3.2 in relation to the Old Testament Scriptures. Some have suggested that Matthew the apostle may have put together a collection of the teaching of Jesus, or a collection of Old Testament texts seen to be fulfilled in Jesus. Then as these were used in the writing of the Gospel, Matthew's name was given to the Gospel.

Because this Gospel greatly depends on and uses Mark's Gospel (and Mark was not an apostle), some people reasonably ask whether an apostle would have done this in writing. It is perhaps more likely that Matthew was associated with a source that people used in the writing of the Gospel than have been the final author of the Gospel as we have it. Some modern scholars have thought that the Gospel may have been drawn together in a Christian community which trained those who were themselves to teach others in the ways of Christ.

As to the place of writing, the fact that we read so much about the Jewish people and Jesus' relationships with the Sadducees and Pharisees suggests that it is likely to have been written in or near Palestine. Gentiles, however, are also in view, and we read of the vital importance of the preaching of the good news of Jesus to them (28.18–20). So some have suggested Syria as a possible place of writing, and because Antioch was the greatest centre of early Christianity in Syria, some have thought that our Gospel may have been written there. Certainly Ignatius, bishop of Antioch very early in the second century, seems to have known it well. But Antioch is really only an intelligent guess at what may have been the place where the Gospel was written.

As we think of the date of writing, we have some indication if we believe that the writer knew and used Mark and if we can date that Gospel to about the year 65. Especially from the way that the Gospel refers to the synagogues where Jesus preached as 'their synagogues' (4.23; 9.35; 10.17; 12.9 and 13.54), some have thought that the Gospel may have been written at a time when the Jews excluded Christians from their synagogues, as happened about the year 85. There are those, however, who argue that Matthew was written before Mark, and they would put the Gospel very early. We have a wide range of possibilities, from AD 50 to AD 90. All that we can say with confidence is that it came from those early decades of the Church's life, and that is enough.

# 9.14–17 Jesus' Response to a Question about Fasting

## See also Mark 2.18–22; Luke 5.33–39

A third criticism of Jesus comes here in the same sequence in Matthew as we have in Mark and Luke. Fasting was a spiritual discipline among the Jews, observed by the Pharisees and by John the Baptist's followers. It was John's disciples who asked Jesus why his disciples did not observe that discipline of regular fasting. Jesus' reply, as was often the case, was in parable form. In fact there are three little parables here.

1 A wedding is a time of feasting, not fasting. Even the rabbis allowed people to break the rule of fasting for wedding celebrations. Jesus came to bring the joy and celebration of God's kingdom, to bring the blessings of God's rule into human lives. There would be a time of deep sorrow for Jesus' disciples, like a bridegroom suddenly being taken away from the wedding celebrations. The shadow of opposition and rejection already hung over Jesus' ministry, but at this time he called disciples to the joy of God's kingdom.

2 You cannot patch an old garment effectively with a new strong piece of cloth, or the old will soon quickly tear again. What people needed, and what Jesus was offering, was like a new garment, not a patched-up system of fasts and other religious observances.

3 In those days people stored wine in flasks made of animal skins, but if they put new wine that was still fermenting into old skins, the skins might burst and the wine be wasted. New wine needed new wineskins. What Jesus offered by his life and teaching needed to have new ways of expression, not just the old Jewish religious observances. Above all it was a new way of love and mercy that the legalistic lifestyle of the Pharisees could not contain.

---

### 📖 Study Suggestions

1 Look back to 6.16–18 (and the notes there) and see how that passage fits in with what 9.14–17 says about fasting.

2 Compare the teaching of Jesus in verses 16–17 with what the New Testament Epistles say about the newness of the life of God's kingdom. See especially 2 Corinthians 5.17; Galatians 6.15; Ephesians 2.13–16; 4.22–24 and Colossians 3.9–11. How should this affect the life and teaching of the Church today?

3 What can we learn from Matthew 11.2–6 and 14.1–12 about the disciples of John the Baptist, and from John 1.35–42 and 3.22–30 about those of his disciples who followed Jesus and those who did not? See also Acts 18.24–25 and 19.1–5, which show that many years later there were still followers of John.

4 What is the importance of the fact that Jesus several times spoke of weddings in his parables? Along with 9.15 see 22.1–14 and 25.1–13.

5 Are there customs or practices in the life of your Church that hinder the full expression of the new life that Christ gives? If there are, what should be done about them, and how?

# 9.18–26 Raising a Young Girl to Life and Healing a Woman

## See also Mark 5.21–43; Luke 8.40–56

After the further teaching on discipleship (9.9–17), we have (as in 8.1–17 and 8.23—9.8) three more incidents in which we see Jesus as healer and life-giver. The first of these links together the raising to life of the daughter of a ruler of the synagogue (a person who would have been responsible for the religious and social life of a synagogue), and the healing of 'a woman who had suffered from a haemorrhage for twelve years'. As we have seen in other instances, the record in Matthew seems to depend on Mark's (5.21–43, and compare Luke 8.40–56), but is briefer, lacking descriptive detail and concentrating on essentials. This incident in Mark also follows the record of the stilling of the storm and the exorcism in Gadara (Mark 4.35—5.20). For Matthew the following things are the essentials of the story:

1 The 'ruler' came humbly and in faith. Mark tells of his coming first when his daughter was grievously ill, but then receiving the message that she had died. Here Matthew presents him as pleading for a person who has already died.
2 Jesus willingly 'followed' the man, together 'with his disciples'. Mark tells of the encouragement this gave to the man's faith as they went.
3 On the way this woman, suffering from a condition that made her ritually unclean, approached Jesus. Understandably she wanted to avoid publicity in coming. Doubtless because of what she knew about Jesus' healing ministry, she believed that if she could touch 'the fringe of his garment', she would be healed.

4 Jesus does not criticize her for hesitating to approach him more publicly, but neither does he let her go away without encouraging her and assuring her that her faith had had its part in her healing.

5 When they reached the home of the leader of the synagogue, the professional mourners were already there. Custom had it that even a poor family should have two flute-players and one wailing woman. A synagogue administrator would probably have had many more.

6 The crowd mocked the statement of Jesus that the girl was 'sleeping', but he demonstrated that death held her no longer. 'And the report of this went through all that district' – the sick healed, the dead raised (see 11.5) by the hand of Jesus.

# 9.27–31 Restoring the Sight of Two Blind Men

In Mark 10.46–52 we have, in similar terms to these verses, the record of the restoration of the sight of a blind man near Jericho, but clearly Matthew 20.29–34 (with Luke 18.35–43) is parallel to that. There is no parallel to this narrative in Mark or Luke. As in the Jericho story, however, Jesus is addressed with the Messianic title, 'Son of David'. The Old Testament records no case of the restoration of a person's sight, but there was the hope of a coming day expressed in the words of Isaiah 35.5, 'Then the eyes of the blind shall be opened, and the ears of the deaf unstopped.' The Messianic hope was fulfilled, but Jesus did not want to be known simply as one who did such miracles. People did 'spread the news about' that he did such things, but not because he wished it so. Verse 30 uses very strong terms when it says that 'Jesus sternly charged them, "See that no one knows it" ' (compare 8.4).

Again the emphasis in this Gospel's record is on faith. 'Do you believe that I am able to do this?' Jesus challenged them; and then he was able to say as he touched their eyes, 'According to your faith be it done to you.'

# 9.32–34 Another Exorcism – a Dumb Man

This last incident in these chapters (8 and 9) which shows us the power of Jesus in action is only in Matthew. There is a similar one in 12.22–24 (paralleled in Luke 11.14–15), and because it leads also to the Pharisees' judgement, 'He casts out demons by the prince of demons', people have sometimes thought that the record of the same incident may have come to the writer of this Gospel through two different sources. The Pharisees may have expressed their verdict, however, more than once in relation to Jesus' ministry of exorcism. Here it stands in sharp contrast to the attitude of those with open minds, who could only acknowledge, 'Never was anything like this seen in Israel.'

# 9.35–38 The Greatness of the Harvest, the Fewness of the Labourers

In our study of the structure of this Gospel we have seen that it has clearly defined divisions, teaching sections and narrative sections, but each section leads into the next. The carefully chosen narratives of the actions of Jesus (and the demands of discipleship) are now to be followed by a teaching section about the disciples' mission (chapter 10). These verses are the bridge between them. They express four things:

1 Verse 35 is a summing up of the work of Jesus as (a) teaching in the synagogues, (b) preaching the good news of the kingdom, (c) healing the sick. The terms are almost exactly those of 4.23, and perhaps Matthew deliberately repeats them here, as all that he has

said between the end of chapter 4 and the end of chapter 9 has served to illustrate that teaching, preaching and healing ministry.

2 The motive of Jesus was compassion. The people were wearied, troubled, oppressed. They were like sheep without a shepherd. The words echo the Old Testament (see Numbers 27.17 and also 1 Kings 22.17), for Israel's kings and priests and prophets were meant to be shepherds for the people. In those Old Testament times they failed in their responsibility (see especially Ezekiel 34.1–10 and Zechariah 10.1–3), and the leaders of Israel in the time of Jesus were still failing. So Jesus was the true Shepherd (John 10), and he wanted the disciples to share his compassion and so to share his shepherding task.

3 Changing the way of speaking, Jesus saw the situation as like a harvest waiting to be reaped (see John 4.35–38), but there were few labourers to work in the harvest. We find these words again in Luke 10.2 in the different context of the sending out of the seventy disciples.

4 Leading up to the sending out of the twelve in the very next section, Jesus tells the disciples to 'pray . . . the Lord of the harvest to send out labourers into his harvest'. Prayer is often answered in and through the lives and the actions of those who pray!

---

### 📖 Study Suggestions

1 On the basis of what the Old Testament says, what would have been the implication of the woman with the haemorrhage coming and touching Jesus (Leviticus 15.25) and what was the significance of the 'fringe of his garment' (Numbers 15.37–41)?

2 What practices and customs associated with death and grief in your own culture truly express the Christian understanding of death and help those who are mourning the loss of a loved one? Are there practices and customs that do not help or that contradict the reality of Christian hope?

3 Especially in the light of the very first verse of the Gospel, what can we learn by putting together the passages in the Gospel which speak of Jesus as 'Son of David'? See 9.27; 12.23; 15.22; 20.30–31; 21.9, 15; 22.41–45.

4 Study other passages in the Gospels that speak of the 'compassion' of Jesus. See 9.36; 14.14–16; 15.32; 20.34; Mark 1.41 and Luke 7.13. What do they indicate were the things that specially moved him to compassion?

5 What in your situation corresponds to the picture in 9.36 of mishandled sheep lying helpless and so in need of a shepherd? What do you see, in the Church and in your country, that needs 'shepherds'?

# PART 4: 10.1–42

## TEACHING: THE DISCIPLES' MISSION

This second teaching section in Matthew begins, like the Sermon on the Mount in chapters 5—7, with a definite setting in the ministry of Jesus, and ends as chapters 5—7 did (compare 7.28 and 11.1). But also like the Sermon on the Mount this section draws together teaching that we find in other Gospels in different places and with different settings. Everything in this chapter, however, relates to the mission of Jesus' disciples. The first part (verses 1–15) relates to the sending out of the twelve in the course of Jesus' ministry. Much of the rest of the chapter applies particularly to what would be their mission later on. We may subdivide this section as follows:

**Analysis**
10.1–5    The apostles and their charge
10.6–15   The sending out of the twelve
10.16–25  Facing hatred and opposition
10.26–33  Nothing to fear except unfaithfulness
10.34–39  Opposition even within families
10.40–42  The reward for receiving a disciple

# 10.1–5 The Apostles and Their Charge

## See also Mark 3.13–19, 6.7; Luke 6.13–16, 9.1

Chapter 9 closed with words that expressed the compassion of Jesus for the crowds that were as sheep without a shepherd, and spoke of the need of labourers in the harvest field. They lead naturally on to this record of the call and sending of the twelve. At first (as in the parallels in Mark 3.14–15 and Luke 9.1) the emphasis is on the authority to cast out unclean spirits and to heal the sick. Mention of the work of preaching comes later. This is the first mention in Matthew of the 'twelve'. All of the Gospels speak of this inner circle of disciples who became the twelve apostles. Matthew 19.28 (= Luke 22.30) suggests the significance of the number twelve by linking them with the twelve tribes of Israel. We also find their names in Mark 3.16–19; Luke 6.14–16 and Acts 1.13. There are small differences in the names in the lists. Matthew and Mark list a Thaddaeus, while Luke and Acts have another Judas (son of James). Matthew and Mark call Simon the Cananaean and Luke and Acts call him the Zealot (but perhaps the two descriptions were similar in meaning).

# 10.6–15 The Sending Out of the Twelve

## See also Mark 6.8–11; Luke 9.2–5, 10.4–12

We might sum up the instructions Jesus gave to the twelve as involving six things (most of which are found in parallels in Mark and Luke):

1 As Jesus saw his own mission largely restricted to 'the lost sheep of the house of Israel' (15.24), so at this time the disciples were not to go by the roads that would lead them to the Gentile world, nor yet to Samaritan towns.

2 As was the case with Jesus himself (see 4.17), so they were to see their primary task as telling the good news of the nearness of God's kingdom. Included with that, however, was to be the ministry of healing the sick, cleansing lepers, casting out demons, and even raising the dead.

3 They were to realize how richly they had received God's blessings and they were to give as freely as they had received.

4 They were to go simply as they were, not to do any fund-raising first, and they could expect support from people of goodwill in the places to which they went.

5 In every place they were to seek out the kind of person who would be willing to receive them, and then stay in the same home as long as they were in the town or village, bringing the blessing of God's shalom (peace and full well-being) to the home.

6 They were messengers of God's word to people whose Scriptures had led them to expect the blessings of which they were now being told. It was a serious thing to reject, and when that happened the apostles were to shake the dust from their feet, as a Jew would do when leaving Gentile territory (see Acts 13.51 and 18.6). People had rejected the opportunity of receiving God's saving message.

---

### 📖 Study Suggestions

1 What is the difference between speaking of the twelve as disciples (= learners) and as apostles (= sent ones)?

2 For the reference to Sodom and Gomorrah as typical instances of God's judgement compare Amos 4.11; Zephaniah 2.9; Matthew 11.23–24 and Luke 17.28–30.

3 What does it suggest to you, that we know a good deal about some of the twelve disciples and very little about others?

4 What do John 1.43–51; 6.5–9 and 12.20–22 indicate about the kind of person Philip was? In a similar way, what would you understand about Thomas from John 11.7–16; 14.1–6 and 20.24–29?

5 Although it is clear that Christians should not apply the instructions in verses 6–15 literally when they go out on the Lord's mission today, what principles are there here that we should still consider as having practical implications?

6 What is the difference between the situation that verses 14 and 15 address relating to the Jewish people, and that of people who

are resistant to the gospel today but do not have the kind of
background that the Jewish people had?
7 What applications are there, in the world and in the Church, of
the principle of verse 10, 'labourers deserve their food'? See also
1 Corinthians 9.1–14.
8 Are there examples in your own area of those who have gone
out with a very simple lifestyle as evangelists or to serve poor
people in their needs?

# 10.16–25 Facing Hatred and Opposition

## See also Mark 13.9–13; Luke 21.12–19

In this section the picture of the scope of the disciples' mission
widens, and the possibility of persecution deepens. The disciples will
be as sheep in the midst of wolves (verse 16 and compare Luke 10.3).
Not only will there be persecution in Jewish synagogues, but from
'governors and kings'. They are no longer to go just to 'the lost sheep
of the house of Israel' (verse 6), but their witness is to be to Gentiles
(as the conclusion to the Gospel (28.18–20) makes very clear).

There are parallels to these verses in other Gospels, but especially
in the chapters that speak of the future (see Mark 13.9–13 and Luke
21.12–19). If Matthew is drawing on Mark's Gospel as a source, he
chose to put these things about persecution here rather than just in
his own chapter about the future (see 24.9 and 13).

There are five points in the teaching here about the opposition
that the disciples must face in their mission:

1 They must be ready for such opposition. Jesus never encouraged
his disciples to think that the way would be easy for them. Following what the Old Testament had said (in Micah 7.6), verse 21
speaks of that opposition coming even from within the family.
2 They should recognize that if disciples are to be like their Master,
they must face opposition as Jesus faced it, even being called

Beelzebul, the prince of the devils (compare verse 25 with Mark 3.22 and Luke 11.15).

3 When the authorities put them on trial for their faith, they do not need to worry about how they should respond, as the Holy Spirit will guide their words. (We have this promise not only in the parallels in Mark 13.11 and Luke 21.14–15, but also in another setting in Luke 12.11–12.)

4 When there is intense persecution, disciples should escape from it rather than throwing their lives away. Perhaps 12.14–15 is an example of Jesus himself doing this. Acts 8.1–4 and 14.5–7 are examples of this in the life of the early Church, and in both cases the result was the further spread of the gospel.

5 Whatever the opposition they have to face, disciples are to 'endure'. Saving faith is the faith that continues and does not turn back (verse 22).

---

## ADDITIONAL NOTE H: THE COMING OF THE SON OF MAN

Verse 23 is one of the most difficult sayings of the Gospels. Passages often link the coming of the Son of man with the end of the world (or the end of the age), as in chapter 24. Some have thought that Jesus expected this to come about in the time of his ministry, but there is much in the teaching of Jesus that makes it unlikely that he thought in this way. Others have linked the coming of the Son of man with the fall of Jerusalem because of the way in which Matthew links the two in parts of chapter 24. Others again think that the Son of man was revealed in a unique way in Jesus' death and resurrection. In Luke 10.1, however, Jesus sends out the disciples 'into every town and place where he himself was about to come', and so the words of verse 23 may mean that the disciples were preparing the way for Jesus himself to come to minister.

# 10.26–33 Nothing to Fear except Unfaithfulness

## See also Luke 12.2–9

These words about fear are linked with the forewarning of opposition and persecution. The fairly close similarity between these verses and Luke's account suggests that Matthew and Luke may have had the same source for this teaching. We do not find similar teaching in Mark, except that there are words like those of verse 26 in Mark 4.22 but in a different setting, and Mark 8.38 (with Luke 9.26 as a parallel) has words about being ashamed to confess Christ that are in essence like the words of verse 33.

This passage gives four reasons why genuine single-minded disciples, faithful to the mission that God has entrusted to them, need not fear:

1 They have nothing shameful to hide, unlike those who plan evil secretly or who are hypocrites, saying one thing and doing another (Luke 12.1). Jesus himself never tried to hide what he was saying and doing (see 26.55). If he said certain things privately to the disciples, it was only because at the time they would be misunderstood in public. Later people could proclaim them 'upon the housetops' (the flat roofs of houses in Palestine were very suitable for making public proclamations).
2 They might have enemies who could even put them to death, but no one could take their real life (their 'souls') from them. A much greater cause for fear is for a person to stand before God as Judge after rejecting the life that he had offered for soul as well as body (who thus could 'destroy both soul and body in hell').
3 Their God is the heavenly Father who cares for the least detail of his creation. The sparrows that are sold for next to nothing in the market matter to him, and their falling to the ground does not go unnoticed by him. God's human creation, those made in the image of God – and not least those whom Jesus sends out in his service – matter more to him than many sparrows (compare 12.12).
4 A promise is given to those who are not ashamed to declare publicly that they belong to Christ (compare Romans 10.9). They will be 'acknowledged' before God as his own. But there is a corresponding warning about denying him.

# 10.34–39 Opposition Even Within Families

## See also Luke 12.51–53

In many ways there are paradoxes or apparent contradictions in the teaching of Jesus. His message was a message of peace, as has been made clear even in this chapter (verse 13). Jesus said, moreover, 'Blessed are the peacemakers, for they will be called children of God' (5.9). Yet now Jesus tells the disciples that they must be prepared to face opposition and persecution. In that way Jesus brought not peace but a sword.

We find another paradox in Jesus' teaching about family. He honoured and supported strong bonds of marriage and family, and respect and loyalty between husbands and wives, children and parents (15.3–9; 19.3–15, 19). Yet the loyalty of a disciple to Christ had to stand higher than even the closest of family loyalties. Sometimes that higher loyalty would involve conflict within the family. Verses 35–36 add to what verse 21 has said already, and now explicitly quotes Micah 7.6. Luke 12.51–53 and 14.26 have teaching similar to that of verses 34–37 but in different settings.

The teaching in this passage relates directly to mission, but it concerns every aspect of discipleship. Thus we find teaching closely similar to verses 38–39 about the cross of discipleship in many places in the Gospels (see 16.24–26 in this Gospel; Mark 8.34–36; Luke 9.23–25; 14.27 and John 12.25). The cross has become such a basic symbol of Christianity that it is hard for us to realize what it must have meant when for the first time people heard preachers compare the call to discipleship with the pain and shame of such a terrible death as crucifixion. The use of such a symbol expresses most powerfully that love for Christ must be set above all love for self. There must be a death to self-centredness and a steadfast following of Jesus, or a person is 'not worthy' to be called a disciple. In fact, Jesus says that to live self-centredly (to find one's life in that way) is to lose real life. To deny self for Christ's sake is to find true life.

# 10.40–42 The Reward for Receiving a Disciple

Finally, this chapter of teaching on the role of disciples in mission turns from the facing of persecution to the thought of those who receive the 'missionaries' (the sent ones). First Jesus himself is the 'sent one', and whoever receives him receives the one who sent him. Whoever receives the disciple whom he sends is reckoned as receiving him.

There were those in Old Testament days who opposed and rejected the prophets and the 'righteous', but also those who accepted them, and these would receive 'a prophet's reward' or 'a righteous person's reward'. But it is not only the receiving of a prophet or one of Christ's messengers that this passage commends, but even the smallest act of kindness (the gift of a cup of cold water), 'to one of the least of these my followers because he is my follower' (as the Good News Bible puts it).

Again we can find this kind of teaching in a number of different settings in the Gospels, which indicates how basic and important it is (see 18.5; Mark 9.37, 41; Luke 9.48; 10.16 and John 13.20). The idea of reward does not mean that we can ever deserve to receive anything from God, nor is there any obligation on God's part to those who are faithful to him. As 25.21 and 23 indicate, the best reward is the Master's commendation, 'Well done, good and faithful servant . . . enter into the joy of your master.'

## 📖 Study Suggestions

1 How does this Gospel apply the word 'wise' to those who are disciples of Christ? See 10.16; 7.24; 25.2–9.
2 With verses 32–33, consider what the New Testament says elsewhere about the confession of Christ or the denial of Christ. See especially Romans 10.9–11 and 2 Timothy 2.11–13.
3 What is the meaning of comparing disciples to sheep, snakes and doves in verse 16?
4 The Gospels often describe Jesus as the 'Sent One' of God. Along with verse 40 see 15.24; Luke 4.43; 10.16; John 13.20 and 20.21. What does this mean for our understanding of Jesus?
5 What examples to you know of Christians who, in the spirit of verses 26–31, have been fearless in the face of great opposition?

What is the right kind of fear, and what is the wrong kind of fear for the Christian to have?

6  What examples do you know from the history of the Christian Church, in early or more recent times, when it has been right to escape from persecution (as verse 23 speaks of this)? When may it be wrong to run away?

7  What would you say to a person who quotes verse 19 as a reason for not preparing in advance for preaching and teaching?

8  In some parts of the world people have said that where one person of a family has come to believe and others have not, it is better for that person to delay baptism and confessing Christ openly, so that others of the family may come to faith and avoid the kind of conflict that verses 34–36 speak of. What do you think about such a policy?

# PART 5: 11.1—12.50

## NARRATIVE: RESPONSE TO JESUS' MINISTRY

We have had the sections in which the teaching (chapters 5—7) and the actions (chapters 8—9) of Jesus' ministry have been shown to us, and then in chapter 10 we have seen the way that the disciples were to share in that ministry. Now we see especially the reactions of people to Jesus' ministry and the consequences of those reactions: faith and unbelief, doubt and opposition. In particular, we begin to see how the religious leaders of Israel were unwilling to believe in Jesus and their unbelief turned to opposition.

We may subdivide this section as follows:

---

**Analysis**

| | |
|---|---|
| 11.1–6 | John the Baptist's question |
| 11.7–15 | Jesus' testimony to John the Baptist |
| 11.16–19 | Attitudes to both John and Jesus |
| 11.20–24 | The unbelief of the towns of Galilee |
| 11.25–30 | Those who respond and what God offers to them |
| 12.1–8 | Criticism of the disciples' action on the sabbath |
| 12.9–14 | Criticism of Jesus' healing on the sabbath |
| 12.15–21 | Jesus' ministry and the fulfilment of Scripture |
| 12.22–32 | The source of Jesus' power to cast out demons |
| 12.33–37 | Good or bad at source |
| 12.38–42 | The request for a sign |
| 12.43–45 | The return of the unclean spirit |
| 12.46–50 | The true family of Jesus |

---

# 11.1–6 John the Baptist's Question

## See also Luke 7.18–23

The first verse here concludes the section of Jesus 'instructing his twelve disciples' about their mission (compare 7.28). Then the writer turns our attention to John the Baptist, and what we have in verses 2–11 is closely paralleled by Luke 7.18–28 but not by Mark.

A question came from John in prison. In 4.12 we read of John's imprisonment and 14.1–12 will give the reason for that imprisonment by Herod and tell of the way he died. According to 3.11 John had spoken particularly of the one who was to come after him, whose way he prepared. But now he had doubts. Perhaps he had doubts because he was discouraged in his imprisonment. He who had preached about righteousness and justice received no justice himself. What was most difficult to him was the fact that he had preached that the coming One would bring in the kingdom of God with the just judgement of evil-doers (3.7–12). But Jesus seemed to be doing very different things from bringing judgement.

Jesus told John's disciples, 'Go and tell John what you hear and see'. He needed to know both what Jesus taught and what he did in order to understand. Moreover, if he heard it reported in the words of the Scriptures (as Jesus expressed his reply), that might help John to understand that it was really the fulfilment both of his own preaching and the hopes expressed by the prophets (see Isaiah 29.18–19; 35.5–6 and 61.1).

The final words in this section applied to John. It was important that he should 'take no offence' at what Jesus was doing. But the words also have a wider application. There is true blessing when people do not take offence or stumble, but genuinely believe.

# 11.7–15 Jesus' Testimony to John the Baptist

## See also Luke 7.24–28

When the people heard the message that came through John's disciples, they might have been left thinking just of John's doubts and weakness. Jesus wanted to leave them with a truer impression of a great and faithful man. People had found the preaching of John so stirring that crowds went out from 'Jerusalem and all Judea and all the region about the Jordan' (3.5) to see and to hear. Did they go to see some very ordinary sight? Did they go to hear a man who would be swayed by popular opinion in what he said? Did they go to see a powerful, royal figure, dressed for the part? The people knew the answer. In 3.4 his dress and lifestyle were described. They went out because they felt that after generations in which no one had heard the voice of a prophet, here indeed was one (see 14.5). Jesus agreed that John was a prophet, but more than a prophet. In him the words from Malachi 3.1 had a special meaning, as he was sent as a messenger to tell that 'the kingdom of heaven is at hand' (3.2), and that the King was coming. One who was far greater than John was coming – of this one he was to be the forerunner. John was great in the task that God had called him to do, but also great in his humility, courage and single-mindedness.

In the last part of this section, however, there are three difficult sayings that we need to look at more closely:

1 Verse 11 speaks of John as greater than any who had been born before him, but then it says, 'the least in the kingdom of heaven is greater than he'. The Gospels see history divided into two by the coming of Jesus. As verse 13 puts it, there was the time of the Law and the Prophets that continued up to John's ministry. Then the new day dawned. The kingdom of God had come into human life in a way that had never happened before. Those who lived in this new day and shared in the kingdom of God might not be greater than John in character or commitment, but they were greater in the privilege that they had (see also 13.16–17).

2 Some have understood verse 12 to mean that there were those who tried to act violently against the kingdom of God, either with deliberate intentions of evil, or trying to turn it into a political kingdom. We read in John 6.15 that there were those who wanted

to take Jesus 'by force to make him king'. Yet is it right to say that violent people would be able to take the kingdom of heaven by force? The New International Version translates the verse, 'the kingdom of heaven has been forcefully advancing, and forceful men lay hold of it.' This would fit with what Luke 16.16 says, and mean that it is those who earnestly seek God's kingdom who find it.

3 Verse 14 speaks of John as 'Elijah who is to come'. There was the prophecy of Malachi 4.5 that God would send 'Elijah the prophet before the great and terrible day of the Lord comes'. According to John 1.21, when people asked John if he was the promised Elijah, he said 'No'. He would make no such claim for himself, though Luke 1.17 speaks of the way that he would act 'in the spirit and power of Elijah'. In the eyes of Jesus John was the fulfilment of that hope of the coming of Elijah (see also Mark 9.11–13).

# 11.16–19  Attitudes to both John and Jesus

## See also Luke 7.31–35

As in Luke 7.31–35 (and in closely similar words), what Jesus said about John the Baptist comes just before a rebuke of the unwillingness of the people – especially the Jewish religious leaders – to respond to either John or Jesus. Both were bearers of the message of the kingdom of God. John bore witness to it with a very simple lifestyle. Jesus lived very differently, offering friendship to people of every kind so that even those whom the religious leaders despised most, 'tax-collectors and sinners', might come to know the blessings of the kingdom. The critics rejected both. Because 'John came neither eating nor drinking', they said, 'He has a demon'. Because Jesus entered into people's festivities 'eating and drinking' with them, they said, 'Look, a glutton and a drunkard'. Yet for those with eyes to see and ears to hear, there was the wisdom of God in the way John lived and in the way Jesus lived. Not for centuries had anyone moved the nation as John had done, and no one had ever shown such concern for the fallen and the neglected and the despised as Jesus did.

In a simple parable Jesus said that the critics were like children quarrelling as they played in the market-place. Some wanted to play weddings and some to play funerals, and as they were unable to agree their play was spoilt.

---

### 📖 Study Suggestions

1 The word English versions translate 'take offence' or 'stumble' or 'fall away' in 11.6 occurs also in 13.20–21, 57; 15.12; 24.10; 26.31, 33. What do these passages indicate as reasons why people turn aside from following Jesus?
2 Read carefully Isaiah 29.18–19; 35.5–6 and 61.1 to see their connection with the words of Jesus in 11.5.
3 In what ways could people describe John the Baptist as a prophet? And in what way was he more than a prophet?
4 In what ways can people criticize Christians today for being at all like John the Baptist or like Jesus in the things that this Gospel describes of them in 11.18–19?

---

# 11.20–24 The Unbelief of the Towns of Galilee

## See also Luke 10.13–15

Sometimes we have the impression that when Matthew speaks of negative attitudes to Jesus, he usually speaks of 'the scribes and Pharisees'. We tend to think in contrast that there was a very positive response to Jesus among the ordinary people in the towns of Galilee. This section (closely similar to Luke 10.13–15, though in a different setting in that Gospel), shows that there was little lasting response in the towns of Galilee 'in which most of his mighty works had been done'. We know the links of Capernaum (near to the northern end of Lake Galilee) with the ministry of Jesus (see 4.13 and 8.5). John 1.44

calls Bethsaida Andrew and Peter's home town, and we read in the Gospels of several things that Jesus did there. They do not tell us of any special events linked with Chorazin, which was about two miles from Capernaum, but according to 4.23 'Jesus went about all Galilee' in his ministry of teaching and healing. So these towns had great opportunities of seeing what Jesus did and hearing what he taught.

The signs of the kingdom should have led these people of the towns of Galilee to realize the blessings and responsibilities of the rule of God, and turn to him in repentance and faith, but they refused to do that. Because of their great opportunities they had less excuse for failing to turn to God than heathen cities like Tyre and Sidon and Sodom. The people of Capernaum might say that knowing Jesus among them was like being 'exalted to heaven', which was the boast of the king of Babylon in Isaiah 14.13 which this passage quotes. 'We ate and drank in your presence, and you taught in our streets' they might say (Luke 13.26). But God's judgement would bring them down very low. The principle of God's judgement stands: 'from everyone to whom much has been given, much will be required; and from the one to whom much has been entrusted, even more will be demanded' (Luke 12.48).

---

📖 **Study Suggestions**

1  What does the Old Testament say about the sins of Sodom (Genesis 18–19) and Tyre and Sidon (Isaiah 23, Ezekiel 26–28, Amos 1.9–10 and Zechariah 9.2–4)? In what ways are their sins less serious than the failures of the towns of Galilee that this Gospel describes in 11.20–24?

2  Follow out the events that the Gospels describe as taking place in Bethsaida and Capernaum (Matthew 8.5–17; Mark 1.21–34; 2.1–12; 8.22–26; Luke 9.10–17 and John 4.46–54) and consider the opportunities that people there were given to believe in Jesus.

3  How do you see as applicable today the principle that the greater the opportunities people have, the greater their responsibilities?

# 11.25–30 Those Who Respond and What God Offers to Them

## See also Luke 10.21–22

In these chapters 11 and 12 we have noted that there is emphasis on the human responses to the ministry of Jesus. At another level, however, we find an emphasis on the fact that to begin with, everything depends on God's revelation and Jesus' invitation. Verses 25–27, speaking of the Son as the revelation of the Father, are almost identical with Luke 10.21–22 (though in Luke the words have a different setting). The invitation in verses 28–30, however, is only in Matthew.

People could never know the truth of God except by God's revelation, but it is God's 'gracious will' to reveal his ways to humankind. From the beginning of the Gospel Matthew has presented Jesus as uniquely 'the Son', Son of God, with a unique relationship with 'the Father'. So he reveals the Father as no one else can, and the Father entrusts to the Son that revelation to the world. But it is available for those who are humble enough to receive it, those who come to Jesus with the trust of 'infants' (18.1–4 will say more about the meaning of this). Those who in the world's way of thinking are 'the wise and understanding', proud of the knowledge that they have and of their reputation for wisdom, can never know God's revealed truth, as they feel no need for it.

So with the words about revelation there are the words of invitation, 'Come to me'. Christian people have applied these words to those who are weary with their 'labour', and who are 'heavy laden' in many different ways. It is important, however, to see its special meaning in this Gospel. Jewish people spoke of the responsibility of keeping the Law as bearing 'the yoke' of the Law as an animal has a yoke put on it when it is taken out to do the work of ploughing or other kinds of work. But in the way that the Pharisees presented it, the 'yoke' of the Law was very heavy and wearisome. In 23.4 Jesus said, 'They tie up heavy burdens, hard to bear, and lay them on the shoulders of others; but they themselves are unwilling to lift a finger to move them.' We can see this in the next two sections of the Gospel in the case of the regulations about keeping the sabbath. Jesus invited those with such heavy burdens to come to him and find rest.

There was a 'yoke' involved in following him, the demands of discipleship, but that yoke was 'easy' and the burden 'light', because it was intended for the highest good of the person who bore it. It was a matter of following one who was 'gentle and lowly in heart', and living like him rather than striving to keep endless regulations.

# 12.1–8 Criticism of the Disciples' Action on the Sabbath

## See also Mark 2.23–28; Luke 6.1–5

We have often noted the importance of recognizing links between one passage and the next in the Gospel. We have noted in this case that Jesus' offer of 'rest' to the weary and those bearing heavy burdens relates to the 'yoke' of the Law as the Pharisees wanted people to bear it. This accounts for Matthew's placing here, after the words of 11.28–30, these two incidents where Jesus was in conflict with the Pharisees about the keeping of the sabbath. In Mark (2.23—3.6) and Luke (6.1–11) the two incidents are together but in a different setting.

Jesus with his disciples went through some grainfields on the sabbath. The Law (Deuteronomy 23.25) allowed people who passed by like that to pluck and eat the ears of corn, though not to use a sickle to cut more than they would eat in passing. But did the disciples break the law by doing this on the sabbath? To the actual Old Testament Law about not working on the sabbath (Exodus 20.8–11 and Deuteronomy 5.12–15) the rabbis added detailed regulations. There were 39 different kinds of work that people could not do on the sabbath. It was possible to say that the disciples had been doing three of these, reaping, threshing and preparing a meal! So the Pharisees said to Jesus, 'Look, your disciples are doing what is not lawful to do on the sabbath.'

There are seven important things about the reply to that criticism here:

1 Jesus used the Scriptures, and, as the rabbis often did, he began by saying, 'Have you not read . . . ?' (compare 19.4 and 22.31).

2 He took the example of what David did (1 Samuel 21.1–6). David's men were hungry, and satisfying their hunger was more important in that case than the rule that the symbolic 'bread of the Presence' in the sanctuary should only be eaten by the priests (see Exodus 25.30 and Leviticus 24.5–9).

3 It was the authority of David as king that the priest accepted, and here was the great Son of David (1.1), the Son of man, who is 'lord of the sabbath'.

4 The priests in the temple had to do work on the sabbath, such as putting out 'the bread of the Presence' and offering the daily sacrifices (Leviticus 24.8 and Numbers 28.9–10), as the temple services were more important than the letter of the sabbath law.

5 If that was true of the temple, now there is the presence of 'something greater than the temple' (see also verses 41 and 42 of this chapter). The kingdom of God has broken into human life. God's Anointed has come.

6 Jesus repeats the words of Hosea 6.6 (which Matthew already records him as quoting in 9.13) as a guiding principle for the religious life: God desires 'mercy and not sacrifice'. In other words, concern for human need is more important than petty legal regulations. The law of God was meant to be a blessing and not a burden. Mark (2.27) adds words that are not in Matthew's record, 'The sabbath was made for humankind, and not humankind for the sabbath.'

7 The Pharisees had used the sabbath regulations to condemn people rather than to help them. If they had followed the spirit of Scripture – in Law and Prophets – they 'would not have condemned the guiltless'.

# 12.9–14 Criticism of Jesus' Healing on the Sabbath

## See also Mark 3.1–6; Luke 6.6–11

The next confrontation between Jesus and the Jewish authorities on the question of the sabbath related to healing. Here the challenge came from them, with the direct question, 'Is it lawful to heal on the sabbath?' They did not ask this question in order to find out what Jesus would teach, but to 'accuse' him, to condemn him as they had condemned the disciples (verse 7). Jesus answered by putting a question to his critics. He used the principle involved in what their regulations would allow on the sabbath. At least under certain circumstances they would allow a person to pull a sheep out of a pit on the sabbath. As in other places (see 6.26 and 10.31) Jesus argues from the special value of human life in God's sight (more than the life of birds or animals, though they are precious to him). But the deepest issue was 'to do good on the sabbath' or to refuse to take the opportunity of doing it. He had changed their question from, 'Is it lawful to heal on the sabbath?' to, 'Is it lawful to do good on the sabbath?'

Jesus' enemies could give no answer to his argument, but they were so determined to reject Jesus' teaching and his actions of love and compassion that they looked for an opportunity to do what was the most desperate evil – whether on the sabbath or any other time – 'to destroy him'. Their way of understanding the Law was more sacred to them than the life of a person, the life of Jesus himself.

---

## 📖 Study Suggestions

1 What sort of people does 11.25 speak of as the 'wise' and 'understanding' who do not receive the revelation of God in Jesus? How are the words of 11.25 like what the apostle Paul says in 1 Corinthians 1.26–29?

2 Look up all the Old Testament references in the notes on 12.1–8 and see how they help to throw light on what that passage says.

3 Compare with 12.9–14 the incidents in Luke 14.1–6 and John 5.1–18 where the authorities judge Jesus by what he did on the sabbath.

4 How do the words of 11.28–30 relate to the methods of Jesus' ministry and how he dealt with people?

5 How do you see people 'weary' and 'carrying heavy burdens' today, and so open to the comfort of Jesus' invitation in 11.28–30?

6 Do you see the Church where you are in danger of having regulations (like those of the sabbath in New Testament times) that are a burden rather than a help to Christian people in their life of discipleship?

# 12.15–21  Jesus' Ministry and the Fulfilment of Scripture

At this point Matthew, in a way typical of his method (and not paralleled in the other Gospels), after summing up Jesus' ministry in a few words, describes it as a fulfilment of Old Testament Scripture. The particular aspects of his ministry that Matthew stresses here are:

1 The crowds that followed him.
2 The healing of all who came to him for healing.
3 The humility and lack of desire for reputation that led him to tell those healed not to make known what he had done for them.

These verses quote Isaiah 42.1–4, one of the passages in Isaiah 40–55 that present the prophet's ideal of the Servant of the Lord. That ideal was fulfilled in Jesus in these ways:

1 He had the anointing of the Holy Spirit (3.16).
2 He proclaimed God's way of justice.
3 He sought no controversy or confrontation even when others confronted him.
4 He was patient and compassionate in dealing with people.
     The 'bruised reed' was a vivid picture of lives greatly hurt by what had happened to them. The 'smouldering wick' was a picture of those in whom the fire of faith burned very low. Jesus did not reject such people, as the Jewish religious leaders tended to do.
5 He would persevere through great difficulties to victory in the end.
6 Not so relevant in this immediate context, but important in the whole setting of the Gospel (culminating as it does in 28.18–20), is the reference to the proclamation to the Gentiles, and Gentiles coming to hope 'in his name'.

---

### 📖 Study Suggestion

In what ways are the words of 12.18–21 relevant to Christian ministry today, as well as being relevant to the ministry of Jesus? What qualities of Christian leadership do those verses indicate? Compare also 2 Timothy 2.23–25 for what it says about ideals of ministry.

# 12.22–32 The Source of Jesus' Power to Cast Out Demons

## See also Mark 3.19–30; Luke 11.14–23

Matthew has already referred to the work of Jesus in dealing with demon-possessed people in 4.24; 8.16; 28–34 and 9.32–34. All three Synoptic Gospels speak of this, leading to the explanation that we have already seen in 9.34, 'He casts out demons by the prince of demons'. Luke 11.14–23 is closely similar to this passage, and both are probably taken from Mark 3.19–30, although Mark does not mention the occasion of the healing of the blind and dumb man. Matthew deals with that actual healing here very briefly. What is important is the argument that follows. Although Matthew's narrative is often much shorter than Mark's, here it is very similar, as each part of the response of Jesus to his critics was important. The crowds saw what Jesus did, and with an openness of mind began to ask, 'Can this be the Son of David?', in other words, the expected Messiah. But, perhaps partly affected by the crowd's reaction, and blinded by jealousy, the Pharisees said, 'It is only by Beelzebul, the prince of demons, that this man casts out demons.' Notice the six points Jesus made to show how wrong this proposal was. All of them would be very meaningful to people in that situation:

1 A kingdom divided against itself cannot stand. In other words, Satan would not be so foolish as to try to cast out demons from people's lives. He would be fighting against himself.
2 If Jesus used the power of the ruler of demons to cast out demons, whose power did Jewish exorcists use? We read of Jewish exorcists in Acts 19.13 and also in the Jewish writer Josephus.
3 If, on the other hand, it is by the power of the Spirit of God that Jesus is casting out demons, then God's kingdom and rule has become a reality in the ministry of Jesus.
4 The little parable of verse 29 says that a strong person can only be overcome by a stronger. In Jesus a stronger power is in operation than the power of evil. Compare Isaiah 49.24–25.
5 Verse 30 has a warning. If people do not side with Jesus in the battle with evil, then they will be working against him. They will not be like good shepherds who gather the sheep, but like enemies who scatter them.

6 There is the danger of an unforgivable sin which Jesus describes as 'blasphemy against the Spirit'. Jesus accepted and forgave many things that were said and done against him. On the cross he prayed, 'Father, forgive them; for they know not what they do' (Luke 23.34). Sometimes people feel afraid that they have committed unforgivable sin. Anyone who has that feeling need not be afraid. When people are conscious of sin and desire to turn from it and seek God's forgiveness, they can be completely confident of God's willingness to forgive. The greatest danger is when people lose a sense of good and evil, and therefore do not recognize their own sins and the need of repentance and forgiveness. Jesus did not say that those opposed to him here had committed unforgivable sin, but the warning of that is given to those who called a work of God a work of the evil one.

---

## 📖 Study Suggestions

1 The name Beelzebul may have originally meant 'Baal the prince', or 'lord of the height' or 'lord of the dwelling', and came to be the name people gave to the prince of the demons. See 2 Kings 1.2 where we have the name of the Canaanite god, Baal-zebub (= 'lord of flies') that sometimes replaces Beelzebul in the Gospel passages.
2 When Jesus began his ministry he took up John the Baptist's message that, 'the kingdom of heaven is at hand' (4.17). What does it mean that he could say in 12.28, 'the kingdom of God has come upon you'?
3 Alongside 12.30 read the words of Mark 9.40 and Luke 9.50, 'Whoever is not against us is for us'. How do the different settings of the two sayings indicate that both can be true, with applications to different settings?
4 In your own situation, what examples do you see of people calling good actions evil, and what do you think is the cause of this?

# 12.33–37  Good or Bad at Source

## See also Luke 6.43–45

In Matthew's deliberate arrangement of what he records, these sayings about the good and bad tree and about the treasure of the heart come straight after the Pharisees have spoken about Jesus supporting Satan's kingdom. There has been similar teaching about good and bad trees in the Sermon on the Mount (in 7.15–20), and there is teaching about the trees and about treasure in a different setting in Luke (6.43–45). There is no parallel in the other Gospels to verses 36 and 37.

Fruit trees are either good trees bearing good fruit or bad trees which can only bear bad fruit. The fruit of what people are in their inner lives comes out – at least partly – in their words. Good words – words that are true and helpful to others – come from an inner life that is true and loving. Or, changing the picture, a person's inner life is full to capacity, but it may be full of good thoughts or evil thoughts, and 'out of the abundance of the heart the mouth speaks'.

In one way we may say that actions matter more than words. Yet in another way we can say that our words show the kind of people we are, especially when our words just tumble out and we have no time to think carefully what we should say that will please others. It follows also that we will be judged by our 'careless words', and either 'justified' or 'condemned'.

# 12.36–42   The Request for a Sign

## See also Luke 11.29–32

Another way in which the Gospels indicate the unwillingness of the Jewish religious leaders to believe in Jesus is in their accounts of their request for a 'sign'. We can understand the word 'sign' in different ways. In John's Gospel the writer calls the healing miracles and other actions of Jesus 'signs', showing who Jesus really is and what was the work he came to do. Here the sign that the Jewish religious leaders requested was some miraculous action like the devil's suggestion that he should throw himself down from the temple and show that no harm came to him (4.5–7).

Jesus said quite bluntly that there would be no such sign, and in Mark 8.11–12 no more is said than that, except for Jesus' deep sigh of disappointment. Here he calls them 'an evil and adulterous generation', unfaithful to the God in whom they should have believed and whose work they should have recognized in the ministry of Jesus. No sign 'except the sign of the prophet Jonah' is what Matthew says here. We have something similar again in 16.4, and similarly in Luke 11.29–32 which says that Jonah was a sign to the people of Nineveh. In the Old Testament Book of Jonah, we have the story of Jonah preaching to the people of Nineveh so that they repented. This Gospel here adds that as Jonah was a sign, appearing to the people of Nineveh after 'three days and nights in the belly of the whale', so the ultimate sign would be the resurrection of the Son of man after three days and three nights 'in the heart of the earth'.

Some have argued that verse 40 must have been a later addition to the Gospel, but there is no direct evidence for this. Some have suggested that this was an addition in the time of the early Church to what Jesus originally said about Jonah (as we have it in 16.4 and Luke 11.29–32). What matters most is the argument (like that of 11.23–24) that compares the judgement of Sodom with that of the towns of Galilee. Here there is a contrast between the people of Nineveh and the 'scribes and Pharisees' who heard Jesus. The people of Nineveh, though Gentiles, responded to the preaching of a Hebrew prophet, and yet the Jewish leaders made no positive response to the preaching of Jesus, though in what he was saying and doing it was clear that 'something greater than Jonah' was present among them.

The next part contrasts the scribes and Pharisees with the queen of Sheba who (according to 1 Kings 10) travelled far to hear the wisdom of Solomon. Jesus was in their midst, but they did not care to heed his words, though they had in Jesus' wisdom the opportunity of knowing 'something greater than Solomon'.

# 12.43–45 The Return of the Unclean Spirit

## See also Luke 11.24–26

Here is a little parable that is also in Luke, immediately following the accusation that Jesus cast out demons by Beelzebul, the ruler of the demons. It is clear that Matthew relates its meaning to the situation that he has been describing, the response or lack of response of that 'evil generation' to Jesus.

An exorcism has taken place. A person has had their life delivered from the presence and possession of evil. But it is not filled with 'good spirit'. The person's life is left like a house 'swept and put in order', but empty. So the one unclean spirit was able to bring seven other demons and come into possession, and 'the last state of that person is worse than the first'. Jewish legalism left people like a house 'swept and put in order'. There was a need for something more than legalism, and that was the presence and indwelling power of the kingdom of God in the lives of men and women.

# 12.46–50  The True Family of Jesus

## See also Mark 3.31–35; Luke 8.19–21

The closing section of this part of the Gospel (paralleled in Mark and Luke) speaks of Jesus' mother and brothers coming to where his ministry was going on. The account gives no reason, but they came to the place where he was and 'stood outside'. They were not directly associated with his ministry and perhaps not really understanding of it. Jesus was not disrespectful to his family, and John 19.25–27 shows the concern of Jesus for his mother even as he was dying on the cross. But in this situation while his mother and brothers stood outside, there were those who were 'inside' with him. There were those who were willing to do the will of the Father, and theirs was the closest relationship to him. In fact his greatest work was to bring people to seek to have God's will done on earth as it is done in heaven (6.10). So this part of the Gospel, concentrating as it has done on attitudes of people to Jesus, ends with a great positive statement. To share with Jesus in the supreme desire to do the Father's will is to have the closest relationship to him.

---

### 📖 Study Suggestions

1  Matthew 12.39 speaks of the people as spiritually 'adulterous' in the way that the prophets often said this of Israel. They spoke of Yahweh, her God, as her husband, and Israel was like an unfaithful wife. See Isaiah 57.3; Jeremiah 3.6–14; 31.32; Ezekiel 16.15–22 and Hosea 2.2–15.

2  Read the different references to people's request for a 'sign' from Jesus in Matthew 12.38; 16.1; Mark 8.11; Luke 11.16, 29; and John 2.18. In 1 Corinthians 1.22 Paul says that while 'Greeks seek wisdom', 'Jews demand signs'. Why do you think that was? Why do we find that sometimes Christian people today want special signs of God's guidance or of God's power? What is the right Christian attitude in such things?

3  People have said that the greatest desire of Jesus was to do his Father's will, and that this was his greatest desire for those who

followed him. Along with 12.50 see 6.10; 7.21; 18.14; 21.28–32 and 26.36–44 for what they indicate about this.

4 Do you think that it is a right application of 12.43–45 for Christians to say that we need not only deliverance from sin and evil but filling with the Spirit of God? How would you support this from New Testament teaching?

# PART 6: 13.1–52

# TEACHING: THE PARABLES OF THE KINGDOM

This section, the third of the five presentations of the teaching of Jesus in Matthew, has a central position in the Gospel, and parables certainly had a central place in the teaching of Jesus (see Essay on pp. 264–8). Verse 34 says that Jesus never taught without using parables. On any reckoning the parables of Jesus are some of the most wonderful stories ever told. As we think of the parables and what is said about them in this chapter, we can see three purposes in Jesus' using parables. At first sight it might appear that these three contradict each other, but further thought shows how they belong together:

1 Jesus told stories about things in the lives of ordinary people, so that people did not need to have great intellect or great education to understand them. They came from the experience of the farmer, the housewife, the shepherd, the trader. So the parables made it possible for 'babes' (as 11.25 says) to understand the deep things of the kingdom of God. People can argue that some of the apostle Paul's teaching in his letters needs a good intellect and background understanding to grasp (note 2 Peter 3.15–16). Not so the parables of Jesus.
2 Jesus used the parables to challenge people to think, and so to respond to his teaching. A very good example is the parable of the wicked tenants in 21.33–46, at the end of which it says that 'When the chief priests and the Pharisees heard his parables, they perceived that he was speaking about them.'
3 Jesus' use of parables also meant that some people learnt 'the secrets of the kingdom of heaven', while they were hidden from others. This is the meaning of the rather strange words of verses 11–17 and the quotation there from Isaiah 6. The response of people to parables shows whether or not they have a desire to understand the ways of God and to act accordingly. Parables make a division among hearers. Some, though they may be very limited in learning in the world's eyes, understand and obey. Others, though the world may see them as 'the wise and the understanding' (11.25), do not.

Matthew brings seven parables together here (eight if we take verse 52 as a parable). There are also three sections about the method of teaching in parables (verses 10–17, 34–35 and 51–52), and two explanations of parables. Mark 4 and Luke 8 both have the parable of the sower and its explanation, and (more briefly than Matthew) the part on the purpose of parables and the quotation from Isaiah. Mark 4 also has the parable of the mustard seed. The parables of the mustard seed and the yeast are both in Luke (13.18–21). The other parables in the chapter are only in Matthew. We may subdivide as follows:

---

## Analysis

13.1–9     The parable of the sower
13.10–17  The reason for teaching in parables
13.18–23  The explanation of the parable of the sower
13.24–30  The parable of the weeds among the wheat
13.31–33  The parables of the mustard seed and the yeast
13.34–35  The use of parables
13.36–43  The explanation of the weeds among the wheat
13.44–46  The parables of the hidden treasure and the pearl of
                  great price
13.47–50  The parable of the net with good and bad fish
13.51–52  The householder with treasures new and old

---

# 13.1–9  *The Parable of the Sower*

## *See also Mark 4.1–9; Luke 8.4–8*

The crowd with Jesus by the lake may well have been able to watch a sower at work. At least it was a very familiar sight. As the sower scattered the seed, not all fell into the best soil. In some places it fell where thorns and thistles had seeded. In other places there was rock just below the surface. There were other places where paths crossed over the field. The Old Testament had likened the teaching and preaching of God's word to the sowing of seed (Isaiah 55.10–11). At least the parable means that there are good results, in spite of disappointments, when someone preaches the message of the kingdom of God, as when a sower sows good seed in good soil.

The interpretation in verses 18–23 gives meaning to the four kinds of soil into which the seed fell. Biblical scholars have often emphasized the difference between parable and allegory. A parable normally makes one main point. It is treated as an allegory when there is the attempt to give spiritual meaning to each of the details of the story, as when in explaining the parable of the Good Samaritan (Luke 10.29–37) early Christian teachers made the inn represent the Church and the two coins that the Samaritan gave to the innkeeper the two sacraments. We should not turn parables into allegories, but sometimes a number of parts of a parable may be important for the meaning of the whole. We will look at this more carefully as we come to verses 18–23.

# 13.10–17 The Reason for Teaching in Parables

## See also Mark 4.10–12; Luke 8.9–10, 10.23–24

The answer that is given in these verses to the question, 'Why teach in parables?' might seem to be what theologians call 'predestination' – God gives some the privilege to know, but not others. Yet constantly in the Gospels, and in the whole of the New Testament, there is an emphasis on the responsibility of the choices that people themselves make. Parables in fact test whether a person wants to know the truth and act on it. God will give more to true disciples, those who accept his truth and the gift of understanding. Others see a parable, but do not 'perceive' its meaning because they do not really seek it. They hear the story, but they are not listening for the truth, and so they do not understand (verse 13).

So the words this passage quotes from Isaiah 6.9–10 were relevant to the ministry of Jesus (see also John 12.37–43), as people saw them to be in the ministry of the early Church too (see Acts 28.26–27). There was opportunity for people to hear the word of God through the prophet, and while they may have heard with their outward ears, they did not really want to listen, to understand and to obey. So it was with many who heard the words of Jesus. But those who wanted to see and hear were truly blessed. They, moreover, had the privilege that 'many prophets and righteous people' of past generations would have loved to share. (The words of verses 16–17 appear in a different setting in Luke 10.23–24.)

# 13.18–23 The Explanation of the Parable of the Sower

## See also Mark 4.13–20; Luke 8.11–15

People have often said that Jesus is not likely to have given explanations of his parables such as we have here, but that he would have left people to reflect on them and come to see the meaning. Also, as we have seen, some have felt that this interpretation turns the parable into an allegory. On the other hand, as we think of the parable, of the experience of Jesus and his disciples and the varied reactions of people to the teaching and preaching of the kingdom of God, it is not hard to think of the disciples, with Jesus' help, coming to understand the parable like this.

They would definitely find it true to their own later experience as messengers of God's word. Certainly we can say that these verses are relevant in the context of the ministry of Jesus, in the context of the early Church and the time of the writing of the Gospel, and in our context today. They show very realistically the different ways in which people respond to the teaching and preaching of God's word. So the details repay careful examination:

1 The 'evil one' can snatch away the good seed when a person 'does not understand it'. This links with verses 12–15, where it is clear that understanding depends on the desire to understand and to act accordingly.
2 The message of the kingdom speaks of the blessings of God and so people often receive it with joy (compare Acts 8.8 and 13.52). But it also calls for a willingness to face 'tribulation' and even 'persecution', and then many turn aside.
3 The competing desire for material things can choke the seed of the word. This may happen with those who are poor who have 'the cares of the world', an understandable anxiety about the provision for their needs (a problem dealt with in the teaching of 6.25–34). It may happen with the rich who have a 'delight in riches' if they let the desire for material wealth control them.
4 The good soil stands for those who 'hear', 'understand' and act. The result is the 'much fruit' and the 'more fruit' of John 15.1–2, 5 and 8.

📖 **Study Suggestions**

1 In relation to God's word what does it mean to 'hear', 'see', 'perceive', 'understand'?
2 In verse 22 the word that expresses what wealth does is, in different English translations, 'lure', 'deceitfulness', 'false glamour'. Which do you think best describes the attractiveness of material possessions?
3 Consider the meaning of the words of Isaiah 6.9–10 in their setting in relation to the call of Isaiah, and then the use of the words here and in John 12.37–43 and Acts 28.26–27.
4 Follow out passages in the Bible that speak on the one hand against anxiety about material things (like 6.25–34 and Philippians 4.6–7), and on the other hand against the temptation to seek material riches (like 6.19–21; Luke 12.13–21 and 1 Timothy 6.9–10, 17–19).
5 In what ways do you think that the sowing of seed, the growth of plants and then harvest express truths about the kingdom of God and about the word of God in people's lives?
6 What situations in your life and what stories from your culture would make good parables that would help people around you understand better the teaching of Jesus and the message of the kingdom of God?

# 13.24–30  The Parable of the Weeds among the Wheat

Here is another parable from the life of the farmer. He sows good seed in his farm, and then – as happened often enough in those days for the Romans to have a law against it – someone who had a grudge against him came along, and at night time 'sowed weeds among the wheat'. What was the farmer to do? He could get his workmen to go as soon as possible and pull out the weeds. But then there would be a great risk of pulling out a lot of good plants at the same time. He decided that both should grow together till harvest time, and then the harvesters would separate out the wheat and the weeds.

We have an interpretation of the parable in verses 36–43 that we will study when we come to it, but it is interesting to think what we might have taken from the parable, if we did not have that interpretation. We would most likely take from it that the world is like a great harvest field in which good and bad exist together. There is danger in people thinking that they can separate good and bad. That is God's work and in his own time he will make the separation. 'Do not pronounce judgement before the time,' says the apostle Paul in 1 Corinthians 4.5.

# 13.31–33  The Parables of the Mustard Seed and the Yeast

## See also Mark 4.30–32; Luke 13.18–21

These two parables clearly belong together. They are both about growth, growth from small beginnings. The mustard seed is a tiny seed, but it becomes a large shrub, big enough for birds to come and make their nests in its branches. In different countries people use different materials in making bread to cause the dough to rise. In some countries they use palm wine. Here it is yeast, and it takes only a small amount of yeast to spread its influence through all the dough so that it all rises and makes good bread. We can think of the work of the kingdom of God in an individual person's life as like that, or the work of the kingdom in a group of people, in a society, or in the whole world.

As we have seen, we have to be careful not to treat the parables as allegories and try to give meaning to each detail, but it may be important to realize that there were parables like that of the mustard seed in the Old Testament. They pictured the great growth of a tree, and sometimes took 'the birds of the air' in the branches to speak of Gentile nations (see Ezekiel 17.22–24; 31.3–13; Daniel 4.10–12; 20–22). At the end of this Gospel (28.18–20) it is the Gentile nations whom the first Christians are to disciple and bring into the kingdom of God.

If there is meant to be a difference between the two parables, it may be that the mustard seed indicates extensive growth, while the yeast indicates inward transformation.

# 13.34–35  *The Use of Parables*

## *See also Mark 4.33–34*

Now for the second time this chapter speaks of Jesus' use of parables. 'He said nothing to them without a parable' does not mean that literally everything that he said was in parables, but that he regularly used this method of teaching the 'crowds'. Then, as in verses 10–17 (and as so often in Matthew), we have an Old Testament quotation. This one comes from Psalm 78.1–2, and a psalmist can be called a 'prophet' because he speaks words from God. Like the psalmist Jesus spoke in parables, and like the psalmist he revealed in that way the deep truths of God, the things of 'the kingdom of heaven', things 'hidden since the foundation of the world'.

# 13.36–43  *The Explanation of the Weeds among the Wheat*

We can say similar things about this explanation as we said of the interpretation of the parable of the sower. Certainly detailed points of the parable have meaning here: the sower, the enemy, the field, the good seed, the weeds. Then the emphasis is on judgement at 'the close of the age'. We have to be aware that when the Gospels speak of 'the kingdom of heaven' or 'the kingdom of God', they are sometimes talking about the realization of God's rule now (what theologians call 'realized eschatology'). At other times what they are describing is the final realization of God's rule in judgement (spoken of as 'futurist eschatology'). Such is the case with this interpretation, as also with the parable of verses 47–50. Good and bad exist together now, but the two lifestyles will prove to have two different goals because of the reality of God's judgement. Ultimately, God will remove 'all causes of sin and all evildoers' from his kingdom, and in that kingdom (in words taken from Daniel 12.3) 'the righteous will shine like the sun'. This passage speaks of the judgement of evil-doers, as in Jewish apocalyptic writings, in the imagery of fire, and Matthew repeatedly describes the regrets of the wicked in terms of 'weeping and gnashing of teeth' (see 8.12; 13.50; 22.13; 24.51 and 25.30).

# 13.44–46 The Parables of the Hidden Treasure and the Pearl of Great Price

These two parables obviously belong together, as do those of verses 31–33. Both compare the kingdom of heaven to something of great value, in one case a treasure accidentally discovered, and in the other case a precious pearl that a merchant had been seeking. In both cases it says that to gain what was so valuable was worth sacrificing everything else, the kind of sacrifice that Jesus asked of those who wished to be his disciples (16.24–25).

# 13.47–50 *The Parable of the Net with Good and Bad Fish*

This parable is closely similar to the parable of the weeds among the wheat and the interpretation Matthew gives to that parable in verses 36–43. Some of the words there about judgement are identical with those here. There were two kinds of fish from the fisherman's point of view, the good to be kept and used, and the bad to be thrown away. 'So it will be at the close of the age'. This Gospel says much about compassion, the opportunity for repentance and the gift of forgiveness, but it also includes many warnings of judgement.

# 13.51–52 *The Householder with Treasures New and Old*

These words close this whole section of the Gospel dealing with parables, and they do so in an important way. Scribes had a very important position among the Jewish people in the time of Jesus. The Book of Ecclesiasticus, or Sirach (chapter 39) in the Apocrypha gives us a picture of the devout scribe, giving himself to 'the study of the law of the Most High', 'concerned with prophecies' and 'the wisdom of all the ancients', praying to the Lord, his Maker, and so 'filled with the spirit of understanding'. The Gospel mentions unworthy scribes, those without spiritual authority (7.29) and those who were deeply critical of Jesus (9.3; 15.1) and who finally shared in having him condemned to death. On the other hand there were also worthy scribes (see 8.19), scribes it was right to link with God's faithful prophets and sages (23.34). The work of the scribe presented an ideal for the Christian teacher to follow, and perhaps it was the ideal of the writer of the Gospel himself. The writer of the Gospel certainly had treasure new and old, the wisdom of the Old Testament that he so often quoted and the wisdom of Jesus as in the parables he has just related.

📖 **Study Suggestions**

1 The word that the RSV translates 'trained' in verse 52 is literally 'discipled', and it appears in 28.19 where it means discipling the nations. What do you think is the work of discipling people, in particular of discipling people for the kingdom of God?
2 Compare the words of verses 44–46 with what the Old Testament says about the preciousness of the Law in Psalm 19.7–10 and of wisdom in Job 28.12–19; Proverbs 2.1–5; 3.13–18 and 8.10–11. Compare also what the apostle Paul says in Philippians 3.7–11 about the worth of what he found in Christ compared with all his previous possessions. See also what he says about riches of wisdom and understanding in Colossians 2.3.
3 How do you see the story of the mustard seed and the yeast applying, in the days of the early Church as the New Testament tells its story, in the early history of Christianity in your own country, and in the work of the gospel today?

# PART 7: 13.53—17.27

## NARRATIVE: LEADING TO THE CONFESSION OF JESUS AS THE MESSIAH

After the teaching section that concentrates on the parables of Jesus we now have chapters that largely tell of the actions of Jesus, but also show the reactions of people to him. They lead up to Peter's confession of Jesus as the Christ, and instruction about the necessity of Jesus' suffering and death. Nearly all of the sections in this part of the Gospel are paralleled in Mark chapters 6–9, and they are in the same order. It is interesting to note that two small pieces of the narrative (16.17–19 and 17.24–27) that are not in Mark both have special reference to Peter. (Look back at the note after the study of 4.18–25 where we gave reasons for the view that Matthew used Mark's Gospel as a source.) We may subdivide this part of the Gospel as follows:

---

**Analysis**

13.53–58 The rejection of Jesus in Nazareth
14.1–12  The death of John the Baptist
14.13–21 The feeding of the five thousand
14.22–33 Jesus walking on the water
14.34–46 The healing of the sick at Gennesaret
15.1–20  The clean and the unclean – the tradition of the elders
            and the teaching of Jesus
15.21–28 The faith of a Gentile woman
15.29–31 The healing of many sick people
15.32–39 The feeding of the four thousand
16.1–4   The Pharisees and Sadducees ask for a sign
16.5–12  The yeast of the Pharisees and Sadducees
16.13–20 The confession of Jesus as the Messiah
16.21–23 Jesus' first prediction of his death and resurrection
16.24–28 The cross of discipleship
17.1–13  The transfiguration
17.14–21 A father with an epileptic son
17.22–23 Jesus' second prediction of his death and resurrection
17.24–27 The temple tax

---

# 13.53–58 The Rejection of Jesus in Nazareth

## See also Mark 6.1–6

This major section of the Gospel begins by showing the attitude to Jesus of the people in his own home town of Nazareth. He came and taught in their synagogue as he had done in other parts of Galilee, and they heard of his 'mighty works' in healing and in other ways. But they could only think of him as a person whom they had known from childhood. Joseph his father (who had probably died before this time) was the village carpenter or builder. Mary his mother was still there, and they knew his brothers and sisters. What could be the source of anything special about him? they asked. The proverb (which we find also in John 4.44) applied, 'Prophets are not without honour except in their own country and in their own house.' People always find it difficult to think that one of themselves could have a very special calling, especially in the service of God. The Gospel says that lack of faith is a hindrance to the healing work of Jesus. It does not always show miracles of healing to depend on the faith of the person who is healed, but Jesus constantly commended or encouraged faith (see 8.10–13; 9.20–22 and 28–30), and an atmosphere of faith helps in the operation of the power of God in people's lives. So we can understand that the 'unbelief' in Nazareth meant that Jesus did not do 'many mighty works' there.

# 14.1–12 The Death of John the Baptist

## See also Mark 6.14–29; Luke 9.7–9

The record of the attitude to Jesus of the people of his own home-town of Nazareth is now followed by the record of the attitude of 'Herod the tetrarch' to him. We have seen in the notes on 2.1–12 that the Herod who was 'king' at the time of the birth of Jesus was a local ruler to whom the Romans allowed limited power under their overall rule. Now the Herod here was one of his sons whose power was over Galilee (see Luke 3.1).

What Herod heard about Jesus made him think about John the Baptist whom he had had put to death. With a guilty conscience he feared that the explanation of the works of Jesus might be that John the Baptist had been raised from the dead. So the story of the death of John is told. Herod had put John in prison because he was outspoken about Herod's adultery with his brother's wife (see 11.2). His thoughts about what he should do with John pulled Herod in different ways. He recognized that John was 'a righteous and holy man' (Mark 6.20), and yet he wanted to silence the voice that accused him of adultery. But he also wanted to keep in favour with the people who regarded John as a prophet. The point of decision for him came when, perhaps having drunk too much at his birthday feast, he made a foolish promise to a dancing girl. To fulfil his oath, to please his wife Herodias, and not lose face with his guests, he had John beheaded in prison.

John's disciples buried John's body and came and told Jesus what had happened. We are not told here of Jesus' reaction, but it is clear in 17.12 that Jesus saw in what happened to his forerunner a foreshadowing of what would happen to him.

---

### 📖 Study Suggestions

1 What examples do you see in your situation of the application of the proverb in 13.57?
2 In what ways are the motives of Herod we find in 14.1–12 like the motives that lead people to oppose the Christian Church today?

> 3 What does Herod's situation say to us about the danger of making rash promises? What should a Christian do if caught in a situation of having made a rash promise?

# 14.13–21 The Feeding of the Five Thousand

## See also Mark 6.31–44; Luke 9.10–17; John 6.1–14

This is the one miracle of Jesus (apart from the resurrection) that all four Gospels record. There are slightly different details in the different records but again Matthew follows Mark quite closely. The setting is a 'lonely place' where Jesus had gone with his disciples. He was followed by the crowds, and 'he had compassion on them, and healed their sick'. The disciples, lacking that compassion, wanted Jesus to send the crowds away as evening came to buy food for themselves, but he challenged them, 'you give them something to eat'.

The food available is said to have been no more than five little loaves of bread and two fish, but Jesus took them and settled the crowd as if in preparation for a meal. The words that describe the action of Jesus are striking for the way in which the New Testament repeats them – in this feeding of the five thousand, in the later feeding of the four thousand (15.36), at the Last Supper (26.26), when the risen Lord met with disciples (Luke 24.30), and as Christians celebrated the Holy Communion (the Lord's Supper or Eucharist – see 1 Corinthians 11.23–24). 'Taking' the bread, he 'blessed', he 'broke', he 'gave' it to the disciples and the disciples gave it to the crowd.

There have been different attempts to explain what happened apart from Jesus literally making five loaves and two fish enough to feed thousands of people. One suggestion is that there were really only tiny pieces of food, but they were satisfying to the people because of the meaning that was given to them, like the small piece of bread and small sip of wine that we take in the Communion service. Another suggestion is that the people really had food with them, but it was only after Jesus acted as he did in taking the bread and the fish that they were encouraged to take out their food. The Gospel writers, however, certainly tell it as a miracle, and the people 'all ate and were satisfied', and later Matthew uses it as grounds for believing in the power of Jesus, as Jesus puts the question to his disciples, 'Do you not remember the five loaves of the five thousand, and how many baskets you gathered?' (16.9).

# 14.22–33  Jesus Walking on the Water

## See also Mark 6.45–52; John 6.15–21

Mark and John give details that are not in Matthew, but neither Mark nor John tell the part about Peter that we have in verses 28–33. It has a strange beginning when it speaks of Jesus making the disciples get into the boat, and then dismissing the crowds, while 'he went up into the hills by himself to pray'. John 6.15 suggests an explanation when it says that the crowd that Jesus had fed 'were about to come and take him by force to make him king', and so he 'withdrew again to the hills by himself'.

It is not hard to imagine what this story meant to the first readers of this Gospel and to generations of Christians under pressure or persecution in all parts of the world ever since. The disciples were in the midst of the lake, and though they went in obedience to the word of Jesus, they faced great trouble and danger. But Jesus came to them in their distress, and the words of verse 27 re-echo in the ears of anxious Christians: 'Take heart, it is I; have no fear.'

As for Peter, always daring, devoted to Jesus, but wanting to be out in front, he had a lesson to learn. He failed when he turned his eyes from Jesus and thought about the strength of the wind. He deserved the rebuke, 'man of little faith', but he experienced the strong hand of Jesus holding him up when he was beginning to sink.

We need not give the disciples' awe and worship and confession of Jesus as 'Son of God' the significance of Peter's confession in

16.16. But we can appreciate the disciples' increasing conviction that the one who was their Master was more than an ordinary human person. In what way could they speak of him? 'Son of God' would not have the meaning that it would have on the other side of Jesus' resurrection, but it expressed a growing sense of wonder.

# 14.34–36 The Healing of the Sick at Gennesaret

## See also Mark 6.53–56

This short section (paralleled at greater length in Mark) is one of several parts of the Gospel where we learn of a large number of healings at one time (see 4.23–24; 8.16; 9.35; 12.15 and 15.30–31). This does not mean that the healings became impersonal. The attention Jesus gave to a woman who hoped that she might just touch the fringe of his cloak and escape notice in the crowd shows Jesus' personal concern (9.20–22). Gennesaret was a fertile area between Capernaum and Bethsaida on the north-west of Lake Galilee (see map). Its lake had the same name (see Luke 5.1).

There may be an intended contrast between this section and what follows in chapter 15 in two ways:

1 In Gennesaret people welcomed Jesus with enthusiasm and he was able to bring healing to many in need. From the Jerusalem religious leaders he met with only criticism.
2 The religious leaders were concerned about the defilement of people's touch. Jesus had no such fear and those who touched him found blessing.

---

📖 **Study Suggestions**

1 What should we deduce from the fact (mentioned above) that the New Testament uses the same words about the action of Jesus, in the feeding of the crowd in 14.19, in describing what

he did at the Last Supper (26.26) and in the apostle Paul's account of Holy Communion (in 1 Corinthians 11.23–24): he 'took', 'blessed', 'broke', 'gave'?
2  In this Gospel we read of Jesus at prayer only in 14.23 and 26.36–44. Note the other occasions in which Luke speaks of Jesus at prayer in Luke 3.21; 5.16; 6.12; 9.18, 29 and 11.1.
3  Consider how the story of Jesus walking on the water might call to mind such Old Testament passages as Job 9.8; Psalm 77.19 and Isaiah 43.16.
4  What lessons do you feel Christian people should take from the record of the feeding of the five thousand in 14.13–21?
5  Do you think that the command to gather up the broken pieces left after the feeding of the crowd in 14.20 says something to us about avoiding waste? If so, what kind of application does it have in your situation?

# 15.1–20  The Clean and the Unclean – the Tradition of the Elders and the Teaching of Jesus

## See also Mark 7.1–23

There are two contrasts here, or two controversies, between the attitude of Jesus and the attitude of the 'Pharisees and scribes' who came in a deputation from Jerusalem to question him. One was between the 'tradition of the elders' and 'the commandment of God'. The other was between two ways of looking at what is clean and what is unclean. It begins with the Jewish religious leaders questioning Jesus about his disciples not washing their hands before eating. The question was not one of hygiene and cleanliness for the sake of good health, but that Jesus did not (like a rabbi) teach his disciples to keep the detailed rules (see Mark 7.3–4) that the Pharisees had. These were intended to help wash off the uncleanness of the outside world, uncleanness through certain illnesses, through contact with death, through mixing with Gentiles, the kind of uncleanness that Jesus' contact with the crowds in Gennesaret (in 14.34–36) would certainly have brought him.

In reply, Jesus first expressed his concern that the Pharisees and scribes often set the tradition of the elders (their past teachers) above the commandment of God. He gave an illustration referring to the fifth commandment, the duty of honouring father and mother (Exodus 20.12 and 21.17). In the rules that they had added, there was a way that a person might avoid honouring parents and providing for them in their need. A person could say, 'What you would have gained from me is given to God.' Although that person had made the gift, yet because they had made a vow, that was put first rather than duty to parents. Jesus indicated further that the words of Isaiah 29.13 well applied to them, in two ways. They professed with their lips to serve God, but their hearts were far from God; and they also gave human regulations and teaching a higher place than the basic commandments of God.

Even more important was the teaching about what is clean and what is unclean in the sight of God, and verses 10–11 speak of Jesus giving this as teaching to the people generally for them to listen and understand. Verse 15 calls it a 'parable', not a story kind of parable, but a saying like a proverb. 'It is not what goes into the mouth that defiles a person, but it is what comes out of the mouth that defiles' (verse 11). Jesus really offended the Pharisees (verse 12) by speaking in a way that went against their regulations, but he told the disciples not to worry. Though the scribes professed to be teachers and guides (see Romans 2.19), in this matter they were blind guides.

The way of truth is very plain. Ultimately the food that we eat does not defile the real person that we are. 'Evil thoughts' are what defile, as verse 19 puts it, and the words and actions that follow such thoughts. The sins named in verse 19 are against the sixth commandment, forbidding murder, the seventh commandment, forbidding adultery and fornication, the eighth commandment, forbidding theft, and the ninth commandment, forbidding false witness and slander (Exodus 20.13–16). Matthew seems to be following Mark (7.1–23) in this passage, but does not give the explanations that Mark needed to give for his Gentile readers, nor did he say, as Mark did, that this teaching had the result of bringing the law of clean and unclean foods to an end (Mark 7.19). Matthew adds to Mark's record the words of verses 13 and 14. There is a parallel to verse 14 in Luke 6.39, but Luke does not give the teaching about the clean and the unclean. He wrote for Gentiles, while the first readers of Matthew's Gospel were either Jewish Christians or those living alongside Jewish people, so that it would still be relevant to give Jesus' teaching relating to these regulations of the scribes and Pharisees.

# 15.21–28  The Faith of a Gentile Woman

## See also Mark 7.24–30

We have seen that in this whole section of Matthew's Gospel (13.53—17.27) Matthew follows closely what we have in Mark chapters 6–9 and Mark's order as well. Mark seems deliberately to have put this incident about a Gentile woman's faith immediately after the teaching about the clean and the unclean. Mark saw that teaching as the means of breaking down the barrier between Jews and Gentiles since the law about unclean foods prevented Jews ever eating with Gentiles. Mark (7.24) says that Jesus went to this area north of Jewish Palestine to be away from the crowds, but his reputation as a healer had gone even into that area, and so this Gentile woman came and begged him as 'Son of David' to help her daughter. There are three things about this narrative that are strange, especially in the light of what we know otherwise about Jesus from reading the Gospels.

1  Jesus said he was 'sent only to the lost sheep of the house of Israel', but even so he gave this Gentile woman the help she asked for. We can explain this best by realizing that Jesus saw his main ministry to the Jewish people, whose Scriptures had prepared them for his coming, though they were in so many ways like 'lost sheep'. He instructed his disciples in this way also when he gave them their mission (in 10.5–6). At the same time Jesus refused to accept the way that the Jewish leaders treated Samaritans and Gentiles as outcasts. In 8.10–11 we have seen how he commended the faith of a Gentile army officer and indicated the place for Gentiles in his kingdom, and so he accepted this Gentile woman and commended her faith.

2 When, however, this woman came with her desperate need, crying out, 'Have mercy on me', Jesus 'did not answer her a word', and when she kept on calling out, the disciples asked him to 'send her away'. We must understand his not answering her at first as coming from his desire to help and strengthen her faith, not to discourage it. God's way is not always to answer prayer the moment a person prays. He has a purpose in making the pray-er wait.

3 The Jews often spoke of the Gentiles as 'dogs', but it is hard to think of Jesus, with his love for all people, and especially those whom others despised, speaking of Jews as children of God and Gentiles just as dogs. We may explain this partly by the use (in Greek) not of the ordinary word for 'dogs' but a word for 'puppies' such as the master and mistress of the house would care for. We can understand that there would have been a look and an attitude of Jesus to the woman that made her feel that she could answer Jesus in the way that she does in verse 27.

Finally we must understand the whole incident by what Jesus said, 'Woman, great is your faith! Let it be done for you as you wish', and by what Jesus did, 'her daughter was healed instantly'.

---

## 📖 Study Suggestions

1 The word the RSV translates 'defile' in 15.11, 18 and 20 means literally 'make common'. See its use in Acts 10.15, and think how what Peter had to learn in Acts 10 relates to what Jesus was teaching the disciples here.

2 Should we as Christians make any rules for ourselves about what we eat and drink? How do 1 Timothy 4.1–4; Titus 1.15 and Romans 14.13–23 link with the teaching of 15.1–20? Are there principles that should affect our eating and drinking when we think of our bodies as temples of the Holy Spirit (1 Corinthians 6.19–20)?

3 Do you find rules or traditions in the life of your Church that go against the great principles of the law of God, the call to us to love God with heart and mind and soul and strength, and to love others as ourselves?

4 Are there ways in which we today can make our duty towards God an excuse for not carrying out our duty towards other people?

# 15.29–31 The Healing of Many Sick People

## See also Mark 7.31–37

In many ways these verses are like several other passages in the Gospel which speak of Jesus carrying out a large number of healings (4.23–25; 9.35–36; 12.15; 14.34–36 and 19.2). There is a difference in the way that at the end it says that 'they glorified the God of Israel', thus suggesting that Jesus carried out the actual healing miracles on Gentiles. The section that corresponds to this in Mark (7.31–37), between the story of the Canaanite woman's faith and the feeding of the four thousand, tells of the healing of just one person, but it speaks of Jesus going from the region of Tyre and Sidon to the Decapolis, east of Lake Galilee, and that was a predominantly Gentile area.

So the Gospel shows that what Jesus did for the Canaanite woman was not an isolated miracle among Gentile people. Even if Jesus' main work was to seek 'the lost sheep of the house of Israel', he showed his care and concern for non-Jewish people. He sat down to teach, but he did more than teach, as people with all their needs were brought to him, laid at his feet, 'and he healed them'.

# 15.32–39 The Feeding of the Four Thousand

## See also Mark 8.1–10

This passage is very similar to the record in 14.13–21 of the feeding of the five thousand (see pp. 135), although when Jesus expressed to the disciples the compassion he felt for the crowds, they made no reference to an event that had happened in the past. Both narratives express that compassion of Jesus. In both cases he used loaves and fish (the common diet of people of that area). In the same way he gave thanks, broke the loaves, and gave them to the disciples to distribute to the crowd, and then they gathered up the broken pieces that were left over.

Some people think that the two are records of the same event that have come down in slightly different ways, so that both forms of the story appear in Matthew as in Mark (8.1–10). Yet there are differences in the numbers of the crowds, the loaves available, and the baskets of broken pieces (and the use of a different word for 'baskets'). Certainly the writer of this Gospel, like Mark, believed that there were two separate events, as 16.8–10 indicates. It may be right to see this incident, like verses 21–28 and 29–31, as involving Gentile people, and so showing the concern of Jesus for hungering Gentiles as well as Jews. In this way the readers of the Gospel could understand that Jesus was 'the bread of life' for all people, whatever their race.

The passage closes with Jesus going across Lake Galilee again, but neither the 'Magadan' of 15.39 nor the 'Dalmanutha' of Mark 8.10 are known to us today.

---

### 📖 Study Suggestions

1 Compare 9.8 with verse 31 and notice the things that lead people to glorify God. How do these relate to what Jesus says in 5.16 about his disciples acting in ways that should lead people to glorify God?

2 See the other passages in the Gospel which like verse 32 speak of the 'compassion' of Jesus (9.36; 14.14 and 20.34). How would you explain this word and the kind of effects that it should have if a person really shows compassion for others?

# 16.1–4 The Pharisees and Sadducees Ask For a Sign

## See also Mark 8.11–13; Luke 12.54–56

As we have seen (in the study of 3.1–12), the Pharisees and Sadducees had very different convictions and interpretations of the Jewish Law, but they were prepared to unite in challenging the truth of what Jesus was teaching and the authority of the things that he was doing. Their test was to ask him to 'show them a sign from heaven', something miraculous as in sun or moon or flash of lightning. In fact there had been many signs of the power of God in human lives, signs of transformed lives when the kingdom of God, the rule of God, took effect in men and women. There were, and would be, signs like that of Jonah, because Jonah stood out from the pages of the Old Testament as a person who preached as a prophet and people repented. (In 12.40–41 the meaning of the sign of Jonah has been developed in a different way.)

Verses 1 and 4 are like Mark 8.11–13, but Mark has no parallel to verses 2 and 3. In fact what those verses say about the signs of the weather is missing from some of the early Greek manuscripts of this Gospel. One view is that copyists added them in the spirit of what we read about the signs of the weather in Luke 12.54–56, though the actual words are quite different. Another view is that the verses may have been left out because the signs of the weather were very different in other places where people read the Gospel from those in Palestine. In any case, as in 12.38–39, Jesus saw it as a mark of 'an evil and adulterous generation' to ask for the kind of sign they wanted. There were plenty of signs in those wonderful 'times' when Jesus was meeting the needs of the sick, the hungry, the marginalized, the demon-possessed. Though Jesus welcomed all who came to him in sincerity, when people were not prepared to open their hearts and minds to the love and goodness of God, 'he left them and departed'.

# 16.5–12 The Yeast of the Pharisees and Sadducees

## See also Mark 8.14–21; Luke 12.1

This section also follows Mark's record, except that Mark speaks of the Pharisees and Herod, while here we have the Pharisees and Sadducees. Matthew has just presented the attitude of Pharisees and Sadducees in testing Jesus by asking him for a 'sign from heaven' (verse 1), as a condition of their believing in him. In the case of the Pharisees the Gospel indicates that their influence, that could spread like yeast in the dough when you make bread, was that of legalism. The influence of the Sadducees was that of seeking power and position for themselves. In both cases their attitudes made it hard for them to believe and recognize the word of God in the teaching of Jesus, and the signs of God's kingdom in the lives of people in need.

The response of the disciples to the words of Jesus illustrates what is very familiar in our daily lives. We have some special concern so much on our minds that when someone speaks to us about something completely different, we misinterpret what they say because of what is filling our thoughts at the time. Jesus spoke figuratively about the 'yeast of the Pharisees and Sadducees'. The disciples thought of yeast and so of bread and had the worry that they had gone to the other side of the lake without a supply of bread.

They deserved Jesus calling them people 'of little faith' in the light of all that they had seen Jesus do, providing abundantly for the hungry in the past, and teaching them to be concerned first of all for the things of God's kingdom and trust God for everything else (6.33). All through the time of their discipleship, Jesus had been seeking to lead them to faith, the kind of faith that Peter is to profess in the next section (verses 13–20). They needed to beware of the influence of the Pharisees' and Sadducees' unbelief, as well as their teaching in other respects.

### 📖 Study Suggestions

1 In what way do you think people today look for the kind of 'signs' that the Pharisees and Sadducees asked Jesus to show? What are the real signs of the work of Christ in the world?

2 Yeast in the parable of 13.33 represents the good influence of 'the kingdom of heaven'. Note, however, how Paul uses yeast in 1 Corinthians 5.6–8 and Galatians 5.7–10, in a way similar to Matthew 16.5–12.
3 How is the Church still in danger of coming under the influence of 'the leaven of the Pharisees and Sadducees' as this Gospel indicates what that was?

# 16.13–20 The Confession of Jesus as the Messiah

## See also Mark 8.27–30; Luke 9.18–21

This is a key passage in the Gospel. Jesus has been leading his disciples to faith in him, and now Peter confesses his faith. And from this point Jesus begins to speak of the way that he must suffer, and the Gospel from this point leads on to his suffering and death. Verses 13–16 and 20 follow Mark 8.27–30 (see also Luke 9.18–21), but what we have in verses 17–19 is only in Matthew.

Jesus probably went to the area of Caesarea Philippi where there were not the Jewish crowds among whom he was well known, and perhaps intended to have a time teaching his disciples by themselves. It was an area where people might think of many different ways of worship. There were temples to other gods in the area, and the town rebuilt by Herod Philip and named in honour of the Roman emperor (or Caesar) had a temple for the worship of the emperor.

There are eight important things to consider as we study this passage:

1 'Who do people say that the Son of man is?' Using that term 'Son of man' that we have seen could have little or much meaning given to it (see notes after 8.18–22), Jesus was asking what people were saying about him. To this there were four answers, all of which involved the thought of someone coming back from the dead.

(a) John the Baptist (we have seen this view in 14.2).

(b) Elijah, because of the hope based on Malachi 4.5–6 in the Old Testament, that Elijah would come back and prepare for the coming of the Messiah.

(c) Jeremiah, the prophet who faithfully proclaimed God's word and suffered for it, bringing also the message of a new covenant and of the forgiveness of God.

(d) Any one of the old prophets come back.

2 This led to the most important question, 'But who do you say that I am?' and to Peter's answer. This Gospel has presented Jesus as the Messiah from its first verse, and indicated that Jesus knew from the beginning of his ministry that he was Messiah. Now Peter believes it and confesses it. Matthew adds 'Son of the living God' here (it is not in Mark and Luke), and though Peter could not have understood this in the way that people understood it after the resurrection of Jesus, the Old Testament had spoken of God's Anointed as his Son in some special sense (as in Psalm 2.7).

3 Jesus says that recognizing him as 'the Messiah, the Son of the living God' is not just the result of human understanding ('flesh and blood'), but is God-given understanding and revelation.

4 Who or what is the rock on which the Church would be built? Elsewhere in the New Testament (in 1 Corinthians 3.11) writers speak of Jesus himself as the Church's 'foundation'. Here he is the founder rather than the foundation. Ephesians 2.20 speaks of the Church 'built upon the foundation of the apostles and prophets, Christ Jesus himself being the cornerstone'. The thought here is similar, though Jesus addresses only Peter. But it is Peter as the person who makes the confession of Jesus as 'the Messiah, the Son of the living God', and the Gospel later indicates that the authority was not just Peter's but shared with the other apostles. We should add that there is nothing said here about how that authority was to be handed on to others.

5 Some people believe that 'Jesus intended to build a Church'. There are two points to be made here:

– Scholars question whether Jesus could have referred to 'the Church' at a time when the Church as such was not yet established. They believe that people read back these words into the time of Jesus from the time that the Gospel was written. However, the word English versions translate 'the Church' may come from an Aramaic expression meaning any assembly of people or community, or, specifically, the Old Testament people of God. Jesus may have been thinking of the Messianic community, and used the word to refer to those who were his disciples and followed his teaching.

– Did Jesus really intend to build a Church?

If we think of the Church as it is – with all its organization, buildings, divisions – we might well say, 'No'. But it does seem clear that Jesus gathered around him a community who were to do his work and carry on his mission. The choice of twelve is linked with the twelve tribes of Israel (in 19.28), and so we can think of the words here as the basis of what is developed in other parts of the New Testament where the writers see the Church of Jesus Christ as the new Israel, carrying on God's purpose for his people, but in a new way.

6 What about the meaning of 'the powers of death' not being able to prevail against the Church? Some translations render verse 18 more literally 'the gates of Hades'. 'Hades' is the place of the dead, rather than the place of punishment, and so the thought is of death never being able to hold the Church bound inside its gates. In other words, the Church will never die or be overwhelmed by any powers against it.

7 People have often understood Peter's holding the 'keys of the king-dom of heaven' to mean that Peter has authority to open the door into God's kingdom to people, and to close the door on others. In the Bible the power of the keys goes back to Isaiah 22.22 where it speaks of God entrusting authority in the life of his people to one Eliakim son of Hilkiah. Here, moreover, Matthew links it with the authority of 'binding' and 'loosing', which in Jewish rabbinic teaching meant the authority of laying down rules of conduct. Peter (and other apostles) did indeed, by the preaching of the gos-pel, open the doors of the kingdom to all who believed, as the Acts of the Apostles shows. They did proclaim the forgiveness of sins, the conditions of forgiveness, and the warning of the possibility of missing God's forgiveness (see John 20.23). But the main thought here may be that of oversight in the community of Christ's disci-ples, authority to preach and to teach and to guide, and whatever they said and did on earth in agreement with the will of God would be established in heaven.

8 Lastly, in verse 20 Jesus ordered the disciples not to tell others that he was Messiah. We can understand this in the light of the fact that there were so many different Jewish ideas of Messiahship, and with Jesus people had to understand Messiahship in terms of service and suffering (as the next few verses tell), or they would terribly misunderstand it.

# 16.21–23 Jesus' First Prediction of his Death and Resurrection

## See also Mark 8.31–33; Luke 9.22

When the disciples had acknowledged Jesus as Messiah, it was most important that they should understand what kind of Messiah he must be. So 'from that time on' Jesus began to teach his disciples how he must suffer and die. Following Mark again, we have the first of three predictions of his sufferings (see 17.22–23 and 20.17–19).

Notice the five things that these verses say:

1 Jesus must go up to Jerusalem. He spent much of his ministry in Galilee, but Jerusalem was the centre of his people's life and worship. There he must offer himself to the people, and there they would reject him and condemn him to die.
2 He would suffer 'from the elders and chief priests and scribes'. We have read of the chief priests and scribes together from 2.4, and with the elders they formed the Jewish supreme council, the Sanhedrin.
3 They would cause him to be put to death.
4 He would be raised from death on the third day. Sometimes people have questioned whether Jesus could have predicted his resurrection. But a spiritual understanding of the Old Testament would have brought him the assurance that God's purposes and God's people are not ultimately defeated. Hosea 6.2 speaks of the raising up of the broken and defeated people 'on the third day', and we can understand that Jesus may have taken those words in application to his own situation.
5 Jesus says that these things 'must' be, and the Gospel as a whole makes clear that this is not just because of the opposition that Jesus faced, but for the realization of the purpose of God.

The response of Peter is understandable. Why should the leader whom they had followed have to suffer like that? Why should he submit to such treatment? So 'Peter took him and began to rebuke him'. But to Jesus, Peter's action was like Satan's temptation coming back, as it had been at the beginning, the temptation to be a different kind of Messiah and avoid opposition and suffering (see especially

4.5–6). Peter was a 'hindrance' to Jesus rather than a true disciple when he said such things. He had to see that although he had followed God's revelation in confessing Jesus as Messiah (verse 17), now his response was a very human one and certainly not in line with God's purposes.

# 16.24–28  The Cross of Discipleship

## See also Mark 8.34—9.1; Luke 9.23–27

Again as we have it in Mark, what Jesus has said about his own sufferings is followed by his teaching that true disciples must also be prepared to suffer. (There has been similar teaching, probably from a different source, in 10.38–39, similar to Luke 14.27.) To be a true disciple means three things:

1  To deny self. This does not mean giving up certain things in order to live a better and more disciplined life. It means saying 'No' to all selfish desires in order to say 'Yes' to Jesus and to the will of God.
2  To take up the cross. Christians have become so accustomed to the cross as the symbol of Christianity that we forget what a terrible and shameful death crucifixion was. Jesus' first disciples would have seen people who were condemned to death carrying to the place of their execution part of the cross to which they would be nailed to die. So to carry the cross meant not just bearing a burden but willingly accepting that they must die to the way of life that they had lived before.
3  To follow, as the sheep follow the shepherd, as soldiers must follow their captain, so they must go the way that Jesus led them, following in his steps. This amounts to saying that there are two ways from which a person who wants to be a disciple of Jesus has to choose. One is to hold on to life and live it in a self-chosen way, but that is to lose real life. The other is to give up selfish ambition for Jesus' sake, and be prepared even to suffer and die for him, and that is to find real life. In the first way, a person might gain all that

the world has to offer (as the devil offered Jesus in his third temptation in 4.8–9), but in the process lose true life. (We can translate
the same word in the Greek as 'soul' or 'life', and verses 25–26 play
on the two meanings. To lose one's soul is to lose one's true life.) In
the end, at the coming of the Son of man 'in the glory of his
Father', a person must give account to God for the way that they
have lived their life.

Verse 28 is one of the most difficult verses in the Gospel, and people
have understood 'the Son of man coming in his kingdom' in a number of different ways:

1 It refers to the coming again of Jesus (the Parousia), but people
   mistakenly thought this was going to happen within the lifetime
   of some of the first disciples. Against that is the firm statement (as
   in 24.36) that the time of that event was not known, not even to
   the Son, but only to the Father.
2 It refers to the transfiguration which the Gospel goes straight on to
   record (17.1–8). In 2 Peter 1.16–18 this is linked with 'the power
   and coming of our Lord Jesus Christ'. There is a sense in which the
   transfiguration offered a glimpse of the glory of 'the Son of man
   coming in his kingdom', but the whole reference of the verse
   could hardly be to an event that it would go on to describe as taking place immediately.
3 It refers to the events that would follow the sufferings and death of
   Jesus, that is, his resurrection and ascension, the coming of the
   Holy Spirit and the showing forth of the power of his kingdom in
   the life of the Church. This would seem close to the meaning, and
   it would give the assurance that although Jesus must suffer and
   die, those who witnessed those sad events would not die before
   they had seen the glory of the Son of man and the power of his
   kingdom at work in the world.

---

## 📖 Study Suggestions

1 See how the words 'flesh and blood' speak of human life in its
  weakness and limitations in 1 Corinthians 15.50; Galatians
  1.16; Ephesians 6.12 and Hebrews 2.14.
2 In 16.21 we have 'from that time' as we did in 4.17. Do you
  think that these words show the main stages in the ministry of
  Jesus?
3 In what ways do Isaiah 22.15–25 and Revelation 1.17–18 and
  3.7–8 help us to understand what 16.19 may mean about the
  'power of the keys'?
4 To follow Jesus, as this is put in 16.24, means to follow in his
  steps. See what 1 Peter 2.18–25 says is the meaning of this.

5 Alongside the confession of Jesus as 'the Son of the living God' see how this Gospel presents Jesus as Son of God earlier on in 3.17; 4.3 and 6; 8.29 and 11.27.
6 In the story of the Christian Church in your own country or area, do you see evidence of the failure of the powers of death or evil to overcome the Church? Are there ways in which it is dangerous to boast about such things on behalf of the Church?

# 17.1–13  The Transfiguration

## See also Mark 9.2–13; Luke 9.28–36

We need to approach with reverence this record of what the Gospel calls the 'transfiguration' of Jesus. The word speaks of a change in his natural appearance, and verse 2 says that not only 'his face shone like the sun', but also 'his garments became white as light'. We may not be able to explain it, but the record indicates that, as in a 'vision' (the word we have in verse 9), the three disciples saw the glory of Jesus as never before. Mark and Luke, like Matthew, link this closely with what has gone before. Matthew speaks of it as happening six days after Peter had confessed Jesus as Messiah, and Jesus had spoken of the necessity of his sufferings and of the cross of discipleship. Jesus had told them that he would be rejected, but now they see his true glory, and a voice proclaims him to them as God's 'beloved Son', and tells them to 'listen to him' beyond all others.

The disciples saw Moses and Elijah with Jesus in the vision. They represented the Law and the Prophets which the New Testament repeatedly speaks of as fulfilled in Jesus. Moses was more than the Lawgiver – he foreshadowed the greatest Prophet who was to come (see Deuteronomy 18.15 and its use in Acts 3.22). There was also the prophecy of the coming of 'Elijah the prophet before the great and terrible day of the Lord comes' (Malachi 4.5).

It was typical of Peter to be the first to speak, even if he hardly knew what to say. How wonderful it would be to stay on the mountain with Jesus and Moses and Elijah, to worship together and prolong the vision! He may have been thinking of the Feast of

Tabernacles, and making temporary huts to celebrate it, and perhaps it would be the special celebration of the feast that prophecy predicted (Zechariah 14.16–18). But that was not to be. The vision faded. Moses and Elijah disappeared. The disciples were left afraid, but comforted by the word of Jesus. They had to get up, leave the mountain-top experience behind, and go down to the ordinary life and ministry of the valley below.

As on other occasions, Jesus told people to be quiet about his miracles; here he warns the disciples not to tell others at this stage what they had seen. It could too easily lead to misunderstanding and wrong reactions from those who had misguided Messianic hopes. The disciples, however, had a problem. In their experience on the mountain they had seen Elijah. The scribes, on the basis of their knowledge of the scriptures, believed that Elijah would come before the Messiah arrived. How could this be if Jesus was the Messiah, and Elijah had not come? The answer was that Elijah had come, in the person of John the Baptist. He had come to 'restore' things, to restore people to their right relationships with God and with one another (as Malachi 4.6 puts it). That was the meaning of his message of repentance. The trouble was that people did not accept that message of restoration. The Jewish leaders refused to recognize him (see 21.25–27). To the great pleasure of his opponents, he was rejected and put to death – as indeed would happen to the Son of man.

## 📖 Study Suggestions

1 Note the use of the same word 'transfigured' in Romans 12.1–2 and 2 Corinthians 3.18. What link do you think there is between the use in those passages and this one?
2 In what ways do the Old Testament passages Exodus 34.29–35; Deuteronomy 18.15–19; Zechariah 14.16–17 and Malachi 4.4–6 help us to understand this passage?
3 How should we link together what this passage says here about Elijah and John the Baptist, and what Luke 1.13–17 and John 1.19–27 say?
4 Verse 2 says 'he was transfigured before them'. Do you think that this experience, as this Gospel records it, was primarily for the disciples, or for Jesus?
5 In what way should we link the record here with that of the baptism of Jesus, and the voice from heaven then, 'This is my beloved Son, with whom I am well pleased'? Look back to the comments on 3.17.
6 There were two other occasions when just Peter, James and John were with Jesus (see Mark 5.35–37 and Matthew 26.36–37). Did

Jesus grant some disciples special privileges not granted to the others?

7 What place does the Bible give to special spiritual experiences like visions? What place should we give them today?

# 17.14–21 A Father with an Epileptic Son

## See also Mark 9.14–29; Luke 9.37–43

What a contrast between the scene on the mountain and this scene of human suffering in the valley below! Often enough life is like that, an uplifting spiritual experience and then the needs of the world to which the disciple of Christ returns.

Matthew does not explain the 'crowd' in verse 14, but a comparison with the parallel to this in Mark suggests that once again Matthew has considerably shortened Mark's vivid account. The man probably rightly described his son as 'epileptic', but treated him as also needing deliverance from the demonic. But whereas Mark tells us much about the crowd, about the father's distress, and the son's plight, Matthew focuses attention on the disciples. Jesus longed to find people who would be prompted to faith in God in the face of great human needs. In Mark the father cried out to Jesus, 'I believe; help my unbelief', and he found Jesus' help. Here in Matthew it is the disciples whom Jesus told, in answer to their question, 'Why could we not cast it out?' that it was because of their 'little faith'.

There are two proverbial expressions in verse 20. People of that time thought of the grain of mustard seed, as the parable in 13.32 puts it, as 'the smallest of all seeds'. Moving mountains was proverbial for overcoming great difficulties. So Jesus is saying that a tiny faith in a great and mighty, loving and caring God changes situations and deals with deep human needs. To such a faith nothing – nothing that is within the will and purpose of God – is impossible.

In most modern translations there is no verse 21. Older translations into English (and other languages) followed later Greek manuscripts with the words that we find in this setting in Mark 9.29, 'This kind never comes out except by prayer and fasting'. This is teaching that is true to much in the New Testament, but not originally written in this Gospel here.

# 17.22–23 Jesus' Second Prediction of his Death and Resurrection

## See also Mark 9.30–32; Luke 9.43–45

As the Gospel now moves steadily towards its climax in the record of the death and resurrection of Jesus, we have here the second of three predictions of that death and resurrection (see 16.21 and 20.17–19). As the disciples understandably failed to take in what being raised on the third day might mean, they were naturally 'greatly distressed'. The terms of the prediction are like those of 16.21, but a key word here speaks of Jesus being 'betrayed into human hands' (NRSV), 'delivered' or 'handed over'. The Gospel uses the same word for Judas handing Jesus over to the chief priests (26.15), for the chief priests handing him over to Pilate (27.2), then for Pilate handing Jesus over to the soldiers for them to crucify him (27.26).

# *17.24–27  The Temple Tax*

From a number of points of view this is a rather strange little passage. There are four questions that we should consider:

1 What is its place in the Gospel? It is hard to see a particular connection with what goes before it or with the next main section of the Gospel, chapter 18. Yet it was clearly important for Matthew to include it.

2 What lies behind what this passage tells us about the attitude of Jesus to the temple tax? The temple tax went back to Exodus 30.11–16 where every person in Israel over 20 years of age had to give half a shekel for the service of the sanctuary. This later became an annual tax of half a shekel or two drachmas (about two days' wages) for the upkeep of the temple. Certain people, like the priests, did not have to pay. Was Jesus in the habit of paying this annual tax? Peter said, 'Yes'. Jesus took up the matter by asking the question, 'From whom do kings of the earth take toll or tribute?' The Romans, like other imperial powers, took tribute from subject races rather than from their own people. Or a powerful king might get his citizens to pay taxes but not his own family. In relation to the temple, Jesus and his disciples were not like foreigners. In 12.5–6 Jesus spoke of his presence as 'something greater than the temple'. He was truly the Son of God in a very special way, and his disciples were members of God's kingdom and children of God. By right Jesus should not have to pay temple tax, but in order to identify himself with his people and not to give offence, he would pay the tax.

3 To what situation in Matthew's time would the principle of this apply? The destruction of the temple in Jerusalem took place in AD 70. If the Gospel was written before that time, the principle might have been applied to encourage Jewish Christians to pay the temple tax, even though they realized that their relationship with God through Jesus had taken the place of the temple in their worship. After AD 70 the Romans took this 'temple tax' and used it for the temple of Jupiter in Rome. It is hard to think that the Gospel writer would have encouraged fellow Christians to pay for the upkeep of a heathen temple. Perhaps the application was more general. There are many things that Christians are called to do as citizens of their country, or in their relationships with other people, that they may not see as part of their basic Christian loyalty, but that they should do in order not to give offence or cause misunderstanding.

4 What about the coin in the fish's mouth? Some people have said that this is quite unlike any other of Jesus' miracles. Did he not do it just for himself and his own convenience, and could it not encourage people to try to rely on the miraculous to get them out of a financial difficulty? Some have questioned whether we should take verse 27 as a miracle, especially because it does not tell us that Peter actually went and caught the fish. Could Jesus have been using a proverb or making a humorous remark, 'If you want a stater (the coin you need), you will have to go and get it from a fish's mouth'? Others have suggested that Jesus was saying to Peter that he would have to go back briefly to his business of fishing to get the money he needed. At the same time we may say that because Jesus and the disciples lived by faith and on the gifts that others provided for them (Luke 8.1–3), he may not have wanted to use such gifts for the temple tax. As far as such a 'miracle' is involved, from all over the world there are equally remarkable stories of God's provision for individuals and communities who have looked to God in faith for him to meet their material needs.

📖 **Study Suggestions**

1 The words 'faithless and perverse generation' in verse 17 recall the words of Deuteronomy 32.4–5. How are the backgrounds of the Old and New Testament passages similar?
2 Follow the references in the notes on verses 22–23 to Jesus being 'handed over' to die, but note also the deeper theological sense of the expression in its use in Romans 8.32 and Galatians 2.20.
3 Compare with verse 20 the teaching of Matthew 21.21–22; Luke 17.6 and 1 Corinthians 13.2 about the faith that can 'move mountains' or do what seem to be impossible things. How should we apply this in our own situations? How can we be sure that what we want to ask is what is God's will for us to do?
4 In relation to Jesus' willingness to pay the tax out of a desire not to offend or cause misunderstanding, is there a connection with the kind of things that Paul chose to do or not to do for the same kind of motive? See especially 1 Corinthians 8—10.
5 Follow through the ways in which, in this main section of the Gospel (chapters 14—17), we see the weaknesses of the disciples, and what we can understand as Jesus' desire to lead them to stronger faith. See especially 14.16–21; 26–31; 15.15–16, 23, 32–33; 16.5–12, 22–23.
6 Do you find parallels today with the experience of the father in verses 14–16, unable to find help through Jesus' disciples and wanting Jesus himself? What is the challenge to us when we

realize that some people have lost faith in the Church but not in Jesus himself?

7 Are there things in your situation and society which do not challenge your basic loyalty to Christ, but which you feel you should do in order not to offend others or be misunderstood?

# PART 8: 18.1—35
## TEACHING: FELLOWSHIP IN THE COMMUNITY

In the way that Matthew planned and structured his Gospel, this is now the fourth of the five great teaching sections (see p. 3), ending as the others have done, 'Now when Jesus had finished these sayings . . .' (19.1).

The teaching of this chapter is about relationships in the community of disciples. It is not a series of laws for them to obey, such as the contemporary Qumran community near the Dead Sea had in its 'Manual of Discipline'. Rather we have guiding principles for living and working together, accepting one another, forgiving one another, supporting one another.

We have seen how this Gospel, especially in its narrative sections, appears to follow Mark and the order of things that we have in Mark. Much of chapter 17 in Matthew has followed Mark 9.2–30. Verses 1–9 in this chapter parallel teaching that we find in Mark 9.33–48, but then none of what comes after this is in Mark.

We can divide the chapter into sections as follows:

---

**Analysis**

18.1–5     The way of humility
18.6–9     Not stumbling or causing others to stumble
18.10–14 Seeking the lost sheep
18.15–20 Reproving and restoring the person who offends
18.21–22 Forgiving others
18.23–35 The parable of the unforgiving debtor

---

# 18.1–5  The Way of Humility

## See also Mark 9.33–37; Luke 9.46–48

This section begins with the disciples' question, 'Who is the greatest in the kingdom of heaven?' The question itself shows a wrong attitude, and Mark (9.33–34) tells of the disciples arguing on the road about which of them was the most important. The question may have arisen because of the position that Peter had assumed in the little company of disciples (17.24–27 as well as other incidents show Peter's position). The answer of Jesus was to get them to think about the position of a little child and their attitude to a little child.

Putting a little child among them, Jesus first said that they needed to 'turn and become like children'. Sometimes people have said that Jesus meant becoming innocent like a little child – but little children very soon come to say 'No' and to disobey, and are not really innocent. Others have said that disciples should be humble like a little child, but even children push themselves forward and try to get attention. Rather the point was that in that society in Jesus' time people treated children as unimportant. Even Jesus' disciples showed this when people brought children for Jesus to bless them (19.13–15). The challenge of Jesus to his disciples was thus to 'turn' from the attitude of trying to be important, striving to be greatest, and be ready to be unimportant in the world's eyes. In a way utterly different from the ideas of greatness in the world's kingdoms, Jesus teaches that it is by humility that a person is great in the kingdom of heaven.

It is also the way of the world for us to want to have friends among the great and important. In Jesus' eyes it was the willingness to welcome the unimportant, the little child, that showed who was a person of worth in God's kingdom. 'Whoever receives one such child in my name receives me.' And these words are also the bridge to the next section that speaks of causing a little person to stumble.

# 18.6–9  Not Stumbling or Causing Others to Stumble

## See also Mark 9.42–48; Luke 17.1–2

We are not to take strictly literally the words of Jesus about being thrown into the sea with a millstone round one's neck and about fire for eternity, but neither must we take away from the seriousness of their warning. It is a matter of the utmost seriousness if we cause another person to stumble and to fall into sin! And how determined we should be to avoid stumbling ourselves!

The words about welcoming a little child (verse 5) are appropriately followed by the words about putting a stumbling-block before 'one of these little ones who believe'. Perhaps the 'little ones' now may include not just children but simple believers, perhaps new believers. In a sinful world there are inevitably many pressures against the life of Christian discipleship, many things that can cause a person to stumble, but those who cause others to stumble or to choose the wrong way must answer to God for their actions.

In relation to a person's own situation the issues at stake are 'life' and judgement. The Sermon on the Mount has already given a warning like this in relation to sexual temptation (5.29–30). That reality of judgement calls for discipline, and the removal from a person's life of what Hebrews 12.1 speaks of as 'the sin that so easily entangles' us (New International Version). James 1.14–15 puts it, 'one is tempted by one's own desire, being lured and enticed by it; then, when that desire has conceived, it gives birth to sin, and that sin, when it is fully grown, gives birth to death.' Similarly, the warning of Jesus is, 'Don't give any opportunity for the sinful desire to grow.'

---

### 📖 Study Suggestions

1  In what ways in the Gospels do we see the humility of Jesus himself (see 11.29 and 21.5)? In the Epistles, what do Ephesians 4.1–3; Philippians 2.1–8 and Colossians 3.12–14 say about humility?
2  What place do people give to little children in your society? Are there ways in which it is necessary to change that, because of

the understanding of Christian values that the New Testament gives?

3 What can we learn from the frequency with which this Gospel refers to the things that cause people to stumble or to take offence? See how this Gospel speaks about this in 5.29–30; 11.6; 15.12; 16.23; 17.27; 24.10 and 26.31–33 as well as this passage.

4 As a very personal question, what do you think are ways in which you are in danger of causing others to stumble? And what things are most likely to cause you to stumble yourself? How should you deal with such things?

# 18.10–14  Seeking the Lost Sheep

## See also Luke 15.3–7

Verse 10 takes us back to the thought of verse 6, which speaks of causing 'one of these little ones' to stumble. Here it is a matter of not despising or neglecting 'one of these little ones'. The 'little ones' – whether young children or those the world thinks unimportant – are precious to God. This is the meaning of the saying that 'in heaven their angels always behold the face' of the heavenly Father. That is, there is acknowledgement of them in heaven, even if there is neglect on earth, and they are of concern to God himself.

We then have the parable of the lost sheep. Luke (15.3–7) tells this same parable of the shepherd with the hundred sheep, but with more detail. There, however, its setting is the criticism of Jesus by the scribes and Pharisees for the way that he was willing to receive 'tax collectors and sinners'. Jesus' response was to compare his work to a woman searching for a lost coin, the shepherd seeking a lost sheep, and the concern of a father for his lost son. It may be right to think that Matthew took this parable and used it in another very practical way in this chapter dealing with relationships in the community of disciples. Disciples needed to be concerned for anyone among them who might go astray. But it may be that Jesus himself used the parable more than once with slightly different applications.

The Old Testament has the background for the thought of God as Shepherd of his people, and of kings and priests and prophets with shepherd-like responsibilities. Those who follow Christ are to be like under-shepherds with the same concern as the Chief Shepherd (compare 1 Peter 5.1–4). Because it is not the will of God 'that one of these little ones should perish', the true disciple must be in the business of seeking the straying. As verse 13 puts it, there is no assurance that the shepherd will always be able to rescue and restore the straying, but 'if he finds it', what great joy there is!

(In most modern translations there is no verse 11. Many early manuscripts and translations had, before the parable of the lost sheep, the words, 'For the Son of man has come to save' (or 'to seek and to save') 'the lost'. But some of the most important and earliest manuscripts did not have these words. Scholars think that people probably added them from Luke 19.10 because they were meaningful in this context.)

# 18.15–20 Reproving and Restoring the Person Who Offends

## See also Luke 17.3

The concern of disciples for one another, following the example of the seeking shepherd, should lead to what James 5.20 speaks of as 'bringing back a sinner from wandering'. If someone feels that another person has wronged them, it is important not just to have a feeling of hostility against that person. The right way is to go to the person directly, aiming to 'restore such a one in a spirit of gentleness' (as the apostle Paul puts it in Galatians 6.1). These are the principles to follow:

1 Go first to the person alone, and if they recognize that they have done wrong and deal with it, then there will be restoration of the fellow-disciple and healing of relationships in the family.
2 If that way of person-to-person contact does not succeed in dealing with the matter, then 'take one or two others along with you'. The principle here is 'that every word may be confirmed by the evidence of two or three witnesses'. In the Old Testament that principle was applied particularly in the case of a trial (see Deuteronomy 17.6 and 19.15), but here it is rather that one or two others may help to bring home to the person the wrong that they have done and so bring about reconciliation.
3 If the person still does not take notice, 'tell it to the church'. This is the only use, apart from in 16.18, of the word 'Church' (the Greek word *ekklesia*) in the Gospels, and it is probably not in the same sense as in 16.18. It is the community. Just as the Jewish local community was the synagogue, so the Christians have their local communities, and they are to be prepared to deal with such matters.
4 If the person 'refuses to listen even to the church' the members should treat him or her 'as a Gentile and a tax collector'. It is sometimes thought that Jesus, with his loving concern for Gentiles and tax collectors, would not have spoken like this. Perhaps, however, as in 5.46–47, the thought is simply of those at present outside the community. Indeed, in the mind of Jesus there was hope for Gentiles and tax collectors, and hope for such people as Matthew describes here, if only they were penitent and accepted reconciliation.
5 Verse 18 indicates that when Christians deal with such matters in the right way, God upholds their actions 'in heaven'. The words of this verse are similar to those of 16.19 where we have studied the meaning of 'binding' and 'loosing'.

Verse 19 may seem to be a very big promise in relation to prayer. We should say two things about it:

1 We must understand it in its context, which deals with questions of restoration and reconciliation.
2 The agreement of two in prayer must be about things that are in the line of God's will, or certainly they cannot be sure of the answer to the request.

Both verse 19, however, and verse 20 stress the importance of the fellowship of disciples. The individual Christian can be sure of the Lord's unfailing presence wherever he or she may be (28.20), but we are to know the special blessing and strength of Christians agreeing together, meeting and acting in fellowship (see Hebrews 10.25).

---

### 📖 Study Suggestions

1 In relation to verse 14 note the biblical passages that speak of the angels representing nations (Daniel 10.13–21; 12.1), representing churches (Revelation chapters 1—3), and supporting individuals (Genesis 48.16; Psalm 91.11–12 and Hebrews 1.14). How should we think of the ministry of angels today?

2 Study the following Old Testament passages that speak either of God as the great Shepherd of his people, or the shepherd-like responsibility of their spiritual leaders: Psalms 23.1 and 80.1; Isaiah 40.11 and Ezekiel 34.

3 What New Testament examples can you think of in which people deal with sins and difficult relationships following the principles we find in verses 15–17? See, for example, 1 Corinthians 6.1–6 and Philippians 4.2–3. How do you think that we should apply such principles in the life of the Church today?

4 What special comfort and encouragement can small groups which meet in the name of Christ in places where Christians are a tiny minority gain from verse 20? Do you think that this applies also to the Christian home and family? What does it really mean to gather 'in the name' of Christ?

---

# 18.21–22  *Forgiving Others*

## *See also Luke 17.4*

For right relationships in the community of disciples – the theme of this chapter – it is a vital necessity to forgive others. This is the teaching of Jesus' answer to Peter's question and of a very telling parable that follows. Luke 17.4 has what is partly a parallel to these verses, the similar teaching, 'if the same person sins against you seven times a day, and turns back to you seven times and says, "I repent", you must forgive.'

Here Peter may have had in mind what we know from the later collection of the teaching of the rabbis (in the Talmud), that Jewish teachers said that you should forgive another who wrongs you up to three times, but not a fourth. Peter may well have thought that he was on the side of generosity, in the spirit of what he knew from the teaching of Jesus, when he offered to forgive seven times. Jesus' answer, whether we take it as 77 times or 490 (70 × 7), may refer back to the words of Lamech in Genesis 4.24 about taking revenge on a person who struck him, 'If Cain is avenged sevenfold, truly Lamech seventy-sevenfold'. In other words, instead of unlimited vengeance, followers of Christ have to show unlimited forgiveness.

# 18.23–35  The Parable of the Unforgiving Debtor

This parable (which we find only in Matthew) does not continue quite the same thought of how often we should forgive, but rather emphasizes the teaching in the Lord's Prayer and what follows it (6.12, 14–15) that those who wish to receive forgiveness from God must themselves be forgiving.

The parable says that the debt that the servant owed to the king was 10,000 talents, using in Greek the largest numeral and the largest unit of money in the language. We might say in English, 'he owed a billion'. We need not try to think who in those days might have owed such a sum, nor need we think what kind of person would cancel a debt like that. No debt could compare with that of which the parable speaks. No forgiveness could compare with the forgiveness of which the parable speaks.

The debt we owe relates to our sins and offences against God and against other people, increased year by year and day by day in our lives. We can no more pay that debt than the man in the story could have paid in many years or by selling his wife and family as slaves. The cancelling of the debt is the picture of what God does because in his pity and love he is willing to forgive every sin that we have ever committed.

But there is another debt in the story, the one that another servant owed to the forgiven debtor. As we realize from the parable in 20.1–16, a denarius was a day's wages for a labourer at that time. There were 6000 denarii to a talent, so a talent represented about 20 years' wages for a labourer. So the first debt forgiven was 60,000,000 denarii. That was 600,000 times greater than the debt of 100 denarii (a labourer's pay for 100 days) that the man refused to forgive.

He must have allowed the debt that his fellow servant owed to him to stick in his mind so that he refused to forgive, even though he had received so much forgiveness himself. It is like the person who says, even though he knows the goodness of God's forgiveness, 'I will never forgive that person!'

The end of the story does not mean that God literally does what the king in the parable did, handing the man over for torture till he pays everything. But it does mean that unforgiving people cannot receive forgiveness from God. They have closed their hearts to the love of God. They have realized neither the greatness and seriousness of their sins nor the wonder of God's love and mercy.

---

### 📖 Study Suggestions

1 How does the teaching of Ephesians 4.31–32 and Hebrews 12.14–15 express or develop what we have here in verses 21–35?
2 In your experience how do feelings of resentment, and the unwillingness to forgive wrongs done, harm the fellowship of the Christian Church? How does this also apply in the relationships of a human family?
3 How should we examine ourselves to make sure that we are not like the unforgiving debtor in the parable of verses 23–35?

# Part 9: 19.1—22.46
# Narrative: Jesus' Journey to Jerusalem

This is the next main section of the Gospel between the teaching sections of chapter 18 and chapters 23—25. Its setting is the journey of Jesus from Galilee to Judea and Jerusalem. We have seen how the Gospel often tells of the three groups of people around Jesus, the crowds, the disciples, and those who opposed him. We read of the crowds at the beginning of this section, and at Jesus' entry into Jerusalem, but most of the time he is either teaching the disciples or facing those who challenged and opposed him. This section follows quite closely Mark 10.1—12.37, but there are passages that we find only in Matthew. We may subdivide the section as follows:

---

**Analysis**

19.1–12   Marriage and divorce
19.13–15  Jesus and the children
19.16–22  The rich young man
19.23–26  Riches and the kingdom of God
19.27–30  The rewards of discipleship
20.1–16   The parable of the labourers in the vineyard
20.17–19  Jesus' third prediction of his death and resurrection
20.20–28  The request of the mother of James and John
20.29–34  The restoration of sight to two blind men
21.1–11   Jesus' entry into Jerusalem
21.12–17  The cleansing of the temple
21.18–22  The cursing of the fig tree
21.23–27  The questioning of Jesus' authority
21.28–32  The parable of the two sons
21.33–46  The parable of the wicked tenants
22.1–14   The parable of the wedding feast
22.15–22  The question about paying taxes
22.23–33  The question about the resurrection
22.34–40  The greatest commandment in the law
22.41–46  The question about David's son

---

# 19.1–12 *Marriage and Divorce*

## *See also Mark 10.1–12*

The first verse here gives the setting for the next main section of the Gospel. We have finished another teaching section, and we are now to read of Jesus' movement from Galilee to Judea. Then it goes on (as in Mark) with the Pharisees coming with a question that they often discussed among themselves, 'Is it lawful to divorce one's wife for any cause?' They intended this as a 'test' for Jesus because there were two different schools of thought among the Jews. There were those who followed Rabbi Shammai and said that it had to be a serious 'matter of shame' for a wife to be divorced. Those who followed Rabbi Hillel allowed divorce for very small things. The Pharisees knew that Jesus would not please everyone by his answer.

Using the words 'Have you not read . . .' that the rabbis often used, Jesus, instead of directly dealing with divorce, took them back to God's intention for marriage. That purpose was expressed in the words of Genesis 1.27 and 2.24, God's creation of male and female, and the saying that 'a man shall leave his father and mother and be joined to his wife, and the two shall become one'. God bonds them together, and so it falls short of God's purpose if any human being breaks the marriage bond.

The Pharisees' response was to say, 'Why did Moses command one to give a certificate of divorce . . . ?', referring to the words of Deuteronomy 24.1–4. Jesus rejected their word 'command', and replaced it with 'allow'. The Old Testament Law, like the law of any country today, had to allow divorce. Relationships break down, but it is because of human weakness and failure, and 'hardness of heart'. It is a falling short of God's intention for marriage as a lifelong commitment.

The words of verse 9, with the exception of 'unchastity', are similar to those of 5.31–32, and we have studied their meaning there, and the possible reason for the exception being given while the parallels in Mark and Luke give no exception.

Did Jesus set an impossibly high standard for marriage, higher than the rabbis of the time? The disciples seem to have thought so from their words in verse 10, as they wonder if it is better not to marry. As we have often found in this Gospel (especially in chapters 5–7), Jesus sets before his disciples God's highest ideal, the ideal of the kingdom of God, but at the same time he reckons compassionately with human weakness and failure.

In some societies quite a number of people remain unmarried, while in other societies this is unusual. It is certainly true that while most people will marry, it is possible to have a full and satisfying life unmarried. In Jesus' own situation he spoke of three classes of people who were 'eunuchs', unable to marry and have children, or willing to forgo marriage:

1 Those who did not have physical sexual ability to have children.
2 Those who, as punishment or because of their work in harems with many women, were sexually incapacitated.
3 Those who, for the sake of the work of God's kingdom, remained unmarried. Jesus made clear that not all who served God had this calling, but it was for those 'able to receive' it. (The apostle Paul writes about this in 1 Corinthians 7.25–35.)

# 19.13–15  *Jesus and the Children*

## See also Mark 10.13–16; Luke 18.15–17

It is significant that this section which shows Jesus' concern for children (as in Mark) follows directly on from the section on marriage and divorce.

In the society in which Jesus lived people loved to have children, but people felt that they were unimportant. There were those who, knowing the great blessing Jesus brought to many people, brought their children for him to lay his hands on them and pray for them. The disciples, acting in a way typical of their society, felt that Jesus had no time to give to children. But they were very wrong. It was another of those ways in which Jesus acted differently from what his society expected of him. He welcomed the children, and said to those who would have prevented them, 'Let the children come to me'. And he spoke in the way that we have seen in 18.2–4, that to such as these children – unimportant in the world's eyes – the kingdom of heaven belongs.

The preciousness and importance of children should influence our thinking about marriage and divorce. A good marriage means tremendous support for children, while divorce often brings great suffering to them.

---

### 📖 Study Suggestions

1 What are the standards and ideals of Christian marriage as the New Testament presents them? What rules do you think the Church should have about marriage?

2 How does Genesis 2.24 (which Matthew quotes in 19.5) relate to the question of polygamy? How should the Church deal with polygamy?

3 What are the laws for divorce in your country? Do you think that they make divorce too easy or too difficult? What attitude should the Church take to divorce and remarriage?

4 What things can and should be done in your situation to support and strengthen Christian marriage and family life?

5 How should Christians who have homes and families try to support those who live a single life? How can single people support those who are married and have families to care for?

6 What do you think about the way that Genesis 2.24 speaks of a man leaving father and mother to cleave to his wife? Should it also work in the other way, for a woman to leave and to cleave like this? What is the point of this cleaving?

7 What lessons should we learn from verses 13–15 about our attitude to children, and about the place that children should have in the life of the Church?

---

# 19.16–22 The Rich Young Man

## See also Mark 10.17–22; Luke 18.18–23

The story of this rich young man's encounter with Jesus involves three questions from the man and three answers from Jesus.

His first question, 'What good deed must I do, to have eternal life?' showed a spiritual concern. He wanted to have eternal life, but he thought that he could gain it by some 'good deed'. Jesus' answer made him think about the word 'good'. Did he think that he was good or that he could be good enough to be accepted with God? Only God is truly good, and it follows that we must admit that we are sinful. But if it is a matter of doing something in order to have eternal life, then we must 'keep the commandments'.

That led the man to another sincere question. Which commandments must I be sure of keeping? Jesus in answer listed five of those of the Ten Commandments that concerned relationships with others. Four were the negatives, not killing, not committing adultery, not stealing, not bearing false witness. The fifth involved honouring father and mother. Then came the words of Leviticus 19.18 that summed up so much of the Law, but in a positive sense, 'You shall love your neighbour as yourself.'

The man replied, 'All these I have observed', and yet he had a feeling that he still had not done enough. 'What do I still lack?' He lacked the understanding of what the Law really required. He might have been able to say truly that, at least in terms of his actions, he had killed no one, stolen from no one, not committed adultery, not borne false witness. Had he done everything possible to honour his father and mother? But, most important of all, had he really loved others as himself? Jesus touched a nerve and showed him what he lacked. Would he be concerned enough for his neighbour to sell what he had and give to the poor, and then come to be Jesus' disciple?

Jesus put the man to a hard test, but he wanted eternal life with God, and Jesus showed him the way to that life, serving the Lord and loving others. Jesus did not put the same demand before everyone who wanted to be a disciple, but along with the requirement of committing life to him, he always requires anything that comes between a person and their living in truth and in love to be set aside.

# 19.23–26 Riches and the Kingdom of God

## See also Mark 10.23–27; Luke 18.24–27

This teaching about riches follows on naturally from the account of the rich young man who 'went away sorrowful'.

On the basis of what this Gospel has said already about entry to the kingdom (5.3, 7.21 and 18.1–4), we can see why it must be 'hard for a rich person to enter the kingdom of heaven'. Jesus, probably with a smile, used a familiar proverb when he said that it would be easier for a camel (the largest beast of burden known in Palestine) to go through the eye of a needle (the smallest hole one could imagine).

The astonishment of the disciples was understandable. Would all the great and powerful people in the land have no place in God's kingdom? And were not riches the sign of God's favour? 'Who then can be saved?' The answer of Jesus makes it clear than in every respect it is not a matter of human abilities, position, possessions, qualifications. For human beings, in and of themselves, 'it is impossible'. The possibility of entering the kingdom rests with God. God is able to draw people to forsake their dependence on possessions or human power and position and bring them to rely on him. A Matthew could leave a job where he could earn good money and respond instead to the call of Jesus (9.9). A Zacchaeus could show that Jesus mattered more to him than money, by paying back all that he had taken dishonestly and by giving generously to the poor (Luke 19.1–10). A Joseph of Arimathea could show courage in going and asking Pilate for the body of the crucified Jesus to give it decent burial (27.57–60).

## 📖 Study Suggestions

1 Do you think that the words of Jesus to the rich young man, 'if you would be perfect' is meant to suggest that there are two classes of Christians, those who want to live the 'perfect' life and those who are content with a more 'ordinary' standard? Does the use of the word 'perfect' in 5.48 help us to answer this?

2 How do you link together the different ways of speaking in

verses 16–21, 'having eternal life', 'entering life' and 'having treasure in heaven'?

3 Do you think that the attitude to the Law of the apostle Paul before his conversion was like that of the rich young ruler? Why did Paul change his attitude? See especially Philippians 3.4–11 and Romans 7.7–25.

4 How do other passages in the Bible indicate why it is hard for the rich to enter the kingdom of God? See, for example, 1 Timothy 6.6–10, 17–19; James 4.4, 13–16 and 1 John 2.15–17.

# 19.27–30 The Rewards of Discipleship

## See also Mark 10.28–31; Luke 18.28–30

Just as it is understandable that the teaching about riches should follow the story of the rich young man who turned away from being a disciple, so we can understand Peter feeling how different the twelve who had followed were from the rich who refused. Peter could say with some pride, 'We have left everything and followed you. What then shall we have?' What is the end of the road for the faithful disciple who has sacrificed family life, possessions and comforts for Jesus' sake?

There are rewards for faithful following. In the spirit of this passage Hebrews 6.10 says, 'God is not so unjust as to overlook your work and the love which you showed for his sake in serving the saints, as you still do.' This passage mentions three things:

1 Faithful disciples will share the kingdom with the Son of man. There will be a 'new world', as the prophets describe it (Isaiah 65.17 and 66.22), and in the New Testament in the Book of Revelation (21.1–5), as 'new heavens and a new earth'. Those who have endured suffering for Christ's sake will 'reign with him' (2 Timothy 2.12), 'judging' as the Old Testament judges ruled over the people.

2 Faithful disciples will know the blessing of family. They had been willing to forgo many of the comforts and joys of family life, but in the fellowship of the family of God, they will find great compensations.

3 They will surely know the 'eternal life' that the rich young man sought (verse 16), but failed to find.

Yet Peter needed a warning, which is spelled out more in the parable that follows. Human reckoning, about those who have sincerely made the sacrifices and will receive the blessings, is not the same as God's reckoning. In the end people will see that 'many that are first will be last, and the last first'.

# 20.1–16 The Parable of the Labourers in the Vineyard

This parable (found only in Matthew) begins as a familiar story but then has a very unexpected ending. Its purpose is not to teach right relationships between employers and employees, right labour conditions or rates of pay. Rather it teaches something about 'the kingdom of heaven', about the way God deals with people in his kingdom.

It was probably the time of the grape harvest when the owner of the vineyard needed labourers to gather in the grapes. He went to the market-place where in that situation in Palestine he would find those seeking employment. At the beginning of the day he employed some with the agreement that they would receive the normal daily wage. He needed more help and went out at 9 in the morning, at mid-day, at 3 and even at 5 in the afternoon and recruited others to work, perhaps needing to gather in the grape harvest before a change in the weather.

Then came the time for the labourers to receive their pay at the end of the day, as the Law provided that no labourer should go home without pay (Leviticus 19.13 and Deuteronomy 24.14–15). Those who had worked only one hour must have been surprised to receive a full day's pay. Then those who had worked right through and 'borne the burden of the day and the scorching heat' expected on those terms to receive more than those who had worked only one hour. But the employer pointed out that they had no reason to be envious because he was generous.

Such then are the principles of 'the kingdom of heaven', the ways of God who never gives less than we could expect, but above all is ruled by grace and generosity. Such a story would certainly have been appropriate as a lesson to those who complained that Jesus welcomed 'tax collectors and sinners' and offered them the riches of the kingdom of God. But it was also appropriate as an answer to Peter's question which was like saying, 'We have given faithful service and borne the burden and heat of the day.' The link between the parable and Peter's question is made clear by the repetition in verse 16 of the words of 19.30, 'the last will be first and the first last.' 'What shall we get?' is never the right question when we realize that it is entirely through God's generosity that he invites us into the kingdom and to work for the kingdom.

---

## 📖 Study Suggestions

1 Compare with 19.27–30 the parallel passage in Mark 10.28–31. What difference do you find?
2 To what kinds of situations do you think that the early Church might have applied the parable of the labourers in the vineyard? To what situations does it apply now?
3 How do other parts of the New Testament teach that we should always think of the generosity of God in his dealings with us, and that it is always a mistake to think that we can earn or deserve the gifts of God?

# 20.17–19 Jesus' Third Prediction of his Death and Resurrection

## See also Mark 10.32–34; Luke 18.31–34

We have had predictions of Jesus' suffering and death in 16.21 and 17.22–23 (and an allusion in 17.12). This one has more details than the earlier ones, in that it says that the chief priests and scribes would hand Jesus over 'to the Gentiles to be mocked and scourged and crucified'. It also emphasizes the journey to Jerusalem, and so the importance of the reality that it would be in the 'holy city' that these things would happen to him.

People often ask how Jesus could have predicted these things, and whether those who handed down the Gospels might have added at least some of the details to the record after the events had taken place. We must take into consideration what Jesus' meditation on the Old Testament, in relation to his vocation, must have meant, especially passages such as those that spoke of the calling of the Suffering Servant. Then, added to his spiritual insight, he would have been aware of what the Jewish leaders were wanting to do, but what they would be limited in doing apart from having the Romans take action against Jesus. Jesus knew well that the regular way that the Romans dealt with those they regarded as trouble-makers was by crucifixion. In the time of his boyhood the rising of Judas was stamped out with the crucifixion of 2000 Jews.

# 20.20–28  The Request of the Mother of James and John

## See also Mark 10.35–45; Luke 22.24–27

We have seen what a strong contrast there was between Jesus' first prediction of his passion, and the ideas that Peter had (16.22). There is a similar contrast between this renewed prediction of what Jesus must face, and the desire which two of his disciples now express for places of honour in his kingdom. Matthew speaks in a way that Mark (10.35–45) does not about the role of the mother of James and John. She may well have been ambitious for her sons, but this did not remove their responsibility, and Jesus addressed his response to them.

Mother and sons alike probably believed in the things that Jesus had said about the coming kingdom, but they failed to understand what the lifestyle of the kingdom would involve. To bring in that kingdom the Lord must suffer, and it is significant who were on his right and his left when he brought in that kingdom by his death on the cross (27.38).

Would James and John be 'able to drink the cup' of suffering that Jesus drank? In the fullness of time they did do this. According to Acts 12.1–2 James met a martyr's death in the early years of the Church's life, and though there is a story that John also became a martyr early in the life of the Church, the more likely tradition is that he died after a long life of sacrificial service.

Jesus was not in the business of saying who would be in the places of greatest honour in his kingdom. There would be people in those places, but for the present other considerations were more important. Verse 24 tells of the anger of the other ten disciples. They were just as keen for the places of greatest honour. (Compare what Luke 22.24–27 says about a quarrel among the disciples about which of them should 'be regarded as the greatest'.) They had to learn that there were two very different understandings of leadership. The one in the world at large ('the Gentiles', as Jesus put it) was that great ones have many servants to wait on them, and they lord it over their people. In the kingdom of God the one who wants to be first and to lead must serve others, even be their slave.

Such was the example of Jesus, but set alongside the statement about his coming 'not to be served but to serve' is something more, especially relating to his death. He came 'to give his life a ransom for many'. The term 'ransom' is linked with redemption, and speaks here of one life given so that many might go free, free from the bondage of sin, as has been indicated from the beginning of the Gospel (1.21). And since the ransom is redemption's price, it speaks of the costliness of our freedom, as do such passages in the Epistles as 1 Corinthians 6.20 and 1 Peter 1.18–19. The one for 'many' may reflect the words of Isaiah 53.11–12 saying what the Suffering Servant there would do for the 'many'.

---

### 📖 Study Suggestions

1 Is it right to understand the request for chief places for James and John as an example of spiritual ambition? What would you see as a right spiritual ambition, and what is an unspiritual kind of ambition?

2 From this and other passages that give us the teaching and example of Jesus, how should we understand the ideals of Christian leadership? What are the special temptations that may come to those in positions of Christian leadership?

3 In relation to the meaning of the 'cup' in 20.22, see from 26.39–44 what the 'cup' meant to Jesus. See also the Old Testament background of the expression in Psalm 75.8; Isaiah 51.17–22 and Jeremiah 25.15–16.

4 In the light of the words of Jesus in verses 26 and 27 and the words of the apostle Paul in 2 Corinthians 4.5, what does it mean in practice for us to see ourselves as 'servants' or 'slaves' of others?

# 20.29–34  The Restoration of Sight to Two Blind Men

## See also Mark 10.46–52; Luke 18.35–43

We might read this as just another healing miracle done by Jesus, and we might note the attitude of the two men and the attitude of Jesus. The blind men took their opportunity, were determined to bring their need before Jesus, and showed faith and gratitude. Jesus showed an attitude very different from that of the crowd who tried to silence the blind men's appeals. Jesus stopped in his way, called the two men and, 'moved with compassion', 'touched their eyes' and restored their sight.

But this incident is also important as the last miracle that the Gospel writers record Jesus doing before he came into Jerusalem for the last time before his death (so also in Mark and Luke). It also has special links with what goes before it in the Gospel and with what follows. In the previous section we read about the two disciples, James and John, who lacked enough spiritual sight to realize what discipleship meant in terms of suffering and service. Now we have two blind men, with some insight into who Jesus was, and when he asked them the same question as he had asked the mother of James and John, 'What do you want?' they replied, 'Lord, let our eyes be opened.' Then, with their request answered, they 'followed him'.

We notice also that although the crowds told the blind men simply 'that Jesus was passing by', they knew enough to link Jesus and his work to the hope of Israel, and to cry, 'Have mercy on us, Son of David'. In the next incident it is the crowd who will cry out, 'Hosanna to the Son of David'.

# 21.1–11 Jesus' Entry into Jerusalem

## See also Mark 11.1–11; Luke 19.29–40; John 12.12–19

The importance of Jesus' entry into Jerusalem, and the way it came about, is clear because all four Gospels record it. In Matthew's record the following eight things are significant:

1 The point they had reached was 'near to Jerusalem', Bethphage, like Bethany, was a village on the slopes of the Mount of Olives. Beyond the Mount of Olives there was just the Kidron valley and then Jerusalem, the 'holy city', the centre of the life of the Jewish people.
2 Jesus had planned carefully what he would do. This, rather than supernatural knowledge, seems the best explanation of the disciples being sent into the village ahead (verses 2–3).
3 This passage describes what Jesus did as the fulfilment of Scripture. In all his earlier ministry Jesus had avoided any public demonstrations, and told the disciples to keep secret their confession of his Messiahship (16.20). Now he allows, even encourages, such a demonstration, as he offers himself as the King 'mounted on a donkey' of which Zechariah 9.9 spoke.
4 The donkey, rather than a horse, suggested a 'Prince of peace' rather than a military conqueror or even a political leader. The 'humble' leadership of which the Zechariah passage spoke fits with what has been said in 20.28 about his serving rather than being served.
5 The reference to two animals, the donkey and its colt, is perplexing. The Old Testament passage has the parallelism of Hebrew poetry, the two lines – 'humble and riding on a donkey' and 'on a colt, the foal of a donkey' – expressing the same thing in slightly different words. Of all New Testament writers, the writer of this Gospel has such a strong Hebrew background that he could not have failed to recognize the parallelism. He may have been aware that there were two animals in the triumphant entry and so took Zechariah 9.9 in that way. Or perhaps, as rabbinic interpretation sometimes did, he may have given interpretation to the two parallel statements as if they were separate.
6 The crowds spread their garments in Jesus' way, as we read that the

people did when they made Jehu king (in 2 Kings 9.13), and celebrated with palm branches as in the time of the victories of the
Maccabees 200 years before (1 Maccabees 13.51 and 2 Maccabees
10.7). Now not just two blind men (20.31), but the crowds, greet
Jesus as 'Son of David'.

7 Psalm 118, which verse 9 quotes, was one of the psalms that the
people sang at the great annual festivals of Israel. At the Feast of
Tabernacles the people took branches of palm and myrtle and wil-
low and made what they called 'lubabs', and in singing Psalm 118
when they came to the words of verse 25, 'Save us . . . Lord'
(Hebrew 'Hosanna'), they shook their lubabs and repeated three
times the cry, 'Hosanna'. Now it was the approach to Passover, not
Tabernacles, but the people had palm branches in their hands, and
Psalm 118 probably in their hearts. Their longing was for salvation, and the words people addressed normally to the pilgrim,
'Blessed is the one who comes in the name of the Lord' related
now to the One who was uniquely 'the coming One', coming to
save his people.

8 In Jerusalem the claim that Jesus was the Messianic Son of David
was not as clearly put, because in answer to questions people seem
to have preferred to speak of him as 'prophet' (compare 13.57 and
21.46), the prophet 'from Nazareth of Galilee'.

# 21.12–17 The Cleansing of the Temple

## See also Mark 11.15–19; Luke 19.45–48; John 2.13–22

Like the triumphal entry into Jerusalem this is an incident of such
importance that it has a place in all four Gospels, although surprisingly in the case of John it is near to the beginning of the Gospel.
Some have thought that Jesus must have acted twice in this way in
the temple, others that John rightly places it at the beginning of
Jesus' ministry. More likely John gives it as a sign of what Jesus came

to do without concern for order of events. All of the other Gospels see it as taking place after Jesus had come into his city as 'king'. Now he comes to the centre of the people's worship and challenges what was going on there.

The temple had an outer court, the Court of the Gentiles, the only part of the temple into which Gentiles could come to worship. The temple authorities had allowed this to be used as a market, where people could buy the birds and animals used for their sacrificial offerings, and exchange foreign coins for those coins that were acceptable in the temple.

Jesus acted with authority in the temple and certainly challenged the authority of those who were responsible for worship there. But from the use of the two Old Testament quotations, Isaiah 56.7 and Jeremiah 7.11, it seems clear that he challenged both the misuse of the temple and probably also the exploiting of people by dishonest money-dealing instead of helping them to worship. 'My house shall be called a house of prayer; but you make it a den of robbers.'

His action, however, was not just a negative one. He brought the blessing of healing to blind and lame people in the temple; and perhaps people saw this as a reversal on the part of the 'Son of David' of what king David had said in relation to Jerusalem, 'The blind and lame shall not come into the house' (2 Samuel 5.8).

True to what the Gospel has said earlier about the understanding of 'infants' (11.25), and the place of children in the kingdom of God (18.1–5 and 19.13–14), it is the children who cry out in the temple, 'Hosanna to the Son of David'. 'The chief priests and the scribes saw the wonderful things that he did', but tried to silence the children who acclaimed Jesus, and so 'leaving them, he went out of the city to Bethany and lodged there.'

# 21.18–22  The Cursing of the Fig Tree

## See also Mark 11.12–14, 20–24

Many people have asked questions about this incident which Matthew and Mark report of Jesus' last days in Jerusalem. Is it not unusual for him to use his power to destroy rather than to heal or restore? Should Jesus have expected to find fruit on a fig tree at Passover time of the year? Was it just because he was hungry that he was angry or upset that the tree offered him no fruit? There are different answers to these questions, but the meaning surely is that this is an enacted parable.

Mark has this incident in two parts, taking place one day after the other (Mark 11.12–14 and 20–24). Matthew, as he often seems to do, shortens the record. The fig tree was often a symbol for the life of Israel. The Bible, and not least this Gospel, repeatedly speaks of the 'fruit' of right living that God expected of his people, and judgement on fruitlessness. Here what seemed outwardly to be a healthy tree in fact had 'nothing on it but leaves only'. Luke 13.6–9 has a parable of an unfruitful fig tree, but here Matthew presents a parable in action, and thus a warning to the nation, just as the cleansing of the temple has been a challenge to its leaders.

Verses 21–22 seem to deal with quite a different subject, the power of 'prayer with faith'. This Gospel, however, often presents the disciples as needing more than anything else to learn the lesson of faith. In 16.6 Jesus spoke to them about 'the leaven of the Pharisees and Sadducees', and their minds were preoccupied with the thought of their need of bread. Jesus had been concerned to warn them about the danger of spiritual unfruitfulness, but the disciples wondered at what seemed an amazing miracle. The lesson that they needed to learn was that believing prayer, seeking the outworking of the will of God, can be the means of overcoming mountains of difficulties.

---

### 📖 Study Suggestions

1 This Gospel, especially in 7.7–11, has given teaching about making requests in prayer. What can we learn from Jesus' attitude to

the two different questions we find in verses 21 and 22? What teaching about prayer does this suggest?

2 The incident of the cleansing of the temple shows the anger of Jesus and the anger of the chief priests and the scribes. What was the difference between the two kinds of anger, the reasons for them, and the expression of them?

3 The chief priests were largely of the Sadducees' party and the scribes were largely Pharisees (see notes on these on p. 18). See how they come together in 2.4; 16.21; 20.18 and 21.15. What do you think brought them together to take action against Jesus?

4 Look up the Old Testament passages that this Gospel quotes in verses 12–16 and also Malachi 3.1–2. In what way do you think that what these passages say is appropriate to what this Gospel describes as taking place in the temple?

5 Link with verses 18 and 19 what other parts of the Gospel say about the 'fruit' that God expects in the lives of his people. See 3.7–10; 7.15–20; 13.1–9, 18–23 and 21.33–41.

6 The idea of faith to move mountains comes both in 21.21 and 17.20, and also in 1 Corinthians 13.2. What do you think is the meaning of the expression and of the promises that these texts link with believing prayer?

# 21.23–27 The Questioning of Jesus' Authority

## See also Mark 11.27–33; Luke 20.1–8

We can see the whole of the next part of the Gospel (21.23—22.14) as challenge and counter-challenge, the challenge to Jesus about his authority for what he was doing, and his challenge to the Jewish leaders which he expressed in three powerful parables.

It was very understandable that after Jesus 'drove out all who were selling and buying in the temple' and now proceeded calmly to teach

there, that the chief priests and elders would question his authority
for his actions. Were they not the ones who had responsibility for
what happened in the temple? Who gave him this authority? It was a
very important challenge and Mark and Luke record it in very similar
words.

It might seem to be an attempt by Jesus to avoid the question that
he answered it by putting a question to them. Two things, however,
make us realize that this was not the case.

1  It was a common method used by the rabbis to answer one question with another question, and we have seen how Jesus did this
   in 12.9–11 and 15.1–3.
2  At a deeper level, if they had answered Jesus' question honestly
   they would have found the answer to their own question. There
   were close links between the ministry of Jesus and the preaching
   of John the Baptist, both in the basic principles of their preaching
   and in what John said about the One who was coming after him
   (3.11 and 11.3).

The unwillingness of the Jewish leaders to give a straight answer
to Jesus' question revealed their deepest motives. Although John
preached about the central things of Jewish religion, the kingship or
rule of God, repentance and 'the way of righteousness' (verse 32),
they were not willing to heed his message. Nevertheless, they were
not willing to say that John's message was just 'of human origin',
because they were afraid of what the people might do to them,
because the ordinary people in a fair-minded way recognized that
John was a prophet.

So these chief priests and elders, who should have been able to
guide their people about what was true teaching and what was false,
had to say to Jesus, 'We do not know'. With good reason, then, Jesus
would say no more in answer to their question to him. They would
have been totally unwilling even to consider the right answer.

# 21.28–32  *The Parable of the Two Sons*

Like so many of the parables of Jesus, this one is very simple but very powerful in its application. This one and the next are both vineyard parables, but the point of this one is simply the difference of attitude of the two sons. One refused his father's sending him to work in the vineyard, but 'later he changed his mind and went'. The other answered very politely, 'I go, sir', but did nothing. Jesus asked his hearers to decide which 'did the will of his father'.

In some cultures it is more important to be polite in answering a request than to be sincere and true to one's word. The standard of Jesus is that a person's 'Yes' should mean 'Yes' and their 'No' mean 'No' (5.37), and saying should be supported by doing (7.21–27). But in its setting the parable meant more than that. Who were those who said 'No' to God and then repented of it? They were the tax collectors and prostitutes who responded to the preaching of John the Baptist and later to the ministry of Jesus (9.10). The professionally religious were polite and professed to say 'Yes', but what attitude were they showing now in relation to the will of God?

We find this parable only in Matthew, but we may set alongside this one the famous parable of the two sons in Luke 15.11–32, while Luke 7.29–30 speaks of the tax collectors who were baptized with John's baptism, and the Pharisees and the lawyers who 'by refusing to be baptized by him . . . rejected God's purpose for themselves'.

## ADDITIONAL NOTE I: THE TEXT OF THE NEW TESTAMENT

There are some places in the Gospel, as in other books of the New Testament, where there is some uncertainty about the original text. Our various English translations, as well as translations into every other language, are translations from the Greek language in which all the New Testament was originally written. There are a great number of Greek manuscripts that have come down from the time of the fourth century onwards, a few fragments even earlier. There were also early translations into languages like Latin, Syriac, Coptic (in Egypt) and Ethiopic. With all of these that come from the early centuries there is never any serious doubt about what was written, but in some places there are variations between different Greek manuscripts or texts of translations or biblical quotations in early Christian writers. There are some variations in the manuscripts in the case of this parable, although the main variant only changes the order in which the story tells of the two sons.

# 21.33–46  The Parable of the Wicked Tenants

## See also Mark 12.1–12; Luke 20.9–19

The challenge of Jesus to the Jewish leaders continues in this second parable. It was a parable so plain in its meaning that it could be said that 'the chief priests and the Pharisees . . . perceived that he was speaking about them'. The power of the parables of Jesus often lay in the combination of everyday circumstances with something unlikely. It was a common enough thing for a landowner to let a vineyard out to tenants whom he would expect to pay as rent an agreed part of the produce of the vineyard. It was an unlikely thing in Jesus' story that the landowner would allow the tenants to mal-treat or kill one servant after another and take no action against them, but rather send his son in the hope that they would respect him.

This parable raises a question for us that we have discussed in our study of the parable of the sower in 13.1–9 and 18–23. Can we some-times treat a parable as an allegory? That is, does it sometimes have more than one point? It seems clear here that there is meaning in the sending of the different servants, then the sending of the son, and then in what happened at the end.

The beginning of the parable was not only what was familiar in life in those times. The words of Jesus recalled the parable of Isaiah 5.1–7. The vineyard was planted with a 'fence' or 'hedge' around it. The owner dug a wine press. This involved two basins, one lower than the other. The workers threw grapes into the upper one and trod them out there so that the juice flowed into the lower basin where the fermentation began. He built a watchtower, a flat-roofed building from the roof of which a watchman could be on the look-out for animals or thieves; the building itself was used for storage.

But at this point the similarity with Isaiah 5 ends. In the Old Testament parable the point was that the vineyard failed to yield a good harvest. Here it is what was done to the servants sent by the owner expecting produce. So God had sent the prophets of old to Israel, and people might have asked the question which was later on the lips of Stephen in Acts 7.52, 'Which of the prophets did your ancestors not persecute?' One after another had faced opposition and some faced death.

Then comes the climax, the sending of the owner's son. Some people have asked whether Jesus would have spoken in such a way with reference to himself. Questioning this, some have taken the developed parable as coming from the early Church rather than from Jesus himself. Yet two things are clear in this Gospel (as, in different ways, they are in the other Gospels). Jesus was conscious of a special relationship with God the Father (shown especially in 11.25–27), and, particularly as he came into Jerusalem, he claimed to be the Messianic Son.

The parable closes not only with the judgement of the tenants, but with the clear warning that the owner will 'let out the vineyard to other tenants who will give him the fruits in their seasons', a point that verse 43 gives a plain meaning.

Often in Hebrew (and similarly in Aramaic) people took pleasure in plays on words of similar sound, and the Hebrew for 'son' (*ben*) was very close to the Hebrew for 'stone' (*eben*). This may account for the way in which what these verses say about the 'son' is followed by the quotation from Psalm 118.22–23. A stone rejected at first by builders became the most important stone in all the construction of the building, the cornerstone in the foundations or where two walls met. In the psalm this applied to Israel. Here it applies to the 'son' whom the Jewish leaders were rejecting and even now plotting to kill. That 'stone' would indeed cause the breaking of many and the crushing of others.

Those who despised and rejected Jesus might indeed take warning. They knew what they were doing. In their hearts was the desire to arrest him, but again (as in verse 26) they were afraid of the action of the crowds against them, because they regarded Jesus as a prophet just as they had regarded John the Baptist before him.

# 22.1–14  *The Parable of the Wedding Feast*

## See also Luke 14.16–24

In Mark's Gospel the parable of the wicked tenants is followed directly by the series of questions that we have in Matthew 22.15–46. Matthew adds this third parable, which is like the two that have gone before (21.28–32 and 21.33–46) because it also speaks about an opportunity rejected and that opportunity then offered to others. As with the parable of the wicked tenants, this parable makes more than one point, but we must still be careful not to give meanings to details where this is not intended.

This parable compares the opportunity of sharing in the blessings of the kingdom of heaven to a wedding invitation, and an invitation to a royal wedding feast it was. Jewish hopes, based on passages like Isaiah 25.6, were of a Messianic feast at the end of the age, but in this parable the wedding feast is in the 'now' and not the 'hereafter'.

At the heart of the parable is the response made by those invited. The invitation had gone out and the would-be guests had received it, but then when the time had come and the feast was ready, those invited 'made light of it' and said that they had more important things to be concerned about. They missed their opportunity, but the king was determined to have guests at his son's wedding. So the king ordered his servants to take the invitation to anyone and everyone whom they could find in the streets. They gathered them in, whether their background was good or bad, and 'so the wedding hall was filled with guests'.

Verses 6–7 read strangely in the midst of a parable about wedding invitations, even rejected invitations. In the parable similar in outline, but different in detail, that we have in Luke 14.15–24, there is nothing that can compare with these verses. It may be that the surprise in the story was Jesus' intention. We could say the same of the strong words of 21.40–41. Jesus was deeply conscious of what the rulers of the people were doing in rejecting him, and what in the long term would be the consequences for Jerusalem (chapter 24 is to spell this out). On the other hand, some see the verses as added, as it were in the margin, and then finding their way into the parable itself.

Verses 11–14 are also an addition that we do not find in the parable in Luke 14. There are some puzzling things about it, whether we see it as a second parable or part of what has gone before. There are some similar parables recorded from Jewish rabbis. When the king had invited 'good and bad' alike to the feast, was it not harsh for him to have a poor man without a wedding robe thrown out? At least there are some biblical examples of the provision of festal robes for those invited to a feast (Genesis 45.22; Judges 14.12, 19 and 2 Kings 10.22). The story only makes sense if the man refused to do what he was able to do and so came into the feast in an inappropriate way. It is not hard to find an application, whether it is the requirement of repentance, or the desire to be made clean and, kept clean and righteous, to stand before the King. The filthy rags of our own best moral efforts (Isaiah 64.6) and God's provision of a robe of righteousness (Isaiah 61.10) both have a place in the biblical background. The parable as a whole makes clear what verse 14 expresses: many are invited but there are few who accept the invitation and become members of the 'elect', the 'chosen' people of God.

## 📖 Study Suggestions

1  In the light of 21.23–27, when do you think it may be right for you to answer a question or a challenge about your faith by another question or a challenge?

2  Do you see around you situations in which the fear of what people may say or do affects both people's understanding of a situation and their attitudes and actions?

3  For the actions taken against prophets in the Old Testament see 1 Kings 18.4; 19.1–3; 2 Chronicles 24.20–21; 36.16; Jeremiah 20.1–2; 26.11; 20–23 and 38.1–6.

4  Compare with 21.41 the words of 8.11–12. What other things does the Gospel say about the rejection of opportunities of knowing the blessings of the kingdom of God?

5  How should we compare 22.8–10 with our situation today, in which the invitation of the good news of God's kingdom goes out to people all over the world? Considering 22.5 and Luke 14.18–20, what reasons for rejecting the invitation do we find today?

6  In 22.5 it says that the people the king invited 'made light of' the invitation. We find the same word in 1 Timothy 4.14 and Hebrews 2.3; in those places, what do the writers warn the people not to 'make light of'?

7  How can we compare the role of members of the Christian Church with that of the king's servants in the parable of the wedding feast?

8  The king invited 'both good and bad' to his wedding feast in 22.1–10. How should we answer the thought that we don't need to strive after goodness because of the free, forgiving grace of God? See the way that the apostle Paul deals with this question in Romans 3.8 and 6.1–14.

9 Follow out the ways in which the Bible likens the provision of God's forgiveness or the living of a godly life to the putting on of clean and beautiful garments. See, for example, Isaiah 61.10; Ephesians 4.24; Colossians 3.12 and Revelation 7.13–14; 19.18.

# 22.15–22 The Question about Paying Taxes

## See also Mark 12.13–37; Luke 20.20–26

In the rest of this chapter we have three questions that people asked Jesus to try to trap him, and then one question that he asked his opponents. Matthew still follows Mark (12.13–37) quite closely and two of the three questions and Jesus' own question are in Luke (20.20–44).

We have seen (notes on 2.1–12) that in the time of Jesus the Romans ruled Palestine, but they allowed the Herods as local rulers to have some power and authority. Two groups joined together here to try to trap Jesus. There were the Pharisees who as devout Jews were unhappy about Roman rule, and especially the use of Roman coins which pictured the emperor of Rome, thought by many to have divine powers and status. Then there were the Herodians, and although there are no references outside the New Testament to this party we can understand that they supported the rule of the Herods and so the authority of Rome from which the Herods gained the position they had.

As the Pharisees and Herodians came with their question to Jesus, they wanted to make sure that he gave them a clear answer. So they said that they recognized four things about him, as the Good News Bible puts them: he told the truth, he taught the truth about God's will for human life, he did not worry about what people thought, and he paid no attention to a person's status. All those things were true about Jesus, but the Pharisees and Herodians said them in flattery and he rightly called them 'hypocrites'.

Their question was whether people should pay taxes to the Roman emperor, and their thought was probably especially of the tax equivalent to a day's pay (a denarius) which every adult, male or female, had to pay each year. Jesus' opponents realized that if he said

'Yes' to the question, many Jews would oppose him. If he said 'No', they could report him to the Roman authorities.

When Jesus in reply asked to see a coin, they brought the denarius which showed the emperor's head and words that gave his name and authority. When they acknowledged these as the emperor's, his answer was, 'Give therefore to the emperor the things that are the emperor's, and to God the things that are God's.' There was wisdom in Jesus' answer far beyond the thinking of the Pharisees or Herodians. No wonder they were amazed and could only go away frustrated in their attempt to trap him. All people are under some earthly state or kingdom. If the state provides reliable currency, roads and other communications, and provides for its people, then people should pay their taxes. But there are claims that a state should not make. There is loyalty and service that people should only offer to God. And while the image of the emperor was on the coin, we as human beings are made in God's image, and we are to give our lives to God in service. We have a heavenly Ruler as well as an earthly one.

# 22.23–33 The Question about the Resurrection

## See also Mark 12.18–27; Luke 20.27–40

The Pharisees together with the Herodians had put their hard question to Jesus to trap him. Now the Sadducees had a question that they felt that Jesus would not be able to answer, and so he might lose influence with the people as a Teacher. In considering the preaching of John the Baptist at the beginning we saw the main features of the party of the Sadducees (p. 18). We saw there that they were anxious to keep the power that the Romans allowed them, and so they would not want anything that Jesus did to cause a political disturbance.

Their convictions were against any belief in resurrection (see also Acts 4.1–3 and 23.8), and they had a question that they had probably tried out on other people and that they felt disproved resurrection. To understand it, we need to appreciate the custom of 'levirate marriage' which the Law provided for in Deuteronomy 25.5–6. If a married man died without leaving a child, his brother married the widow to 'raise up children for his brother' so that his line might continue. In the Sadducees' question a woman had seven husbands one after another and there were no children from any of these marriages. 'In the resurrection', they asked, 'to which of the seven will she be wife?' An impossible situation, they thought – therefore there cannot be a resurrection. They might have thought of a man having seven wives, but never a woman having seven husbands!

Jesus' answer indicated that their wrong thinking had two causes:

1 They did not reckon with the power of God. Surely God who is Creator and Lord can find a way to deal with such a problem. In fact, Jesus added, the life to come is not exactly like our present life, in which birth, marriage and having children all have their place. 'For in the resurrection they neither marry nor are given in marriage, but are like angels in heaven.'
2 They did not know the Scriptures. The Old Testament has a number of hints and some clear statements (like Daniel 12.2) of the resurrection. The Sadducees only accepted with full authority the five books of the Law. So Jesus took them to a very familiar statement in the Law, 'I am the God of Abraham, the God of Isaac, and the God of Jacob' (Exodus 3.6). Jesus' argument is that God is their God and they are thus related to him. He is the God of the living. Those who are his people, with a relationship with him, are alive and physical death cannot be the end for them.

The Sadducees did not discredit the Teacher in the eyes of the people as they intended. Rather, when the crowd realized the wisdom of Jesus' answer, they were astonished at his teaching.

# 22.34–40  The Greatest Commandment in the Law

## See also Mark 12.28–34; Luke 10.25–28

The third of the questions put to Jesus followed on when 'the Phari sees heard that he had silenced the Sadducees'. It was their turn, and they wanted to prove themselves superior both to their rivals, the Sadducees, and to Jesus. The passage describes the questioner as a 'lawyer', but not in the sense that we give to the word today. He would have been an expert in the Old Testament Law, and the parallel passage in Mark speaks of him as 'one of the scribes'.

It was a question put to 'test' Jesus, and no doubt the questioners felt that Jesus would fail to give an answer that would satisfy all his listeners. 'Which commandment in the Law is the greatest?' The rabbis often debated the question. They said that there were 613 commandments in the Law, and some people would have liked to single out one particular law as the greatest of them all. Others divided the laws between the 'light' and the 'heavy', the more important and the less important. Some probably thought that Jesus would speak against the whole Mosaic Law or set himself above it, and so they would catch him.

Jesus answered in words that came from the Law (from Deuteronomy 6.5 and Leviticus 19.18) and that covered everything in relation to God and in relation to people. They summed up not only all the Law but the prophets as well, and did so in the great positive demand of 'love'. No one has ever given a better summing up of what God seeks from human lives. It stands for us today, whatever our culture or circumstances, giving us what is most basic for those who would live as God's people in the world.

# 22.41–46  The Question about David's Son

## See also Mark 12.35–37; Luke 20.41–44

After the Pharisees had put three questions to Jesus to trap or test him, we have here (as in Mark and Luke) a question that Jesus put to them. We can understand the question best if we realize two things about the rabbis' use and interpretation of the Scriptures. First, they thought of all the psalms as coming from David. Second, it was a method that they often used, to put together two things from Scripture that seemed to contradict each other and then show how both could be true.

Jesus wanted people to think more deeply about the Messiah whom they expected. In answer to the question about whose son the Messiah should be, they could readily say, 'the son of David'. When they answered like this Jesus turned their thoughts to one of the royal psalms, Psalm 110. Such psalms originally referred to a historic king of Israel, perhaps at his coronation, but even before the time of Jesus some took Psalm 110 (as well as some of the other psalms) to refer to the Messiah.

No one could deny that the Messiah would be the son of David, and this Gospel has expressed this from its very first verse. But was the usual Jewish understanding of the Messiah, as a king and conqueror like David, big enough? Does not the psalm mean that the Messiah is David's Lord as well as David's Son?

This section ends, and so does the part of the Gospel that has taken us from the beginning of chapter 19 to the end of chapter 22, by showing how Jesus had answered the questions his opponents put to him with undisputed wisdom, and they were unable or unwilling (as in 21.24–27) to answer his questions.

## 📖 Study Suggestions

1 How does the teaching of Romans 13.1–7 and 1 Peter 2.12–17 support Jesus' answer to the question about paying taxes in 22.21?

2 At the time of the writing of Matthew's Gospel, the authorities in some places in the Roman Empire asked Christians to offer worship to the Roman emperor. How do you think that they would have applied the words of Jesus in 22.21? What should be the attitude of Christians today in situations where there are laws that prevent Christian worship or which call Christians to give the kind of loyalty to the state that is due only to God? Are there situations in which Christians have reasons not to pay taxes?

3 Are there customs in your country which are anything like the 'levirate marriage' we have in 22.24? In the light of New Testament teaching relating to marriage, what should the attitude of Christians be to such customs?

4 How does the teaching of Paul in 1 Corinthians 15 about the resurrection life develop what we have here in 22.30?

5 Why is it so significant that Jesus sums up the commandments in the word 'love'? How does this great positive demand relate to the negatives of the Law put in the terms 'You shall not . . .'?

6 How should we see the two great commandments of 22.37–39 as separate and yet, in practical living linked together? See what 1 John 4.20–21 says about this.

7 Look up the following passages in the Old Testament that led to or expressed the hope of a Messiah of the house of David: 2 Samuel 7.11–16; Isaiah 9.6–7; 11.1–10; Jeremiah 23.5–6; 33.15; Ezekiel 34.23–24; Micah 5.2–4 and Psalm 132.11–12.

8 Because the early Church could see Psalm 110.1 to be true of Jesus as Lord, at God's right hand, and conqueror of sin and death, it often used this verse in its preaching and teaching. See how Acts 2.34–35, 1 Corinthians 15.25; Ephesians 1.22; Hebrews 1.13; 10.13 refer to it.

# PART 10: 23.1—25.46
# TEACHING: THE FUTURE KINGDOM AND JUDGEMENT

This is the last great teaching section of the Gospel, and the three chapters are linked by their presentation of Jesus' warnings and prophecies of the judgement that lay ahead. In a number of ways they correspond to the first teaching section (chapters 5–7). Both that section and this begin by speaking of what Jesus presented in the hearing of both 'the crowds and his disciples'.

We have seen that Matthew in 22.15–46 appears to follow Mark quite closely. After Mark has told of Jesus' question about David's Son and David's Lord, he has a brief denunciation of the scribes (Mark 12.38–40). This is greatly enlarged in Matthew for reasons we will consider as we study chapter 23. We may subdivide the section as follows:

## Analysis

| | |
|---|---|
| 23.1–12 | The pride of the Pharisees and the call to humility |
| 23.13–36 | Seven 'woes' on the scribes and Pharisees |
| 23.37–39 | Jesus' lament over Jerusalem |
| 24.1–2 | Jesus foretells the destruction of the temple |
| 24.3–8 | The question about signs of the end |
| 24.9–14 | Warning of persecution |
| 24.15–22 | A climax of suffering |
| 24.23–28 | Warning of false Messiahs |
| 24.29–31 | The coming of the Son of man |
| 24.32–35 | The parable of the fig tree |
| 24.36–44 | The need for watchfulness |
| 24.45–51 | The faithful and unfaithful servants |
| 25.1–13 | The wise and foolish maidens |
| 25.14–30 | The parable of the talents |
| 25.31–46 | The parable of the sheep and the goats |

# 23.1–12 The Pride of the Pharisees and the Call to Humility

## See also Mark 12.37–39; Luke 20.45–46

As we begin to study this chapter of denunciations of the scribes and Pharisees we need to consider three difficulties that people have felt about it:

1 We have here some of the sternest words that the Gospels ascribe to Jesus. Does this present a different picture from the caring and compassionate Jesus? Yes, but Jesus had cleansed the temple because of its misuse, and had shown a righteous anger against those who caused others to stumble (see 18.6–7). He could understandably be grieved and angry because of those who professed to be very religious but in fact missed the whole purpose and spirit of God's law.

2 Because Matthew's Gospel was written at a time and in a situation where Christians and Jews were opposed to one another, people have suggested that some of the things in this chapter may have come from the writer of the Gospel or the Church in his time rather than from Jesus. Yet Mark and Luke, who wrote largely for Gentile situations, have some of the same denunciations of scribes and Pharisees (see especially Luke 11.39–52; 18.9–14 and 20.45–47). We can well believe that Matthew made selection from the things people had handed down from the teaching of Jesus, presenting what was relevant to his situation. He may have seen that Christian leaders faced the same temptations as the religious leaders in the time of Jesus' own ministry did.

3 Some feel that teaching such as we have in this chapter can be taken in a very anti-Jewish sense, and encourage the feeling against Jews that Christians have expressed in terrible ways in different periods in the life of the Church. Yet the writer of the Gospel was probably himself the most Jewish of all the writers of the New Testament books, and, as we have suggested, when he wrote he was not so concerned to condemn the Jewish leaders of the time of Jesus' ministry as to warn the Christian leaders of his own time.

When the passage speaks of the scribes and Pharisees as sitting on 'Moses' seat' it indicates their role as teachers of the Law. People are right to follow them in all that they genuinely teach about that Law, but when their lives do not uphold the Law people should not follow their example.

We have seen in the study of Jesus' words about his 'easy yoke' and the 'light burden' he offered (11.28–30), that this was in contrast to the way that the Jewish leaders made the law of the sabbath an unnecessary burden (12.1–14). The detailed regulations that the scribes and Pharisees had added to the Law was like laying heavy burdens on people's shoulders. At the same time, those who knew those regulations well knew better than others how to avoid the demands that they made (as 15.3–7 illustrates).

Another temptation of religious leaders is to make a show of their religious practices. Jesus has warned about this in his teaching in 6.1–18. Here he mentions the 'phylacteries' which were leather cases worn on the forehead and the left arm as a literal observance of Deuteronomy 6.8. They contained special passages of Scripture (Exodus 13.1–10 and 11–16; Deuteronomy 6.4–9 and 11.13–21), and if people wanted to show how religious they were they had large phylacteries and wore them not just at times of prayer but for the rest of the day. The Law in Numbers 15.37–41 said that people should have 'fringes on the corners of their garments' to remind them of the commandments. These similarly were made specially long by those who wanted to show themselves religious.

There was a great temptation also for the rabbis to delight in the honours that people gave them and to take pleasure in having important places in the synagogues and at feasts. When they chose to have titles of honour they were neglecting the fact that they were really called to honour God with their lives, and they failed to do that when they took honour and praise to themselves. Verse 11 repeats what we have had already in 20.26, and verse 12 is a solemn warning that the proud will surely be humbled (compare Luke 14.11 and 18.14 and the echoing of this teaching in 1 Peter 5.5–6).

# 23.13–36 Seven 'Woes' on the Scribes and Pharisees

## See also Mark 12.40; Luke 11.39–51, 20.47

The word 'woe' (that this Gospel has used earlier in 11.21 and 18.7) appears seven times in this section. (Verse 14 is in some older translations, but it was not in the earliest manuscripts of this Gospel. What it says is in Mark 12.40 and Luke 20.47.) 'Woe' expresses both sadness that people should act in the ways they did, but also the warning of judgement. There were good scribes, as we have seen in 8.19 and 13.52. There were also noble Pharisees at the time, like Gamaliel of whom we read in Acts 5.34–39. But very many of the scribes and Pharisees were 'hypocrites' (a word Matthew uses six times here), because in their outward actions they followed the rules of their strict religion, but the state of their hearts was very different. They made their rules about outward observances more important than a personal relationship with God in worship and love, obedience and sincere service. We will look at the seven 'woes' in turn:

1 At the heart of the message of the Gospels is the statement that with the coming of Jesus 'the kingdom of heaven' has come into human life in a new way. There is the opportunity for people to come into the God's kingdom and become members of it (see 7.21 and 18.1–5). Most of the scribes and Pharisees were themselves unwilling to respond to what Jesus said about the kingdom, and because they wanted to hold to their own spiritual status tried to prevent other people turning to Jesus. John 9.22 and 12.42 say that the Jewish authorities required that anyone who acknowledged Jesus as Messiah would be put out of the synagogue. And we know that this happened in the time of the early Church. It is a serious thing to turn away from the revelation of the truth and love of God. It is even more serious to turn others away (compare 18.6–7).

2 Verse 15 uses the word 'proselyte' for a convert to the Jewish religion. Often converts are even more zealous for the religion they embrace than those who have converted them. Some Jewish people in the time of Jesus worked hard to convert others to their religion, but they did not necessarily really turn them to God. The danger was that these converts would have an even more legalistic religion, and so be even further from the truth and love of God we

see in Jesus, and more likely to be 'children of hell' than members of the kingdom of heaven.

3 The rules about oaths illustrate one of the worst features of the religion of the Pharisees. They regarded one kind of oath as more powerful than another. They made statements as to whether oaths were more or less binding if they were by the temple, the altar in the temple, the gold on the altar and so on. Jewish rabbinical writings give endless details as to which oaths are stronger and which are weaker. Those who taught in this way were 'blind guides' to others, blind to what was really important: that it should be possible to trust a person to speak the truth without there being the need of any oath. This is the heart of the teaching of Jesus about oaths in 5.33–37.

4 The Law said that people should pay tithes of their income. They had to bring a tenth of their income from their land as an offering to the Lord which was used for the support of the Levites (Leviticus 27.30–33 and Deuteronomy 14.22–29). The Pharisees kept this law down to the smallest detail, bringing a tenth of their small garden plants. Matthew mentions 'Mint, dill and cummin' here and the parallel in Luke 11.42 says that they brought tithes of 'every herb'. But Jesus says that while obeying the law of tithes to the smallest detail they neglected the things that the Law and the Prophets showed were most important: 'justice and mercy and faith'. With real humour Jesus says that it is like people straining what they drink to be sure that there is no tiny unclean insect in it (Leviticus 11.20–23), but swallowing down a camel (also unclean according to Leviticus 11.4).

5 The next 'woe' in verses 25–26 emphasizes further the way that the Pharisees treated religion as a matter of outward observances rather than inner attitudes such as Jesus has spoken of in interpreting the Law in 5.21–48. In the parallel to these verses in Luke 11.37–41 we have a setting to this teaching. Jesus was having a meal with a Pharisee and he spoke about the concern to have cups and plates properly washed and cleansed, but not such a concern for inner purity. (Compare the words of Jesus about the clean and the unclean in 15.10–20.) In particular he rebuked the greed and self-indulgence of such people. The parallels in Mark 12.40 and Luke 20.47 speak of them making money even out of widows who less than any others could afford it.

6 Another 'woe' in verses 27–28 rebukes the same contrast between outward appearances and inner reality which made them 'like whitewashed tombs'. The Law said that a person who touched a dead body would be unclean for seven days and unable to take part in religious or social matters (Numbers 19.11–20). For this reason, especially at festival times, tombs were whitewashed in order to be seen easily and so that people would not defile themselves

accidentally by contact with death. People could be like white-washed tombs, appearing very nice on the outside but inside there was only corruption. They outwardly obeyed all the details of the Law, but in reality were 'full of hypocrisy and iniquity'.

7 The last woe also shows up the insincerity and hypocrisy of the Jewish religious leaders for what they really were. They honoured the memory of the prophets of old by what they did to their tombs and graves. They said that they would not have killed them as their ancestors had done. But the test was, What were they doing then to the greatest Messenger of God's word? The challenge is like that of the parable in 21.33–41. The Good News Bible translates verse 32, 'Go on, then, and finish what your ancestors started!' The next verse is a most solemn warning of judgement. Past, present and future – all bring the story of the goodness and patience of God sending his messengers, 'even rising up early and sending them' (as Jeremiah 26.5, Revised Version, puts it). But it was one sad story of people's rejection of God's word and persecution of God's messengers.

So it had been in Old Testament days. So it was when Jesus came. So it would be in the future with the sending of 'prophets, sages, and scribes'. In Old Testament times the murder of faithful men and women began with Abel in the first book of the Bible (Genesis 4) and ended with Zechariah in what was the last book of the Hebrew Bible (2 Chronicles 24.20–22). This passage calls him Zechariah son of Barachiah probably by a slip that linked him with the prophet Zechariah who was son of Berechiah (Zechariah 1.1). The story of the sufferings of the apostle Paul (2 Corinthians 11.23–26) illustrate what future sufferings were to face the messengers of the gospel of Jesus. Verse 36 prepares us for chapter 24 which gives more details of the way that judgement was to fall on that generation because of the constant rejection of God's word. The history of Israel was moving to a terrible climax.

---

### 📖 Study Suggestions

1 What tempts Christian people today to show themselves off as religious? What is the effect of this on those who are not Christians?

2 Is there a temptation for those in positions of Christian leadership in your situation to want places and titles of honour?

3 In your Church situation is there a danger of rules and regulations obscuring the central things of the gospel and the essence of Christian discipleship?

4 How do Hosea 6.6 (which this Gospel quotes twice in 9.13 and

12.7) and Micah 6.6–8 illustrate verse 23? How does Jesus' story in Luke 18.9–14 also illustrate his teaching here?

5 How does the teaching of verses 25–26 link with the teaching about the clean and the unclean in 15.1–20?

6 Thinking of the seventh woe (verses 29–36), how do you think it is possible for people today to honour the memory of godly men and women of the past, and yet in fact to be more like those who opposed them than imitators of their godliness?

# 23.37–39 Jesus' Lament over Jerusalem

## See also Luke 13.34–35

Many of the words of the woes in this chapter may have seemed hard words. But here we see the love and concern of Jesus for the people of Jerusalem, even though they had repeatedly killed God's prophets and stoned his messengers. His longing was that they might turn from the course of action that could only bring them into great danger of judgement. The record pictures his love as like that of a mother hen calling to her chicks to come under her wings into a place of safety.

Because they refused to heed the warning, their house (perhaps the temple, or the city, or the people themselves) would become desolate, as will be made clearer in chapter 24. Their only hope would be in saying sincerely, 'Blessed is the one who comes in the name of the Lord' and acting accordingly. (These words of welcome are from Psalm 118.26, and the crowds had used them in 21.9 at the triumphal entry into Jerusalem, but the Jewish religious leaders had been unwilling to apply them to Jesus as God's Sent One.)

# 24.1–2 Jesus Foretells the Destruction of the Temple

## See also Mark 13.1–2; Luke 21.5–6

Jesus had taught in the temple, but now he came out from it. In the disciples' minds were thoughts of the beauty and grandness of the temple. In Jesus' mind was the sad thought of the destruction of the temple that lay ahead. Mark's Gospel in this context (12.41–44) relates something that happened in the temple, the small but sacrificial gift of a very poor widow. Matthew omits that, and so the words about the temple here follow directly on from Jesus' lament over Jerusalem for the way that its people had rejected God's protection and the salvation he offered. As the prophets had said, a beautiful temple was no use if people were not serving the One to whose worship the temple was dedicated.

# 24.3–8 The Question about Signs of the End

## See also Mark 13.3–8; Luke 21.7–11

In verse 2 Jesus has spoken about the destruction of the temple. In verse 3 the disciples ask about the coming (Parousia) of Christ and the end of the age. This chapter deals with both the Parousia and the destruction of Jerusalem, and one of the difficulties in interpreting it is that it is hard sometimes to know which of the two is meant. The New Testament speaks of both as resulting from the ministry of Jesus. The people's rejection of the salvation that God offered to them in Jesus would have tragic results, and lead to the destruction of the temple. But what he had done would also lead on to his coming at the end of the present age.

The disciples, like many people still today, asked the questions, 'When will this be?' and 'What will be the sign of your coming?' Jesus gave no direct answer to their questions. In verse 36 he will make clear than we cannot know the time. He also shows that there is no sign that will make people see that the Parousia is shortly to take place. He says two things in answer to their questions:

1 They must be on their guard so that no one leads them astray. People will come and even claim to be the Messiah. All down the history of the Church people have been led astray by those who have claimed to be able to predict the future. So Jesus says, 'Beware'.
2 People must be prepared to face great troubles in the world, conflicts between nations, and also natural disasters such as famines and earthquakes. Great blessings came into the world through the coming of Jesus. Great spiritual blessings come now to those who welcome him into their lives. But in the world they must face troubles, and the intensity of these does not mean that the end is just round the corner. Such things must take place. God is still in control. Trials are troubles that we can compare with the pains of child-birth, pains which are very sharp but lead to the blessing of a new life.

# 24.9–14 Warning of Persecution

## See also Mark 13.9, 13; Luke 21.12, 17–19

Most of this chapter is closely similar to the teaching about the future in Mark 13, but verses 10–12 are not closely paralleled by Mark. In the 'mission charge' of Jesus to his disciples in 10.17–22 we have had teaching that they must expect persecution. Here there are warnings of four things to expect, and then an emphasis on two things that disciples must be prepared to do.

1 Disciples must expect to face hatred in every nation to which they go with the gospel. That hatred will result simply from the name that they bear, the fact that they are Christ's men and women, and that hatred will lead to suffering and even death.
2 There will be increasing 'lawlessness' in the world with all the disorder and confusion that results from that in any society.
3 There will be 'false prophets' who will lead many people astray, just as verse 5 has spoken about false Messiahs.
4 The love of many who have been disciples will grow cold. They will turn away from their faith and even become traitors of those who still hold to the faith. Two things are vitally important for those who are genuine disciples. It is those who endure to the end who will be saved. From one point of view salvation is the gift of God, but it is a gift received by faith, and true faith is faith that endures whatever the difficulties and temptations faced. The one great task of disciples is to share the good news of God's kingdom that the coming of Jesus has brought into human life, and they are to share that good news with people of all nations. God's purpose for the world will only be fulfilled with the completion of the mission he has given to the Church, the mission for which Jesus commissions disciples in the last verses of the Gospel (28.18–20).

# 24.15–22  A Climax of Suffering

## See also Mark 13.14–20; Luke 21.20–24

This section clearly seems to refer to the fall of Jerusalem and thus links with what has gone before in verse 2. It begins with a reference to the Book of Daniel. That book (in 8.13, 9.27, 11.31 and 12.11) speaks of the trampling of the temple by enemy forces, the halting of the usual sacrifices and the setting up of heathen worship. Daniel speaks of this as 'the desolating sacrilege . . . standing in the holy place'. The Daniel passages also speak of the destruction of the city. Luke (21.20) does not speak of Daniel in the way he puts this teaching (because that would not have been very meaningful to his

Gentile readers), but says, 'When you see Jerusalem surrounded by armies, then know that its desolation has come near.'

The words of Daniel related to what happened in the year 168 BC when the Syrian ruler, Antiochus Epiphanes, set up a pagan altar in the temple, and did all that was in his power to stop the normal Jewish worship. Now verse 15 says, 'let the reader understand'. These things that the Book of Daniel had spoken about would happen again. They would happen in fact when the Romans came and besieged Jerusalem. It would be a time of great distress, greater, it might be said, than any the world had seen before (with verse 22 compare Daniel 12.1 and Joel 2.2). People would be wise to escape from Jerusalem to the security of the mountains, and not to stop to think of gathering up their possessions from their homes. It would be a hard time for pregnant women and mothers with little children. It would be hard if the flight was in winter when roads would be difficult. Jewish people would find it hard to have to flee on the sabbath because they felt bound by the detailed regulations that the Pharisees had added to the Law.

It was some comfort for this passage to say, as earlier Jewish writings had said, that the days of such trials would be cut short. Otherwise 'no human being would be saved'. The teaching of Jesus makes very clear that disciples cannot avoid trial and suffering, but there is a limit. The spirit of verse 22 is the same as that of the words of the apostle Paul in 1 Corinthians 10.13, 'God is faithful, and he will not let you be tested beyond your strength, but with the temptation will also provide the way of escape, that you may be able to endure it.'

The Jewish historian, Josephus, who wrote a little later than the date of this Gospel and 20 years after the fall of Jerusalem, tells of the tremendous sufferings of the people in the city when it was besieged by the Romans for four years.

# 24.23–28 Warning of False Messiahs

## See also Mark 13.21–23; Luke 17.20–21, 23–24, 37

This passage seems clearly to move from the thought of the desecration of the temple and the fall of Jerusalem to the coming (or Parousia) of Christ. As we have had the warning in verse 5 about false Messiahs and in verse 11 about false prophets, so we have both here. Those who are truly God's people will be on their guard. The writer uses the word 'elect' in verse 24, as also in verses 22 and 31, for those who have put their trust firmly in the true Christ and belong to him.

People will be deceived by 'great signs'. They should realise that apparent 'signs and wonders' are not always proof of the power of God at work. Some will say that you can find the Christ in the wilderness, the place to which men and women determined to serve God have gone to avoid the evil influences of society. Others will say that you can find the Christ 'in the inner rooms', that is, that there are secrets about him that only special people know. In both of these ways people could be deceived.

What verse 27 says here is that when the climax of history comes and the Parousia of the Son of man takes place, everyone will know it. It will not be hidden any more than anyone can hide a flash of lightning.

Verse 28 is a proverb. Those who live in countries where there are vultures or other birds that feast on dead animals know what the proverb means. The gathering of a large number of these birds is a sure sign that there is a dead animal on which they are feasting. The application is not quite so clear, but it is probably linked with the verse before. The coming of the Son of man 'will be as obvious and unmistakable as the gathering of vultures to a carcass; you can see the birds concentrating on the one spot from many miles away' (M. Green).

---

### 📖 Study Suggestions

1 With verse 2 compare what the prophet Jeremiah (7.1–15; 26.1–15) said about the destruction of the temple, and what

Ezekiel (10.1–19) said about the glory of the presence of the Lord departing from the Jerusalem temple.

2  To fill out what verse 4 says about being on guard against being led astray, see 2 Thessalonians 2.

3  What verse 8 says about the birth-pangs of the new age has a background in the words of the Old Testament prophets and later Jewish writings. See Isaiah 13.8; 26.16–19; Jeremiah 4.29–31; 6.24–25 and Micah 4.9–10.

4  People applied the 'name' of Christ to disciples who 'were for the first time called "Christians" in Antioch' (Acts 11.26). Why do you think they gave the name like that? With verse 9 compare what 1 Peter 4.12–16 says about suffering as a Christian.

5  What does it mean when the New Testament calls the subject of Christian proclamation the 'good news of the kingdom' (see 4.23 and 9.35) and 'testimony' or 'witness' (see Acts 1.8)?

6  Often the first Christians in any place are the most zealous, or people when they have first become Christians. What reasons are there for that first love growing cold? With verse 12 read Revelation 2.4–5 and 3.15–22.

7  What today may correspond to the 'great signs and wonders' which can in fact lead people away from the truth rather than towards understanding God's truth and God's purposes?

8  Although we may not exactly think of false Messiahs or false prophets today, what influences are there that can tempt Christians away from their faith in Christ and loyalty to him, and put something or someone else in the place that only he should have in their lives?

# 24.29–31  The Coming of the Son of Man

## See also Mark 13.24–27; Luke 21.25–38

Although some people have taken these verses to speak of 'earth-shaking' events at the time of the fall of Jerusalem, it is more likely that we should understand them as referring to the end of the age, the climax of human history, and the appearing of the Son of man. What this future event will mean is beyond description because it is beyond any experience of the past. But we can best describe it in language that the Old Testament has used to speak of great crises in past history or of future hopes. We can see this use of the Old Testament in five ways:

### 1 Signs in sun, moon and stars

It is uncertain how literally we are meant to understand these, but the language of verse 29 appears in relation to the fall of Babylon in Isaiah 13.10, and the judgement of the nations is spoken about in similar terms in Isaiah 34.4 and Ezekiel 32.7, as is a plague of locusts in Joel 2.10.

### 2 The Son of man coming on the clouds of heaven

Daniel 7.13–14 speaks of one like a son of man coming 'with the clouds of heaven' in relation to the time when God would be truly worshipped and his people reign with him. 26.64 records such words on the lips of Jesus at the time of his trial before Caiaphas.

### 3 All the tribes of the earth will mourn

Zechariah 12.10–14 speaks of people mourning for what they have done to 'one whom they have pierced' (compare Revelation 1.7). This day of the Son of man will be a day of exposing the follies and sins of people's past lives leading to their discomfort and sorrow.

### 4 The gathering of the elect

We have had Matthew use this term 'the elect' for God's faithful people in verses 22 and 24. The Old Testament often speaks of the scattering of Israel as God's judgement on them for their unfaithfulness. But then their restoration was their 'gathering' from far and near in the places where they had been scattered (see Deuteronomy 30.4, Jeremiah 23.3, Ezekiel 34.13).

### 5 The sound of the trumpet

People blew the trumpet in Old Testament days in times of religious celebration (Numbers 29.1, Isaiah 27.13), political celebration (as 2 Kings 11.14), to warn of danger (Numbers 10.5–6), or to call the people together (Numbers 10.2–3). Moreover, since there was a blast of the trumpet that grew louder and louder at the time of the awe-inspiring event of God's revelation at Mount Sinai (Exodus 19.19), so the sounding of the trumpet can well be associated with the future appearing of the Son of man in glory.

# 24.32–35 The Parable of the Fig Tree

## See also Mark 13.28–31; Luke 21.29–33

We have noted that this chapter draws together teaching about the future, (a) related to the fall of Jerusalem (which took place in AD 70), and (b) related to the coming again of the Son of man. It is sometimes hard to know which one the teaching refers to. Some have taken verse 34 to mean that Jesus expected his Parousia to take place within the lifetime of those who were with him in the days of his ministry, or was understood to have taught them – and was mistaken or misunderstood. This, however, would be a contradiction of what immediately follows in verse 36 about his not knowing the time.

It may help us to determine the meaning of these verses if we realize that earlier in this chapter Jesus has said two things about 'signs' of the future:

1 People are not to take wars and conflicts, famines and earthquakes, as signs of the nearness of the end – they are only 'the beginning of the birth pangs' (verses 6–8).
2 On the other hand there are signs for people to recognize when the fall of Jerusalem would shortly take place (verses 15–22).

This makes it more probable that the fig tree getting new leaves being a sign of summer applies to the signs of the approaching fall of Jerusalem. It is true that the word 'generation' can have a number of different meanings. Its most common use, however, is such as we have in 12.41–42 and 23.34–36, speaking of the whole body of people alive at one time. Also we should note that we can translate verse 33 as either 'he is near' or 'it is near'.

Verse 33 stresses the authority of the word of Jesus to which this

Gospel has often referred (compare the repeated, 'But I say to you' in 5.22, 28, 32, 34, 39 and 44, and the conclusion of the Sermon on the Mount in 7.28–29).

# 24.36–44 The Need for Watchfulness

## See also Mark 13.32; Luke 17.26–27, 34–35; 12.39–40

These verses have parallels in Luke (though in different contexts from Matthew) but only verse 36 is paralleled in Mark. The section is all about the coming of the Son of man, and its emphasis is on the certainty of the fact that he will come, but that to us, and even to Jesus himself, the time is not known. Some of the early manuscripts omitted the words 'nor the Son' in verse 36. They probably omitted them out of the desire not to speak of Jesus being ignorant of anything, but we can accept such ignorance as part of the limitation of his incarnate human life (note Philippians 2.7). The stress on the time being unknown should turn Christian people away from trying to make predictions about the future. Above all, it should challenge them to be ready at any time, or the Parousia will certainly be unexpected when it comes.

This passage describes the Parousia as involving judgement and the necessary division between those who will experience the ultimate blessing of God's kingdom and those who will miss it. The Christian gospel, and not least the presentation of it in Matthew, is good news of the love and compassion of God and his offer of forgiveness and acceptance. But this Gospel nevertheless presents the reality of judgement. It is sadly possible to miss the life that God offers. This reality is clear in the Sermon on the Mount (especially in 7.13–27). It is in the three parables of chapter 25. It is here in this section. We are shown it vividly but simply in the picture of two people working in the field together, and of two women grinding corn together. One is taken and the other is left behind.

Jesus reinforces the teaching by a lesson from the Old Testament and a parable from life.

In the Old Testament the story of the Flood in the days of Noah was the most startling presentation of God's judgement, and Jewish writings often referred to it. Normal life went on, eating and drinking, marrying and giving in marriage. These were things good in themselves, but dangerous when carried out by people living a God-neglecting, God-rejecting life. When people are living such a life, the day for giving to God an account of their lives takes them by surprise. 'As were the days of Noah, so will be the coming of the Son of man.'

Then the picture of the thief coming in the night is another example of a person taken by surprise. The only way to meet unexpected events of the future, and especially the coming of the Son of man at an unknown time, is to be ready at all times, ready to meet the Lord himself.

---

### 📖 Study Suggestions

1 What examples do you see around you of things that are good in themselves but keep people away from God and from a readiness to meet with him?

2 The word 'watch' (which some English versions sometimes translate 'keep awake' or 'keep alert') is a key word in Christian instruction. See its use in Acts 20.31; 1 Corinthians 16.13; Colossians 4.2; 1 Thessalonians 5.6; 1 Peter 5.8; Revelation 3.2–3; 16.15, and also in the warning of Jesus to his disciples in the Garden of Gethsemane (Matthew 26.36–46).

3 Note the use of the parable of the thief coming in the night elsewhere: in 1 Thessalonians 5.1–8; 2 Peter 3.8–10; Revelation 3.3; 16.15.

# 24.45–51 The Faithful and Unfaithful Servants

## See also Luke 12.42–46

Question: What does it mean to be ready for the Parousia? Answer: To be continuing faithfully in the work one has been assigned to do. This is illustrated by another parable which pictures wise and foolish, faithful and wicked servants.

Their master entrusts each of them with responsibility in his household, for the care of his property and provision for fellow-servants.

The one servant acts faithfully, and so can gladly give account of his stewardship at whatever time his master returns. The other puts the thought of his master's return out of his mind. His thought is only of his own enjoyment and he has no care for his fellow-servants. His master's return and his challenge to account for himself and for what he had done was a rude shock for him.

The master rewarded the first servant with greater trust and responsibility. The second met a fate that this Gospel describes in similar terms in various places (with verse 51 compare 8.12; 13.43; 22.13 and 25.30). And it is 'with the hypocrites', those who professed to be very religious but who lived lives that were in reality displeasing to God.

# 25.1–13 The Wise and Foolish Maidens

Some parables are difficult to understand, and down the history of the Christian Church people have interpreted this parable in many different ways. There are six points, however, that may help us in understanding it as it was probably intended to be understood.

## 1 Its setting in the Gospel

It follows on what chapter 24 has said about the future, especially about the crisis of the Parousia of the Son of man, the coming again of Christ, and the judgement that this will involve. All three parables of chapter 25 speak about being ready for the future coming of the Lord through taking the opportunities of the present.

## 2 The parable is about wedding celebrations

We have wedding celebrations also in the parables of 22.1–14 and Luke 12.35–38. Jesus clearly rejoiced in the happiness of weddings, but this parable, like others, indicates that people may share the joy, or miss the opportunity of sharing it.

## 3 The Lord as the bridegroom

The Old Testament often speaks of God as Husband or Bridegroom, and Israel as Wife or Bride (see Isaiah 54.4–8; 62.4–5; Ezekiel 16 and Hosea 1—3). So the New Testament speaks of the Church as the Bride of Christ (see 2 Corinthians 11.2, Ephesians 5.23–32 and Revelation 19.6–8 and 21.1–6).

## 4 The wedding customs of the time

Although we do not know the details of Palestinian wedding customs in New Testament times, it seems that there were two parties involved, the bridegroom and his supporters, and the bride and her supporters. Translations of this passage sometimes call the bride's supporters 'bridesmaids', but they were not quite the same as bridesmaids in many marriage customs today. They would have been waiting for the bridegroom with his party when he went to claim his bride in her house.

## 5 Details in the parable

As with many parables, we should not try to take meanings from details that are just part of the story. For example, when verse 5 speaks of all the maidens sleeping, it is not saying that none of them were watchful. When verse 9 says that the 'wise' would not give oil to the 'foolish', it does not mean to say that they were selfish. There are certain things in life, like the opportunities that come to people, that they cannot share with others. Oil is sometimes understood as a symbol of the Holy Spirit, but this may not be the intention here. Having lamps burning well, however, is taken (as in Luke 12.35–36) as a mark of being prepared. There is probably no special point in the number ten, nor is there necessarily a suggestion that the wise and the foolish are equal in numbers. Some have thought that this parable arose in the early Church out of the situation in which people felt that there was a delay with the Parousia (compare 2 Peter 3.1–4), but the concern of Jesus seems to have been that his disciples should be ready whether their time was shorter or longer.

### 6 The main lesson

The final verse of the section indicates what should be a main point in our understanding of the parable. True disciples should continue in a state of watchfulness. The foolish maidens thought only of their immediate situation. The thoughts of the wise were kept on the hope of the coming of the bridegroom, and they were determined to be ready to meet him when he came, whatever the time of day or night.

# 25.14–30 The Parable of the Talents

## See also Luke 19.12–27

While the emphasis of the previous parable was on waiting for the Lord, the emphasis of this one is on working for the Lord, and so being ready for his coming. There is a similar parable in Luke 19.12–27, which is known as the parable of the pounds, but it differs especially in that the master entrusts each of the servants (or slaves) in that parable with the same amount. Although the two might represent different ways in which people handed down the same parable in the life of the Church, Jesus may well have told two similar parables but with slightly different themes. We can easily see a meaning in saying that each of God's servants receives the same gift, the same opportunity of life and the knowledge of God's love and purpose. It is also true, as this parable indicates, that people receive different abilities, some greater, some lesser.

Originally a talent was a very large sum of money, as we have seen in the parable of the two debtors in 18.23–35. The use of the word 'talent' in English for natural gifts and abilities is a derived meaning, perhaps helped by this parable. The parable shows that there are two ways of dealing with the gifts that people entrust to us. The first and second servants, with the five and two talents, acted in the same way and received exactly the same commendation from their master. The third acted very differently. He made his choice not to use the talent, but to bury it. The way that he thought about his master (verse 24) affected what he chose to do (verse 25).

The conclusion of the parable in verse 29 does not give a principle that we can apply to business dealings! It is a spiritual principle in almost exactly the same words that 13.12 used. Those who have talents of any kind – personal gifts, abilities and opportunities – and fail to use them, as a result lose them. On the other hand, those who use such gifts and abilities and opportunities find that they increase in the using of them. That is what goes on all the time in our lives. But there is also a future time when each person must give account to God. Verse 30 speaks of judgement in the same terms as 8.12; 13.42, 50; 22.13 and 24.51.

# 25.31–46 The Parable of the Sheep and the Goats

This third parable of the chapter gives us a picture of a farmer separating off his sheep from his goats (as in Ezekiel 34.17). It is a picture of divine judgement that people of 'all nations' must face. 'The Son of man' is both King and Judge, and (as 13.41; 16.27 and 24.31 say) he appears with 'all the angels with him'.

What is striking here is that the one thing that is the basis of the Son of man's judgement is how a person has acted, or failed to act, towards the hungry and thirsty, the sick and the naked, the stranger and the prisoner. There is, however, something even more striking, both to those who have acted in kindness and compassion and those who have failed to act in that way.

What people have done to the most insignificant person in need is taken as done to the Son of man himself, and the neglect of that insignificant person in need is treated as neglect of the Son of man himself.

There is thus the strongest possible motivation for Christian service, the realization that to help a person in need is to help the Lord himself. To fail a person in need is to fail the Lord himself. It increases the sense of responsibility, but also the sense of the privilege of such service of those in need.

There are two questions that this parable raises when we set it alongside other aspects of teaching in the Gospel and in the New Testament generally:

1  When the king's words in verse 40 (as in the New Revised Standard Version) are, 'just as you did it to one of the least of these who are members of my family, you did it to me', is the reference only to good deeds done to those who are Christ's disciples? It is true that such passages as 10.42 and 18.6 express special concern for 'little ones who believe'. On the other hand the teaching in the parable of the Good Samaritan (Luke 10.25–37), and Jesus' attitude to Samaritans or Gentiles, tax collectors or prostitutes, makes it unlikely that he intended to restrict his honouring of acts of kindness to those that people had shown to his own disciples. Moreover, through his own suffering Jesus is in solidarity with all those who suffer, and this means that whenever we serve them, we are in effect serving him.

2  Does this parable mean that our salvation is dependent on the good that we do to those in need? Does it not depend rather on God's grace and forgiveness? This Gospel from its beginning speaks of Jesus as coming into the world to save his people from their sins (1.21), and many passages in the Gospel illustrate the reality that people find salvation by the grace and mercy of God rather than by what they do (see 9.10–13; 11.25–30 and 20.28). One way of bringing the two aspects of New Testament teaching together is to say that we are saved by grace but judged according to our works. We have acceptance with God on the basis of his love and what Jesus Christ has done for us. But our acceptance of that salvation, in repentance and faith, is shown to be real and effective only as we express it in love (Galatians 5.6 and 1 John 3.14–17) and in care for those in need (James 2.14–26).

## 📖 Study Suggestions

1 What ways does the parable of 24.45–51 suggest that disciples of Christ today can describe the work that God entrusts to them?

2 In the light of the parable of 25.14–30, how can we think of the different gifts that the man entrusts to the servants? Consider the passages in the Epistles that speak of spiritual gifts, especially Romans 12.3–8; 1 Corinthians 12.1–11, 27–31 and Ephesians 4.11–16.

3 Compare the use of the word 'wise' to describe the servant in 24.45, the bridesmaids in 25.1–13 and also in 7.24 and 10.16. Compare also the use of the word 'foolish' in 25.1–13 and 7.26.

4 Follow up the use of the word 'faithful' in 24.45; 25.21, 23, and see also Luke 12.41–44; 16.10–13 and 19.16–17.

5 Consider other passages which, like 24.47; 25.21 and 23, suggest that if a person is faithful in carrying out their responsibilities, they will get greater ones. See Luke 16.10–13 and 22.28–30.

6 What would be a right application of the parable of 25.1–13 in your society today?

7 Compare the emphasis in these parables on the future giving account to God with the teaching of the Epistles in such passages as Romans 14.10–12; 1 Corinthians 3.10–15 and 2 Corinthians 5.9–10.

8 How does the emphasis come out in these parables on sin involving not only wrong things that a person does but also the good that a person fails to do? Note the linking together of the words 'wicked' and 'slothful' in 25.26.

9 In the light of 25.23–25 how do you think that a failure to understand the goodness of God must affect a person's desire to serve him? On the other hand, what does it mean to appreciate the goodness and love and wisdom of God?

10 If we take seriously the teaching of the parable of 25.31–46, who are the people in our society in particular need, for whom we have special responsibility and the privilege of helping as we would help the Lord himself? In particular, who are the 'strangers' in our situation whom we should specially want to help?

11 What should we understand by the New Testament speaking of our future share in God's kingdom as an 'inheritance'? With verse 34 compare 19.29; Ephesians 1.14, 18 and 1 Peter 1.4.

# PART 11: 26.1—28.20

# NARRATIVE: THE ARREST, TRIAL, DEATH AND RESURRECTION OF JESUS

We have come to the end of the last teaching section of the Gospel. So we have in 26.1 words like those we have had in 7.28; 11.1; 13.53 and 19.1, but now it is 'When Jesus had finished all these sayings'. The sustained teaching that has been a distinctive mark of this Gospel is complete. Now we have only words of Jesus that explain his actions or what was being done to him in the culmination of his ministry, his death and resurrection.

In general terms these chapters are parallel to the concluding chapters of Mark and Luke and John, and are closer to Mark than the others. There are a few details here that are not in any of the other Gospels: the death of Judas (27.3–10), the dream of Pilate's wife (27.19), Pilate's washing his hands (27.24–25), the appearance of the saints who had died (27.52–53), and the guards at the tomb of Jesus (27.65–66, 28.4, 11–15). Most important, there is a great emphasis on the fulfilment of Scripture in the death of Jesus and the things associated with it. This is not lacking in the other Gospels, but, as we would expect from what we have seen of Matthew's Gospel in other ways, it has a greater place here than with any of the other evangelists.

We may subdivide this final major section of the Gospel as follows:

---

## Analysis

26.1–5     Plans for the death of Jesus
26.6–13    The anointing at Bethany
26.14–16   The treachery of Judas
26.17–19   Preparations for the Passover
26.20–25   Jesus' prediction of his betrayal
26.26–30   The institution of the Lord's Supper
26.31–35   The prediction of Peter's denial
26.36–46   Jesus' prayer in Gethsemane

# 26.1–5 Plans for the Death of Jesus

## See also Mark 14.1–2; Luke 22.1–2; John 11.47–53

What we call the Passion narrative – the story of the events leading to the arrest of Jesus, his trials and then his crucifixion – is full of contrasts.

The words of Jesus show him determined to give his life. At the Passover time the Son of man will be 'delivered up to be crucified'. The chief priests and elders were determined to take Jesus' life. They feared the popular support for Jesus, perhaps particularly among those who came as pilgrims to Jerusalem to keep the Passover. So they 'made plans to arrest Jesus secretly and put him to death' (Good News Bible). (Compare Mark 14.1–2 and Luke 22.1–4.)

All of the Gospels emphasize that the death of Jesus took place at Passover time, and imply (what the apostle Paul states in 1 Corinthians 5.7) that in an important way it was the fulfilment of the meaning of the Passover. The Jews kept the Passover year by year, with the sacrifice of a lamb and with other rituals, in remembrance of the deliverance of Israel from their slavery in Egypt (Exodus 12, Deuteronomy 16.1–8). They kept it not only as people looking back to the past, but with the hope of a new and greater deliverance in the future.

Another of the great contrasts in the Passion narrative is that the enemies of Jesus acted with fear. Jesus acted openly and unafraid. His enemies were the ones who in the eyes of the world had power in their hands, but at a deeper level it is Jesus who controls the events that take place, and they are fearful of what might happen.

# 26.6–13 The Anointing at Bethany

## See also Mark 14.3–9; John 12.1–8

Between the record of the plans of hatred against Jesus in verses 3–5 and 14–16 we have the record of this action of loving devotion. The account in Mark is very similar. John speaks of the Bethany anointing as something that Mary did in the home of her brother Lazarus.

Although Jesus was declared from the first verse of this Gospel as the 'Christ', the anointed one, he had never had his head anointed with oil, as kings and prophets did in Old Testament times. This woman, in love and gratitude, poured her costly ointment on his head.

The criticism of the disciples (John 12.4 speaks of it as Judas's criticism) was that it would have been possible to put the value of the precious ointment to more practical use, giving it to help the poor. Jesus, however, accepted what the woman had done and honoured the motive that inspired her action. She would not have such an opportunity again. It was as if to prepare him for death and for burial.

People have often misunderstood the words of Jesus in verse 11. There were always the poor to help, and Jesus may have alluded to the words of Deuteronomy 15.11 which state this together with the command to be generous to them. We know how Jesus often showed concern for the poor, and that he and his disciples gave to the poor from the small resources they had (see John 13.29). But this was a special act of devotion that people would tell wherever they told the good news of Jesus. And in fact it has inspired many acts of devotion to the Lord himself, and led many to give their lives in the service of the world's poor. Christians do not need to decide between devotion to Christ and care for the poor. Both should have their place in Christian living.

# 26.14–16 The Treachery of Judas

## See also Mark 14.10–11; Luke 22.3–6

The woman who anointed Jesus had thought about what she could give to show her love and gratitude. Judas asked, 'What will you give me if I deliver him to you?' She looked for and took the opportunity to express her love. Judas, according to Matthew, sought 'an opportunity to betray' Jesus.

In practical terms the betrayal meant telling the Jewish authorities where they could find Jesus at a time when the crowds who might rise up to support him were not around him.

We can ask many questions about why Judas who had been a disciple – 'one of the twelve' as the New Testament regularly reminds us – decided to betray Jesus. Was he trying to force Jesus to act in a particular way to declare himself to the people? Was he disappointed that Jesus was not turning out to be the kind of Messiah for which he had hoped? Whatever other reasons there may have been, the one reason that the Gospels give is that he came to love money more than he loved Jesus as his Master. John (12.6) adds that he actually stole from the money box in which their little community kept its funds.

In this passage there is no actual quotation of the Old Testament, but we should note that Zechariah 11.12 speaks of thirty pieces of silver as the price paid there for the faithful shepherd of the flock; and Exodus 21.32 reckons the same amount as the value of a slave.

### 📖 Study Suggestions

1 There is a word in Greek that appears several times in the Passion narrative which English versions sometimes translate 'handed over' or 'delivered up' and sometimes 'betrayed'. See its use in 26.2, 16; 27.2, 26. See the use of the same word in Romans 8.32 and Galatians 2.20.
2 In the light of 26.6–13, how should Christian people think of the relationship of love and devotion to Christ and care and concern for the poor?
3 Considering what this Gospel says about Judas in 26.14–16, do you still see it as a temptation for even those who are trustworthy

disciples and even church leaders to turn aside because of their love of money? See the warning about this in 1 Timothy 6.3–19.

4 In what sense should the disciples' question in verse 22, 'Is it I, Lord?' still be on the lips of Christians? See 1 Corinthians 10.12 and 2 Corinthians 13.5.

# 26.17–19 Preparations for the Passover

## See also Mark 14.12–16; Luke 22.7–13

The Passover was associated with the Festival of Unleavened Bread. The connection went back to the Exodus, because in hurrying to escape from Egypt the people had no time to make leavened bread (Exodus 12.39). The Old Testament speaks of the celebration of the Passover on the fourteenth day of the first month of the year and the celebration of the Feast of Unleavened Bread from the fifteenth to the twenty-first day of the same month (Exodus 12.1–20, Leviticus 23.4–8 and Deuteronomy 16.1–8). So it was possible to speak of celebrating the Passover on 'the first day of Unleavened Bread'.

The disciples' question about Jesus' plans for keeping the Passover is understandable, as that would be in the mind of every devout Jew as the time approached. The record here is similar to the records of Mark and Luke but briefer, not telling what the other Gospels do about the way the disciples were to meet a man carrying a jar of water.

What is important in Matthew is the message of Jesus to the owner of the home in which he and the disciples were to meet. 'My time is at hand . . .' The Greek language had two words for 'time', one which usually speaks of the passing of time, hours and days and years. The other speaks of an important time when something is to happen. This was the 'time' so vitally important to Jesus, the time to which all of his ministry and life on earth had been moving.

The preparations that the disciples had to make for the Passover would have included a number of things. They had to kill the Passover lamb. They had to have bitter herbs, the reminder of the experience of bitter slavery in Egypt. They had to make a paste of apples, dates, pomegranates and nuts to remind them of the clay of Egypt that they had to make into bricks. They had to prepare the wine for the four cups that they would pass around at the feast.

## ADDITIONAL NOTE J: THE PASSOVER AND THE TIME OF JESUS' DEATH

If we try to piece together what each of the four Gospels say in relation to the time of Jesus' death and the observance of the Passover we find a number of difficulties. Matthew, Mark and Luke all present Jesus as eating the Passover with his disciples and then going out from it to Gethsemane, to his arrest and then his trials and his death. John's Gospel (18.28) speaks of the time of the trials of Jesus as that of preparation for the Passover, not after it had taken place. There are four main ways of explaining these differences:

1 In the matter of the date of the Passover, the Synoptic Gospels are right, and John for theological reasons has linked the death of Jesus with the killing of the Passover lambs to indicate his fulfilment of the meaning of the Passover by his redemptive death as 'the Lamb of God' (John 1.29 and 36). One of the main difficulties with this view is that if the Thursday night (rather than the Friday) had been the time of the celebration of the Passover, it would be hard to think of the Jewish elders and high priest doing all that they did to bring Jesus to trial at the time of the Passover.

2 In the dating of the Passover John's Gospel is right, and the Synoptic Gospels wanted to link the Passover with the Last Supper as being in a special way the fulfilment of the meaning of the Passover. Some have thought that the meal that Jesus had with his disciples was not literally the Passover, but had much of the meaning of the Passover linked with it.

3 Another suggestion is that both may be right, as there is some evidence (though not altogether convincing) that different sections of the Jewish population may have kept the Passover on different dates.

4 Perhaps the best suggestion is that the Friday night, after the crucifixion of Jesus, was the night for keeping the Passover, but Jesus was conscious that this would be too late. As his words in Luke 22.15 express it, 'I have earnestly desired to eat this Passover with you before I suffer.' There may be the same tone of urgency and strong desire in the words of verse 18 here in Matthew, 'My time is at hand, I will keep the Passover at your house with my disciples.'

# 26.20–25 Jesus' Prediction of His Betrayal

## See also Mark 14.17–21; Luke 22.21–23; John 13.21–30

Each of the Gospels gives an important place to the record of what Judas did. Each of them stresses that it was one of the twelve who 'betrayed' Jesus, 'handed him over' (see notes on verse 2) to his enemies, perhaps as a warning to all who follow Jesus that it is possible even for one of the inner circle of discipleship to be unfaithful in the end. When in verse 23 Jesus speaks of 'the one who has dipped his hand into the bowl with me', there may be an allusion to Psalm 41.9 (which John 13.18 actually quotes) where the psalmist says, 'Even my bosom friend in whom I trusted, who ate of my bread, has lifted his heel against me.'

There are two things which this Gospel – and in many different ways the whole Bible – puts together. There is the purpose of God which must come to pass, a purpose that the Scriptures often reveal. As verse 24 puts it, 'The Son of man goes as it is written of him'. It was the Father's purpose that Jesus should give his life – even that his disciples should desert him and one of them should hand him over to his enemies. But men and women are responsible for their actions. They can never say, 'It had to happen like this, so it is not my fault.' Very solemnly Jesus said of Judas, 'Woe to that one by whom the Son of Man is betrayed! It would have been better for that one not to have been born.'

All the disciples were distressed at what Jesus said about his betrayal. All of them said, 'Surely not I, Lord?' Judas also asked, and we can understand that Jesus' words to Judas at the meal were (as John 13.26–30 puts it) a final appeal to him to remain loyal. Though Judas understood what Jesus was saying, it seems that Jesus did not show him up before the other disciples for what he had already planned to do.

# 26.26–30 *The Institution of the Lord's Supper*

## *See also Mark 14.22–26; Luke 22.15–20*

Here we have the record (told for us also in Mark, Luke and by the apostle Paul in 1 Corinthians 11.23–25) of the beginning of what Christians regard as the central act of their worship. Our different churches speak of it as the Lord's Supper or the Eucharist, Holy Communion or the Breaking of Bread. There are details in one record that are not in another, but the main points are the same in all. Matthew does not have the actual command to 'do this in remembrance' of Jesus (as in Luke 22.19 and 1 Corinthians 11.24–25). Clearly, however, Matthew did not intend this to be taken as the record of something that happened only at that time (like the washing of the disciples' feet in John 13). Acts 2.42 indicates that the early Church celebrated the Lord's Supper from the beginning. We can assume that it had a regular place in the Church which first knew Matthew's Gospel.

So the 'feast' with bread and wine was clearly intended to recall the sacrificial death of Jesus. The broken bread spoke of his body that he was about to give and have broken on the cross. The wine spoke of the outpouring of his blood, the offering of his life in death. When people made a covenant in Old Testament times, they offered a sacrifice (as we see in Exodus 24). Here was the making of a covenant, which Luke 22.20 and 1 Corinthians 11.25 speak of as a 'new covenant'. It was the fulfilment of the 'new covenant' of which Jeremiah (31.31–34) had spoken, a new covenant based on the forgiveness of sins, the restoration of right relationships with God.

The Church was thus to celebrate the Lord's Supper looking back to what Jesus did through his death on the cross, realizing his continuing presence with his people, but also looking forward. Verse 29 speaks of the final realization of the 'Father's kingdom' which Jesus saw beyond the cross. 1 Corinthians 11.26 links past and future with the words it addresses to those who share in the Lord's Supper, 'as often as you eat this bread and drink the cup, you proclaim the Lord's death until he comes'.

The meal that Jesus had with his disciples closed with the singing of a hymn. The custom of the Jews was to sing Psalms 113 and 114 at the beginning of the Passover celebration, and Psalms 115—118 at the end.

# 26.31–35 The Prediction of Peter's Denial

## See also Mark 14.27–31; Luke 22.31–34; John 13.36–38

We have read Jesus' warning that one of the disciples would betray him (verse 21). Now the warning was that all of them would 'fall away' and that very night none of them would remain standing by him. We again have the use of words of Scripture, this time Zechariah 13.7 which spoke about the striking of the Shepherd which would result in the scattering of the sheep.

Yet this prediction gave a comfort that the prediction of the betrayal could not give. There would be a scattering of the disciples, but Jesus saw beyond this to a gathering together again, which would be in Galilee where they had first lived with him as disciples.

We can understand the response of Peter, and we should see both strength and weakness in it. He desperately wanted to remain loyal to his Master. He was determined that he would never 'fall away' and become disloyal. Yet he failed to realize his human weakness and that under the pressure of temptation, with everyone around him against Jesus, he would prove unfaithful.

The need to warn all future disciples was so great that all the Gospels tell of this prediction of Peter's denial. Mark (14.27–31) tells it in terms very similar to this passage, Luke (22.31–34) and John (13.36–38) rather differently.

### 📖 Study Suggestions

1 As background to the keeping of the Passover and the Festival of Unleavened Bread read Exodus 12.1–28; Leviticus 23.4–8 and Deuteronomy 16.1–8.
2 With the thought involved in the words of verse 18, 'My time is at hand', follow out the way that Jesus speaks in John's Gospel of his 'time' or his 'hour', as the climax of his ministry. See John 7.6, 8, 30; 8.20; 12.23, 27; 13.1 and 17.1.
3 In what ways should Christian people still take the story of Judas's betrayal of Jesus as a warning!
4 How do the different parts of the Passion narrative show both

the loving purpose of God being carried out by Jesus, and also
the responsibility of people for their actions against him? What
do Acts 2.23; 3.13–19 and 13.27–29 have to say about this?

5 Compare the records of the institution of the Lord's Supper in
the three Gospels (in Matthew, in Mark 14.22–26 and Luke
22.18–20) and see what details each one adds that are not in the
others.

6 What teaching about the meaning and importance of the Lord's
Supper do we find in 1 Corinthians 10.14–22 and 11.17–34?

7 In what ways is it possible for Christians today, like Peter, to
make public promises of loyalty, but to fail to keep them?

8 In this Gospel the word English versions translate as 'deny' in
verses 34 and 35 also means denying self (in 16.24). Are there
situations in which Christian people have to choose between
denying self and denying their Master?

# 26.36–46 Jesus' Prayer in Gethsemane

## See also Mark 14.32–42; Luke 22.40–46

In this passage, more than any other in this Gospel, Matthew presents us with Jesus' feelings as he approached what he knew would be
the culmination of his ministry. In one way that culmination meant
the handing over of Jesus, 'betrayed into the hands of sinners' (verse
45). At a deeper level it was accepting a 'cup' that he had to drink,
accepting the Father's will. We need to have both in mind as we try
to understand what this involved for him.

The place was Gethsemane, according to Matthew and Mark
(14.32–42). Luke (22.39–46) speaks of Jesus going, as his custom was
in those last days in Jerusalem, to the Mount of Olives. John (18.1)
speaks of a garden across the Kidron Valley from Jerusalem. The
name 'Gethsemane' means 'olive press', and the traditional place of
Gethsemane is on the slopes of the Mount of Olives where today
there are very ancient olive trees.

Jesus went there at this time, above all, to pray (verse 36). He had to be alone in his communion with the Father in prayer, but he wanted his disciples near. He took three of them nearer than the others, Peter and the sons of Zebedee, James and John. They had been close to him at the time of the transfiguration (17.1) and when he raised to life the daughter of Jairus (Mark 5.37). James and John had said (20.22) that they were 'able to drink the cup' that Jesus drank, and Peter had just said (26.35) that he would die with Jesus rather than deny him. Jesus asked them now to 'watch' (perhaps we should translate this as 'stay awake') with him.

Verse 38 describes his own feelings, as he says to them that his 'soul is very sorrowful, even to death', in 'deep distress' or 'greatly troubled' (in other translations). The distress, as his prayer shows, was because of the 'cup' that he felt that he must drink. In his humanity he shrank from what that 'cup' meant, but he was determined above all, as each repeated prayer expressed it, to do his Father's will.

Each time after Jesus had agonized in prayer, he came back to find the disciples asleep. He had spoken first about their watching with him. He then urged them to 'watch' ('stay awake') and 'pray' for their own sakes, that they might not 'enter into temptation'. They would soon face a great trial, testing their promise never to deny or forsake their Master. They needed to realize that though they had a willing spirit, their human strength ('the flesh') was small. Their only hope of standing was in prayer. Still they found themselves unable to stay awake. The past days had been days of strain and fear for them, and Luke (22.45) says that they were sleeping for sorrow. Finally Jesus said to them, 'Are you still sleeping and taking your rest?' (as the RSV puts it), or perhaps we should translate his words, 'you can sleep on now and take your rest' (Jerusalem Bible). It was now too late to pray. The time of the final crisis had come.

We should set Jesus' words 'the hour is at hand' alongside the words of verse 18, 'My time is at hand', that time when he would be 'betrayed into the hands of sinners', but also the time when he would accept the 'cup' and do the Father's will. But the time for prayer alone, and the disciples' opportunity for prayer, was over. The time for action had come. 'My betrayer' – the one who would hand him over to his enemies – 'is at hand'.

---

## ADDITIONAL NOTE K: THE 'CUP' AND THE ANGUISH OF JESUS

People have often commented that the attitude of Jesus facing death, as the Gospels describe it is very different from that which we see in martyrs about to die in a great cause. So they ask why the record describes Jesus as shrinking from death. His fear of physical pain or the shame of rejection can hardly be the reason, nor even what it would mean to have his disciples deserting him and one of them handing him over to his enemies. If we take the following three things together they may help us at least in part to understand.

1 From the beginning, this Gospel has spoken of the role of Jesus as his coming to 'save his people from their sins' (1.21). His message was a message of forgiveness (9.2–6) and the restoration of those who realized they were sinners (9.10–13).

2 As we have seen (for example, in the study of 4.1–11), although Jesus was conscious of a Messianic calling, he knew that his role was not to be the kind of Messiah that many of the Jewish people expected. All the Gospels often stress that the hopes and promises of the prophets were fulfilled in Jesus, and that Jesus saw himself as fulfilling the Scriptures. We have seen the indications earlier in the Gospel that Jesus saw the fulfilling of Messiahship in terms of the Servant, the Suffering Servant, that Isaiah 40—55 pictures. In verses 54 and 56 Jesus sees the fulfilment of Scripture as applying specially to his giving himself to die, and we can appreciate the place that Isaiah 53 must have had in that expectation. That helps us to understand also that when Peter confessed Jesus as the Messiah, Jesus went on immediately to teach the disciples about the necessity of his suffering and death (16.16–21). If Isaiah 53 was in the mind of Jesus as he realized his own vocation, the words of that chapter about the Servant bearing the sins of others must have sunk deeply into his soul. That chapter spoke about someone wounded for the transgressions of others, the iniquity of his people laid on him, making himself an offering for sin.

3 We then need to add to the relevance of Isaiah 53 for Jesus the way that the Old Testament spoke of 'the cup'. The 'cup' might refer to an experience of joy (as in Psalm 23.5), or of sorrow or suffering. But its most frequent use was in terms of God's judgement on people's sin (Psalm 11.6, Isaiah 51.17 and 22, Jeremiah 25.15, 49.12, Lamentations 4.21, Ezekiel 23.33, Habakkuk 2.16 and Zechariah 12.2).

The basic proclamation of the gospel from the early days of the Church was that 'Christ died for our sins in accordance with the scriptures' (1 Corinthians 15.3), and the fact that his was a death which bore the sins of others helps our understanding of what the Gospels record, and not least his anguish as he approached his arrest and handing over to die.

# 26.47–56 Jesus' Arrest

## See also Mark 14.43–50; Luke 22.47–53; John 18.2–11

We have the record of the arrest of Jesus in all four Gospels. Matthew's account is closest to that of Mark, but what is most distinctive in Matthew is the place it gives to the words of Jesus, which in fact show him in control of the situation, rather than those who came to arrest him.

1 Acts 1.16 speaks of Judas as 'guide to those who arrested Jesus'. His part was to show the band 'from the chief priests and the elders of the people' where they might find Jesus in the hours of darkness and to identify him with the sign of the kiss. Judas made that mark of respect and affection the sign of betrayal. Jesus still responded to him with the word 'Friend'. He was no longer a disciple, but he did not cease to be a friend. The other words of Jesus to Judas are hard to translate from the Greek. RSV, 'why are you here?' may be right, or the NRSV and New English Bible, 'do what you are here to do'. At least Jesus without protest allowed Judas to do what he had planned and promised to do.

2 The 'crowd' that Judas brought came 'with swords and clubs', but Jesus rightly challenged them about why they came with such weapons to arrest him as if he were a robber, when in fact 'day after day' he had 'sat in the temple teaching' (compare John 18.20). He exposed them, or those who had sent them, for their unwillingness to act openly but only under the cover of darkness.

3 'One of those who were with Jesus' – John (18.10) says it was Peter – took out his sword and used it to try to prevent Jesus' arrest, and merely sliced the ear of the high priest's slave. Jesus would have no violent action in his defence, for two reasons.
   – Violence was not his way. The saying 'All who take the sword will perish by the sword' may not be meant for us to take absolutely literally, nor yet be the answer to all questions of war and peace. What it means is that violence leads to more violence, and violence is not the way for disciples of Jesus to act in his support.
   – A deeper reason was that, as he had finally resolved in Gethsemane, it was the Father's will that he should give himself. Only in this way could the purpose of God expressed in the

Scriptures be fulfilled (as verses 54 and 56 state twice). He, whose kingdom is not of this world (compare John 18.36), could have called for thousands of the hosts of heaven to come to help him and prevent his arrest – if that were the Father's will.

So Judas's work was done, the 'crowd with swords and clubs' did their work, but the deepest reality was that Jesus gave himself over to them.

---

📖 **Study Suggestions**

1 In what ways do you think that verses 36–46 help us to understand how Jesus faced the death that lay before him?
2 What lessons for prayer can Christians find in the way that Jesus prayed in Gethsemane? In particular how should we see the desire for the will of God as basic to the meaning of all prayer and in fact all Christian living? See 6.10; Acts 21.13–14; Romans 1.10; 12.1–2; Ephesians 5.17 and Hebrews 13.20–21.
3 In what ways do the words, 'the spirit indeed is willing, but the flesh is weak', describe what is often the experience of Christians?
4 In the light of verse 52 can we say that the use of violence is never right for those who follow Christ?
5 What is the connection between the emphasis on the fulfilment of Scripture and Jesus' acceptance of the Father's will in Gethsemane?

---

## ADDITIONAL NOTE L: THE TRIALS OF JESUS

The accounts of the trials of Jesus in the four Gospels are mostly independent of one another, but largely complementary. Matthew is in part dependent on Mark, but there are details in Mark that are not in Matthew, and Matthew has some details that are not in Mark. In all the Gospels there were both Jewish and Roman trials, though there is some doubt whether we should see what was done before Caiaphas as an official Jewish trial.

As we have seen, all the Gospels speak of the role of Judas in handing Jesus over to the Jewish authorities. There is a view that what Judas betrayed was the claim of Jesus to be Messiah ('the Messianic secret'). It is much more likely that Judas simply told the Jewish authorities where they might find Jesus in the hours of darkness, so that they could do what they were determined to do: arrest Jesus without the knowledge of the crowds who might have come to his support (verses 3–5).

So Judas led the 'crowd with swords and clubs' to arrest Jesus, and they took him to appear before the high priest. What John (18.13) says about a trial before Annas is understandable, since in the eyes of devout Jews Annas was still high priest. What was politically important, however, was the trial before Caiaphas because he alone was the high priest that the Romans recognized.

We may be right in imagining that after having made their bargain with Judas the Jewish authorities would have waited for him to bring Jesus to them, and then tried to gather together as many of the 'scribes and elders' (members of the Jewish Sanhedrin) as they could during the night. Then there seems to have been a more official meeting of the Council at daybreak. They certainly did not follow the rules for Jewish trials that we know from a slightly later date, but the Jewish leaders were so determined to dispose of Jesus that all they needed was the kind of meeting and inquiry from which they could send Jesus to the Roman governor for trial.

There has been considerable debate about whether the Jews could have condemned Jesus to death without involving the Romans. The Romans had ultimate authority in Palestine. They delegated certain powers to the local Jewish leaders, especially in religious matters and matters relating to the temple. It seems that in the early days of the Church the Jewish Sanhedrin condemned Stephen and had him stoned (Acts 7). They may have taken the law into their own hands in that case, while actually they had no power to do so (see John 18.31). The fact of the matter in any case was that Jesus was such a public figure with a strong following among the people that any attempt to put him to death might have caused an uproar for which the Jewish leaders would have to give account. It would thus have been highly desirable, even if not actually necessary, to involve the Romans. It may well be that in the hours of darkness the Jewish leaders made an arrangement with Pilate to have Jesus put on trial in the early hours of the morning (this would also give a good explanation of the dream of Pilate's wife that 27.19 reports).

The inquiry before Caiaphas may have taken many different directions as the authorities sought sufficient evidence to condemn Jesus to death. At the heart of the trial, as Matthew, Mark and Luke all record it, is the claim of Jesus to be the Messiah. Rejecting this claim without further thought, this was enough for Caiaphas to propose that they condemn Jesus as deserving to die for blasphemy. Such religious grounds for condemnation would have no weight with Pilate, and so we can understand the political twist the Jewish authorities gave to it when they took their accusation against Jesus to the Roman court. It was possible to say that he claimed to be 'king' (see 27.11). In Luke (23.2) the accusation is put with more details, 'We found this man perverting our nation, and forbidding us to give tribute to Caesar, and saying that he himself is Christ a king.'

Pilate sees no adequate reason to condemn Jesus to die. Luke (23.6–12) tells of his sending Jesus to Herod because it was possible to say that he was under 'Herod's jurisdiction' in Galilee, but Herod only sends him back to Pilate. Matthew and Mark tell of the custom of releasing a prisoner to the people at the time of the festival. So Pilate thinks that it will satisfy the Jewish leaders' action on the basis of their jealousy of Jesus (27.18) to condemn Jesus and then release him. They remain unsatisfied and, according to John (19.12), they force Pilate's hand by political blackmail: 'If you release this man, you are not Caesar's friend; every one who makes himself a king sets himself against Caesar.'

# 26.57–68 Jesus before Caiaphas

## See also Mark 14.53–65; Luke 22.54–55, 63–65, 67–69; John 18.19–24

Behind the beginning of this section we can understand the preparations that the Jewish authorities made. Caiaphas must take the lead because only he could hand Jesus over to the Roman authorities. As many as possible of the Sanhedrin ('scribes and elders') gathered in the high priest's house.

The scene is set for the 'trial' of Jesus, but also (verse 58) for the 'trial' of Peter that would follow. It was courageous of him to follow as far as he did 'to see the end', but he was in a place where it would be hard to confess himself as a disciple of Jesus who was facing condemnation.

There was no question of the authorities giving Jesus a fair trial. If this was an official trial they should have held it in the daytime, and if there was to be a guilty verdict, it had to be on a second day. All that 'the chief priests and the whole council' wanted was to have the agreement of at least two witnesses, as the law required (see Deuteronomy 17.6 and 19.15), to condemn Jesus – no matter whether the evidence was true or false. It is significant that the evidence that becomes most important is that Jesus had spoken of destroying the temple and rebuilding it in three days. We may see three things lying behind this:

1 Jesus had predicted the destruction of the temple (24.2 and perhaps 23.38).
2 He may have spoken about the role of the temple being superseded as Stephen later taught (Acts 6 and 7), and as people might have taken from the words of 12.6, 'something greater than the temple is here'.
3 John 2.19 gives the words of Jesus at the cleansing of the temple, 'Destroy this temple, and in three days I will raise it up', which that Gospel says the Jews misunderstood when Jesus really 'spoke of the temple of his body'.

Jesus was silent in the face of the accusations, and his followers would come to see his silence as fulfilment of the words of Isaiah 53.7 (see Acts 8.32–33), but he would not oppose the human proceedings, unjust as they were, that would lead to his death. There was no point in stating the truth to those who had already determined not to listen to or follow it.

The high priest was then determined to get Jesus to speak so that he might condemn himself by his own words. 'I adjure you by the living God' involved the greatest pressure that he could bring on a person to make him speak (see Leviticus 5.1). Jesus could still have chosen to be silent, but he chose to give his response to that demand, 'tell us if you are the Christ, the Son of God'. The difference between his and Caiaphas's understanding of the terms made his answer, 'You have said so' a little less direct than a straight 'I am'. We need to recognize four points in order to understand both Caiaphas's question and Jesus' answer:

1 In 16.20 we have read about Jesus telling the disciples 'to tell no one that he was the Christ'. Some believed that Jesus was the Messiah. Others rejected the idea. The authorities wanted to know what Jesus himself was really saying (see John 10.24). The triumphal entry had made a much more public statement, but now Caiaphas wanted to hear the claim from Jesus' own lips.
2 People have sometimes thought that 'the Son of God' may have been a later Christian addition to 'the Christ'. Christians came to reckon Jesus as 'Son of God' with a depth of meaning that could not exist at this time. Nevertheless, 2 Samuel 7.14 and Psalm 2.7 made possible the linking of the two titles 'Christ' and 'Son of

God'. There was certainly a link between the two in the hopes of the Qumran community at this time. From the parable in 21.37–38 Jesus' hearers could have understood that he indeed claimed to be 'Son of God' as well as 'Christ'.

3  In the minds of many Jewish people, the high priest included, the understanding of Messiahship was very different from that which Jesus saw himself as fulfilling. Jesus would accept the title, but not other people's understanding of it. As his response to the question of Caiaphas continued, Jesus used the term he preferred, 'the Son of man', but he spoke clearly of the coming exaltation to the right hand of God (compare Psalm 110.1), and he used the words of Daniel 7.13–14 that he has already referred to in 24.30.

4  Caiaphas took the words of Jesus as 'blasphemy', which merited the death penalty (Leviticus 24.16). Strictly speaking, blasphemy involved the use of the name of God, and the claim to be Messiah was not itself blasphemy, though to state that one would be exalted to the right hand of God might be taken in that way.

The section closes with the mockery of Jesus, their spitting in his face and striking him (compare Isaiah 50.6). He claimed to be a prophet, so they blindfolded him (Mark 14.65 adds this detail) and asked him to tell who had struck him.

# 26.69–75  Peter's Denial

## See also Mark 14.66–72; Luke 22.56–62; John 18.15–18, 25–27

All four Gospels tell of Peter's denial. The records agree about the situation, the fact that there were three denials and the cock-crow at the end. They differ in the details of the people involved, the words they spoke to Peter and the words he said in reply. We can understand that Peter told and retold the story, perhaps with slightly different details, and that Christians would have told and retold it in the life of the early Church. People would have told it to show that even a close disciple could fail, but there was a way of repentance, and there was the forgiving grace of the Lord.

The failure of Peter is more shameful because it was not the result of fear of people who might have had power to arrest him but of the taunts of servant girls. They probably knew little about Jesus, but as people of Jerusalem they despised him as a Galilean, coming from Nazareth. Then Peter failed to take warning from the first failure. He moved 'out to the porch', no doubt wanting to get into a safer place, but then he denied more emphatically, first 'with an oath' (like those 5.33–34 and 23.16–22 refer to), and then 'cursing' also, perhaps with some words like, 'May God strike me down, if I know him at all.'

The crowing of the cock, however, reminded Peter of Jesus' warning (verse 34). He had failed in the way that he had promised he never would fail his Master. But 'he went out and wept bitterly'.

---

### 📖 Study Suggestions

1 In verses 59–66 what are the things that indicate that 'the chief priests and the whole council' had no desire to give Jesus a fair trial?
2 From the study of the whole of Daniel 7.9–27, how can we understand more fully what it meant to refer to 'the Son of man . . . coming on the clouds of heaven' as it is put in Daniel 7.13?
3 How does the record of the trial of Jesus and his sufferings illustrate the words of 1 Peter 2.22–23?
4 What does it indicate to us when we compare the words 'before all of them' in verse 70 with the words of 5.16 and 10.32–33?
5 What does it say about the character of Peter who, as a great leader in the early Church, would still tell against himself the story of his denial of Jesus?

# 27.1–2 Jesus goes to Pilate

*See also Mark 15.1; Luke 22.66—23.1;*
*John 18.28–32*

This reads more like an official meeting of the Jewish Sanhedrin than
does the description of the trial in 26.57–68, but there is no more
thought here of a fair trial than there was there. They simply 'took
counsel against Jesus to put him to death'. Putting him to death, as
we have seen, required their handing him over to the Roman authorities. This leads to the first mention of Pilate, who was 'the governor',
the procurator in charge of the Roman province from AD 26 to 36.
His headquarters were at Caesarea, but he would come to Jerusalem
at times when there was any threat of trouble there, as at this Passover time. From what historians know of Pilate he ruled harshly and
had little sympathy with the Jews.

What this Gospel says here is closely similar to Mark 15.1. Luke
22.66 says that 'When day came, the assembly of the elders of the
people gathered together, both chief priests and scribes; and they led
him away to their council'; then Luke 23.1 tells of their bringing
Jesus to Pilate. John 18.28–32 enlarges on the way that 'they led Jesus
from the house of Caiaphas to the praetorium' (the residence of the
Roman governor), where they handed him over to Pilate.

# 27.3–10 The Suicide of Judas

This Gospel records the death of Judas at this point, not necessarily
because it belongs here in order of time, but Matthew saw the handing over of Jesus to the Romans as the decision that he should die,
and so that decision made Judas realize the seriousness of what he
had done. When verse 3 says 'he repented', it does not use the normal New Testament word for 'repent', but one that expresses a
change in his feelings. Peter's attitude when he realized his failure in

denying Jesus was one of repentance, a sorrow for the wrong he had done and a turning back to ask forgiveness. Judas realized that he could not undo what he had done, but he did not turn back to ask forgiveness.

The action he took was to go to the chief priests and the elders and throw back at them the money they had paid him. He knew he had done what was terribly wrong 'in betraying innocent blood'. Though they were religious leaders, the chief priests showed no responsibility, no spiritual concern for Judas in his despair, but they only responded, 'What is that to us? See to it yourself.' So he went out and took his own life.

Mark and John tell us nothing about Judas after his action of betraying Jesus. Luke tells us nothing in his Gospel, but in Acts 1.15–20, at the point where the apostles are choosing a twelfth member in the place of Judas, we have the record of his suicide. The records here in Matthew and in Acts 1 are quite different in detail. They both make three main points, but differ in the ways they describe them:

1 They both say that Judas took his own life. Matthew says he 'hanged himself'. Acts 1 speaks of his 'falling headlong' to his death.
2 Both associate a field called 'the Field of Blood' with his death. Matthew speaks of the field as bought by the Jewish leaders with the thirty pieces of silver and used to bury strangers. Acts speaks of Judas buying the field and meeting his death there. Some commentators on the New Testament have tried to bring the two records together, but perhaps we should be content to take the main point of both records to be the tragic end of one who had been among 'the twelve'.
3 Both records see the death of Judas as the fulfilment of Scripture. Acts 1 quotes Psalm 69.25 about the desolation of the house of the wicked man and Psalm 109.8 about another taking over his office. Here in Matthew we have a reference to the fulfilment of 'Jeremiah', but the reference is mostly to Zechariah 11.13. This Gospel has quoted Zechariah 9.9 about the king coming to Zion in 21.5, and Zechariah 13.7 about the striking of the shepherd and the scattering of the flock in 26.31. Here the main point is the payment of thirty pieces of silver as the price of the shepherd. The Hebrew of Zechariah 11.13 speaks of the money being 'thrown to the potter' (though another early rendering has 'Cast it into the treasury'). The reference to the potter seems to have called to mind what Jeremiah says, and we need to realize that when people did not have written scriptures in front of them, they depended on memory and associations in the mind. Jeremiah learned lessons in a potter's house (Jeremiah 18.1–11) and about a potter's earthen flask (Jeremiah 19.1–13) and he had to buy a field and put the

sealed deed of purchase in an earthenware vessel made by a potter (Jeremiah 32.9–15). This is the kind of way people might link Zechariah 11.13 and Jeremiah and understand the fulfilment of Jeremiah. Once again the details may not be clear, but what Matthew so often stresses is that God realized his purpose and fulfilled the Scriptures in all that relates to the life and the death of Jesus.

# 27.11–14  Pilate's Questioning of Jesus

## See also Mark 15.2–5; Luke 23.2–5; John 18.33–37, 19.9–10

Verse 11 takes up where verse 2 left off. Jesus now stands before Pilate, and, as in all the other Gospels, his question is, 'Are you the King of the Jews?' (see Mark 15.2, Luke 23.3 and John 18.33). The reason for the question must have been that the Jewish leaders gave Jesus' claim to be Messiah the kind of political twist that would lead Pilate to condemn him. In the Greek the 'you' of Pilate's question is emphatic, 'Are *you* the King of the Jews?' It was as if he said, 'You don't look much like a king, or a person trying to get political leadership.' The answer Jesus gave was not a direct 'No', nor was it a direct 'Yes', because being a 'king' meant quite different things to Jesus and to Pilate. The word was right, but not with Pilate's meaning. Kingship belonged to him, and this Gospel has called Jesus Messiah from its very first verse.

The Jewish leaders made many accusations against Jesus, but Pilate was amazed now not just that such a person should be claiming to be king, but that he made no answer to all that they said against him. Most people would defend themselves with loud claims of innocence. Jesus knew that there was no real case to answer, and his silence also bore witness to the fact that he was giving himself to die. He would say nothing to prevent either Jews or Romans from doing what they wished. By their actions Jesus was fulfilling what he knew to be the Father's purpose.

# 27.15–26 Jesus or Barabbas for Crucifixion?

## See also Mark 15.6–15; Luke 23.17–25; John 18.38–40; 19.4–6

All four Gospels tell of Barabbas and of the choice that lay between him and Jesus: free one, crucify the other. Matthew largely follows Mark (15.6–15), but what he records in verses 19 and 24–25 is not found in any other Gospel. Luke (23.6–25) tells more briefly of Barabbas (verses 17–25), but no Gospel other than Luke tells of Pilate sending Jesus to Herod (verses 6–16). John (18.29—19.16) gives more of the dialogue between Pilate and the Jewish leaders, tells of the custom of releasing a prisoner at the Passover, the clamour for the release of Barabbas instead of Jesus, and simply says, 'Now Barabbas was a bandit.'

Apart from a possible reference in a Jewish rabbinic writing, we have no knowledge from outside the Gospels of this custom of the release of a prisoner, but prisoners were released for various reasons, and it would be an understandable way of helping people to look with greater favour on an unpopular government.

It was a strange choice to have to make. There were two men of similar names, but utterly different characters. We do not have an explanation of the meaning of the name 'Barabbas' here, but anyone who knew even a little Aramaic would know it to mean 'son of a father', perhaps meaning that he was the son of one who in a good sense was a noted father, though the son had become a 'notorious prisoner'. Jesus, the Gospel tells us (as in 11.27) was the Son of the Father. The New Revised Standard Version, like some other modern translations, gives the other name of Barabbas as 'Jesus'. Many ancient manuscripts do not have 'Jesus', but some do, and the Christian writer Origen (about AD 200) indicates that most manuscripts he knew read 'Jesus'. It is more likely that copyists would have dropped the word from manuscripts because Christians would not like to have thought of anyone other than their Lord bearing the name of Jesus, than that they would have added it if it was not there originally. The choice, as verse 17 puts it, was between Jesus Barabbas and 'Jesus who is called Christ' or the Messiah.

This section shows how and why each made their choice: the chief priests and elders, the crowds, Pilate.

The chief priests and elders knew who they wanted Pilate to crucify and who they wanted him to release, and verse 20 tells how they stirred up the crowds to ask for Barabbas and to have Jesus put to death. Pilate, who was sure to have his informants to tell him what was going on throughout the land, knew that 'it was out of envy that they had delivered him up' (verse 18). They were jealous of the following that Jesus had (compare John 12.19) and his spiritual authority with the people.

The crowds probably clamoured for Barabbas both because the chief priests and elders persuaded them, and because there would have been those who were friends of Barabbas and those who would back anyone who rebelled against the power of Rome (Luke 23.19 says he 'had been thrown into prison for an insurrection'). There is often an unthinking, blind excitement that moves through a crowd. They probably thought very little when, in response to Pilate's desire to accept no responsibility for the death of Jesus, they shouted, 'His blood be on us and on our children.'

Pilate's choice was certainly against his better judgement. He saw the motives of the Jewish leaders. He found no crime in Jesus. He had the warning of his wife's dream. (She may have known of the work and character of Jesus, and it may be that the Jewish leaders had come to her husband the night before and asked him to try Jesus in the morning, and so she would have gone to sleep thinking of that 'righteous man'.) In the end (as Luke 23.23 puts it), the voices of the crowd prevailed. Pilate was more afraid of a riot beginning (verse 24) than of going against his conscience and condemning an innocent person. (Compare how John 19.12 and 15 speak of the argument that Pilate could not be a friend of the emperor if he released one who claimed to be king.) So Pilate handed Jesus over to the cruel flogging that was the custom before crucifixion, then to go to the cross.

As we read the narrative our attention focuses now on Pilate, now on the Jewish leaders, now on the crowd, but we need to stay aware of the central figure in the drama, the silent Sufferer. The Gospel intends us to appreciate the meaning of his going to the cross that the Romans had prepared for Barabbas. They released Barabbas the criminal, and handed over Jesus the bearer of the sins of others for crucifixion.

We should note a final point on this section. People sometimes say that Matthew's Gospel emphasizes the guilt of the Jewish people. Pilate declares himself innocent, demonstrating it by following the Jewish custom of publicly washing his hands, as if he had no responsibility for the wrong done (see Deuteronomy 21.6–7 and Psalms 26.6 and 73.13). But it is obvious to any reader of the Gospel that his washing his hands did not remove his failure to stand for what he knew was right. People have also misunderstood and misapplied the words of verse 25, 'His blood be on us and on our children'. The Jewish people and especially their leaders did indeed have responsibility for the death of Jesus, and in a way they and the next generation suffered the consequences of the rejection of their Saviour, as chapter 24 has indicated. But they did what we, or any people, might have done, and it has been terribly wrong when Christians down the centuries have continued to see Jewish people as the murderers of Jesus and to rejoice in their suffering. Such an attitude is utterly contrary to the way that we learn in Jesus and the responsibility that all humanity alike shares for the sins that led to the death of Jesus.

# 27.27–31 The Soldiers Mock Jesus

## See also Mark 15.16–20; John 19.1–3

Matthew tells of the soldiers' mockery of Jesus in terms very similar to those in Mark. John tells it more briefly, and Luke (23.11) tells of Herod and his soldiers mocking Jesus instead. Compared with what the Jewish leaders and Pilate do, this is a picture of what unthinking people, used to violence, do when there is nothing to restrain them, the violence that the police and the military in too many countries can inflict on those who are weak and defenceless.

'The whole battalion', all the soldiers who would have been in the Roman governor's residence there in Jerusalem, gathered for the fun. They took what they had heard, his claim to be 'king of the Jews', and with this they mocked him, and probably also wanted to mock the Jews for having such a 'king'. The 'scarlet robe' was probably the soldier's red cloak, mockery for the purple robe of the emperor. The crown may have been intended to represent the crown that is on Roman coins, rays going out from it like rays of the sun – but the crown was of thorns. The 'reed' stood for the sceptre, the royal staff that the emperor carried as sign of his office. They pretended to kneel before Jesus, as subjects before a king, but instead of the kiss of respect and loyalty 'they spat on him'.

# 27.32–44 *The Crucifixion*

## See also Mark 15.21–32; Luke 23.26–43; John 19.17–24

Crucifixion was a way of executing criminals practised among the Carthaginians of North Africa and the Phoenicians in Syria and taken over by the Romans. The method commonly followed involved the person who was to be executed carrying the cross-bar to the place of execution. There they nailed him to it with nails through the wrists or hands, and either tied together his feet or nailed them to the upright part of the cross probably already sunk in the ground in preparation for the crucifixion. People in the ancient world regarded this form of execution with horror. The Romans only crucified the worst criminals and people of the lowest classes. The Roman writer Cicero said, 'Far be the very name of the cross, not only from the body but even from the thought, the eyes, the ears of Roman citizens.' Jewish people, as we can realize from Galatians 3.13, regarded a person who thus 'hung on a tree' as under a curse.

What is important to notice is that Matthew, like the other Gospels, places little emphasis on the physical act of the crucifixion of Jesus or on the pain and shame that it involved. This section refers to ten things that take place at the time when the soldiers led out Jesus to crucify him:

1 The soldiers 'compelled' a man named Simon to carry his cross. Mark 15.21 names his two sons, presumably as people familiar to those in the life of the church for which Mark's Gospel was first written. It may be that the naming of Simon here implies that he became a Christian, but we cannot say that with certainty.
2 The place was 'Golgotha', the word means 'place of a skull'. The place may have got its name because it was a skull-shaped hill, or it may have been a common place of execution.
3 Jesus rejected the offer of wine 'mixed with gall', probably because he was determined that his senses should not be dulled as he was giving himself to suffer that death on the cross.
4 As normally happened, the soldiers kept the few clothes that had belonged to those crucified. The casting of lots has more of an explanation in John 19.23–24.
5 The soldiers sat down and kept watch over him, a fact that was perhaps important for Matthew to record as against those who suggested that Jesus did not really die.

6 The title that was written expressed the charge, 'This is Jesus, the King of the Jews'. John 19.19–22 tells of the chief priests' objection to Pilate's putting it the way he did.

7 The Romans crucified two 'bandits' with him, one on the right and one on the left.

8 We have the derision of those who passed by, referring to his claim to destroy the temple and build it in three days, and also the claim to be 'Son of God'.

9 There is the mockery of the Jewish leaders – the passage names them all: chief priests, scribes and elders. They speak of him saving others but being unable to save himself, and reject with derision the thought of him as 'king of Israel' and 'God's Son'.

10 Finally here, there is the taunting of those who were crucified with him. It is Luke (23.39–43) that tells of the one who rejected the taunting of the other, and then asked Jesus to remember him when he came into his kingdom.

When we consider what Matthew does emphasize, having placed no emphasis on the physical suffering of crucifixion, we see two things as most significant:

1 Everyone mocked and rejected Jesus. We have seen the mockery of the soldiers in verses 27–31, and now it is the passers-by, the Jewish leaders and the two crucified with him who are involved in the mockery. Everyone opposed him, and we see the sinfulness of human nature revealed as the One who had lived in absolute integrity and loving concern for all people suffered like this with no one to support him.

But what they say mockingly tells what the Gospel expresses as most true about him:

(a) He was 'King of the Jews' (verse 37), 'King of Israel' (verse 42), and we have seen a great emphasis on his kingship in Matthew.

(b) He would truly build up the temple (of his body) in three days, and the truth of this was soon to be apparent. (See also the comments on 26.61.)

(c) He saved others and he could not save himself. His ministry had certainly been a ministry of saving others, and so that would be his work in his death, but only because he would not save himself.

(d) They said that they would believe if he came down from the cross. In the perspective of the Gospel, people will believe because he did not come down from the cross.

(e) He was truly God's Son, and his delighting in the Father's will led him not to seek the Father's deliverance from the cross.

2 There are allusions to the Old Testament in much that the record says, although there is never a description of a specific quotation:

(a) Verse 34 calls to mind Psalm 69.21, 'They gave me poison for food, and for my thirst they gave me vinegar to drink.'

(b) Verse 35 calls to mind Psalm 22.18, 'they divide my garments among them, and for my raiment they cast lots.'

(c) The crucifixion of Jesus between the two bandits recalls Isaiah 53.9 and 12, 'they made his grave with the wicked', and he 'was numbered with the transgressors'.

(d) Verses 39 and 42 call to mind Psalm 22.7–8, 'all who see me mock at me; they make mouths at me, they wag their heads: "He committed his cause to the Lord; let him deliver him, let him rescue him, for he delights in him!" ' There may also be an allusion to Lamentations 2.15.

(e) It seems probable that Wisdom 2.10–20 (in the Apocrypha, but probably based on Psalm 22 and Isaiah 53) is also in the writer's mind as he describes these events. That passage speaks of opposition to the 'honest man', and the words of those who persecute him, 'Let us tread him under foot . . . He knows God, so he says; he styles himself the servant of the Lord . . . he . . . boasts that God is his father. Let us test the truth of his words, let us see what will happen to him in the end; for if the just man is God's son, God will stretch out a hand to him and save him from the clutches of his enemies . . . Let us condemn him to a shameful death, for on his own showing he will have a protector.'

# 27.45–56  The Death of Jesus

## See also Mark 15.33–41; Luke 23.44–49; John 19.28–30

Again it is important to see the things that the Gospel regards as significant about the way that Jesus died and what happened at the time or as a result of his death. The record here continues to be close to that of Mark, but verses 52–53 in particular have no parallel in other Gospels.

1 There was darkness over the whole land for the three hours before Jesus died. The Old Testament often speaks of such 'supernatural

darkness' (see Exodus 10.22; Isaiah 13.10; 50.3; Jeremiah 13.16; 15.9; Joel 2.10, 31; 3.15 and Amos 8.9). Here it is, as it were, a sign of the rejection of the One who had come to be the 'Light of the world' (John 8.12).

2 The cry from the cross (also in Mark) is the Aramaic of the first verse of Psalm 22. Some people say that we need to think of the whole psalm (in which in the end the sufferer comes to an attitude of confidence and triumph), as being in the thoughts of Jesus as he suffered on the cross. Yet it is the first verse with its expression of being forsaken that is on his lips. He cries out as someone who has lost the sense of the Father's presence with him. We should not say that God did forsake his Son in judgement. The New Testament never states that, but rather has expressions such as that of 2 Corinthians 5.19, 'God was in Christ reconciling the world to himself'. But, as sin deprives us of the sense of God's presence, so we can understand, even if dimly, that Jesus' sin-bearing work led to the cry of forsakenness. People misunderstood the cry and linked it with the belief that the prophet Elijah came to the help of those in deep distress. But someone, in compassion, brought Jesus a sponge full of sour wine, perhaps seen by the Gospel writer as a fulfilment of Psalm 69.21, 'for my thirst they gave me vinegar to drink' (see John 19.28–29). At least the cry of Jesus was still 'My God, my God', and Luke (23.46) speaks of his dying prayer as, 'Father, into thy hands I commend my spirit'.

3 This Gospel, like all the others, speaks of a 'loud cry' coming in the end from the lips of Jesus. John (19.30) records it as a cry of triumph, 'It is finished'. The description of his actual death is in words that we could more literally translate, 'He let go' or 'sent away his spirit' (in John 19.30 'He handed over his spirit'), as if to say that though crucifixion was the physical cause of his death, he in fact gave up his life (as the Gospel has many times indicated).

4 Then Matthew (like Mark) records the tearing of 'the curtain of the temple — from top to bottom'. There were two curtains in the temple. One was between the outer Court and the Holy Place. The other was between the Holy Place and the Holy of Holies, the inner sanctuary into which only the high priest could go and only once in the year (Leviticus 16.11–19). At least in the understanding of the Epistle to the Hebrews (6.19–20; 9.7–8, 11–12 and 24–26), the sacrificial offering of Jesus in his death meant that there is now free access to God (compare Ephesians 2.17–18) that there was not before. It also means that the temple and its sacrificial system no longer had the place that they had had previously in the life of the Hebrew people.

5 Verse 32–33 speaks of an earthquake breaking open the graves of the 'saints' who had died in the past; then after the resurrection they appeared to many people. However we take these verses,

clearly their purpose is to say that the death of Jesus destroyed the power of death and made resurrection possible.

6 The Gentile centurion and those with him supervising the crucifixion of Jesus were amazed, and indeed 'terrified' by what they saw taking place, and they were led to the confession, 'Truly this was the Son of God.' That confession could not have had the full meaning that it was to have later for Christian people (and it is given a reduced form in Luke 23.47), but it is a foreshadowing of what would happen when the message of Christ crucified went out to the Gentile world and unnumbered people would come to confess him as 'Son of God' (see 28.18–20).

7 There were the women who had been and remained devoted disciples to the end. They had been 'ministering to him' from the times back in Galilee, and now they were still there at the cross. There was Mary Magdalene (see Luke 8.2), Mary the mother of James (James the younger in Mark 15.40) and Joseph, and the mother of the sons of Zebedee (Salome in Mark). If we are right in linking the names here with those in John 19.25, the mother of the sons of Zebedee was the sister of Jesus' mother, Mary, and the other Mary was the wife of Cleopas (who, according to Luke 24.18, was with Jesus on the road to Emmaus on the day of Jesus' resurrection) whom the second-century writer Hegesippus spoke of as the brother of Joseph. If these family linkings are true, it is perhaps important to realize that for those who were disciples the spiritual relationship with their Lord meant more than the physical relationship.

---

## 📖 Study Suggestions

1 What do you think were the motives of (a) the Jewish leaders, (b) Pilate, and (c) the soldiers, for what they did to Jesus? What are the parallels to these motives today?

2 In our consideration of verses 32–44 we mentioned that while Matthew does not often quote the Old Testament in the record of the trials and crucifixion of Jesus, he often seems to reflect or echo the language of the Old Testament. Look up the Old Testament passages that the comments refer to (especially in the case of Psalms 22 and 69 and Isaiah 53) and consider the contexts of the passages and how they might relate to our understanding of the crucifixion of Jesus.

# 27.57–61 *The Burial of Jesus*

## See also Mark 14.42–47; Luke 23.50–56; John 19.38–42

All of the Gospels speak of Joseph of Arimathea being responsible for the burial of Jesus. Mark (15.43) and Luke (23.50–51) add that he was a member of the Jewish council, and one who was 'looking for the kingdom of God'. Luke adds that he, 'though a member of the council . . . had not consented to their purpose and deed'. John (19.38–39) says that he was a secret disciple, and adds that Nicodemus was involved with him in the burial. Matthew only adds to the description of him as a disciple that he was 'a rich man', perhaps intending to recall the Old Testament, that Isaiah 53.9 said of the Suffering Servant that 'they made . . . his tomb with the rich'. The Romans often left the bodies of criminals to rot on the cross, though they might be given to relatives or friends. The Jews had a law (Deuteronomy 21.22–23) that the body of a person hanged as a criminal should remain unburied all night. According to the other Gospels this was especially important because of the sabbath coming up. So Joseph asked Pilate for the body of Jesus, and with great respect 'wrapped it in a clean linen shroud, and laid it in his own new tomb', no doubt realizing that the rabbis forbade a tomb to be used in future if a criminal had been laid in it.

As was the way with tombs hewn in the rock (compare John 11.38–41) – and archaeologists have discovered such tombs in Palestine – people rolled a large stone along a prepared groove to shut off the entrance to the tomb. As well as Joseph, the two Marys (that verse 56 mentions) were witnesses of the burial and thus knew the place.

# 27.62–66 *The Guard at the Tomb*

What Matthew records here is not in any other of the Gospels, but, according to 28.11–15, is linked with the realization in Jerusalem that the tomb of Jesus was empty, and the favoured story among the Jews was that the disciples had stolen the body. The statements of this Gospel rule that out as impossible in the light of the precautions that the Jewish leaders had taken.

There are two things that are a little perplexing here:

1 The record describes the action as taking place 'the next day', 'after the day of Preparation' (compare Mark 15.42 and John 19.31 and 42), which would most naturally mean on the sabbath itself. Would the chief priests and Pharisees who had condemned Jesus so strongly for healing on the sabbath (12.9–14) have conferred with Pilate like this on the sabbath? It may be an indication of their determination to have the tomb guarded, though it is possible that they went to Pilate on the Saturday evening when the sabbath was over.

2 Would they have quoted the prediction of Jesus, 'After three days I will rise again' which was in the main given to the disciples (16.21, 17.23 and 20.19), and even they found it difficult to grasp or hope for? In 12.40 the prediction seems to have been made more publicly, and we can understand the difference in this situation between disappointed disciples and the Jewish leaders who had apprehensions about Jesus because of what he had done in his life (compare John 18.1–7).

It is understandable that the Jewish leaders were anxious, and though they may have misjudged Jesus' disciples, they were afraid that they would try to take the body of their Master from the tomb. We could translate Pilate's words to them in verse 65 as 'You have a guard', that is, the temple police, or 'Take a guard', implying that Pilate would provide Roman soldiers. In either case they felt that with the help of men to guard and with the sealing of the stone (compare Daniel 6.17), they had done all they could.

## ADDITIONAL NOTE M: THE RECORDS OF THE RESURRECTION IN THE GOSPELS

Matthew records four incidents relating to the resurrection of Jesus: the earthquake and the angel's announcement of the fact of the resurrection to the women at the tomb, Jesus' appearance to the women and his giving them a message for the disciples, the report of the guard, and the meeting with the disciples in Galilee and their commissioning to teach all nations.

There are differences between the records of the four Gospels of the appearances of Jesus, in Jerusalem and in Galilee, but all four Gospels agree in speaking of the empty tomb, telling of Jesus' appearances to his disciples, and the importance of telling out the good news. Although the differences between the records may make them hard to reconcile in every particular, by the same token the witness to the central facts is strengthened by the evidence of four independent witnesses over and above what would be the case if they were completely dependent on one another.

Some argue that the Gospels were written at a later date than, for example, the Epistles of Paul, and that Paul says nothing in his writings about the empty tomb. However, we need to examine closely what the apostle Paul says in 1 Corinthians 15. He speaks of the third day as the time of the resurrection, and the way he speaks of Jesus having 'died', been 'buried', and 'raised on the third day' would be hard to understand other than as meaning that the body of Jesus that was buried was raised from the tomb. 1 Corinthians 15 goes on to speak of resurrection as a triumph over physical death, and we may add that the analogy of Christian baptism as death, burial and being raised to new life certainly suggests the actual raising of the body of Jesus from the grave (Romans 6.3–11).

Many Christians, especially in Western countries, have felt that a spiritual resurrection of Jesus and the believer's spiritual experience of the risen Christ is what matters rather than a bodily resurrection. We need to say three things about this.

1 In 1 Corinthians 15 the apostle Paul seems to indicate clearly a difference between the experience of those first witnesses to the risen Christ and other Christians who subsequently have a spiritual experience of the living Christ with them. Acts 1 similarly indicates an end to the specific witness to the resurrection that was uniquely the experience of the first disciples.

2 Unlike Greek-thinking people of New Testament times, Jewish people could only think of resurrection in physical terms. To a Jew if there were not a bodily resurrection there could be no resurrection at all. This is significant because the first preaching of

the risen Christ was in the heart of Judaism in Jerusalem and only later did it come to the Greek-thinking world.

3 Not only does the New Testament present the resurrection of Jesus in terms of spiritual victory over the powers of evil and the Lord's spiritual presence with his disciples, but as victory over physical death, so that those who believe in him are not to fear death.

There are many things, such as the nature of the resurrection body of Jesus, that we may not fully comprehend. Christians may differ in some respects in the way that they understand the resurrection. What we can say with great assurance is that without the resurrection of Jesus there would have been no Christian gospel and no Christian Church. The followers of a crucified Jew, who at his death were broken and downcast men and women, went out with their brokenness transformed into great joy and confidence. They were prepared to spend their lives, and some of them literally to give their lives, in the cause of the truth of which they were convinced: Jesus had died for them and for all the world, and Jesus had been raised from the dead.

# *28.1–10  The Resurrection*

## *See also Mark 16.1–8; Luke 24.1–12; John 20.1–10*

It is now after the sabbath, which would have ended on the Saturday evening, but the dawn of the first day of the week must mean the Sunday morning. We have read about the guards (in 27.65–66), and about Mary Magdalene and the other Mary at the tomb when Jesus was buried (27.61). Now they are the characters at the tomb when there is, or has been, an earthquake. The tomb was empty; an angel, brilliant in appearance, rolled back the stone showing that the body of Jesus was no longer there. The guards, whom the authorities had sent to guard the dead, in their fear 'became like dead men'.

The women also were afraid, but the message of the angel to them was that they need not fear. They were looking for the crucified Jesus, but they can know that he is not in the tomb, as they can come and see. He had 'been raised', as verse 6 is most correctly translated, and it is important to notice that this is the most frequent way in which the New Testament speaks of the resurrection. It is not usually 'He rose from the dead', but 'He is raised', or specifically 'God raised him from the dead' (see, for example, Acts 2.24, 32; 3.15, and 1 Corinthians 15.4).

'Go quickly and tell his disciples' is the angel's message to them. Then Jesus himself met them, and they 'took hold of his feet, and worshipped him'. As the angel had said, so the Lord tells them not to be afraid, but 'go and tell my brothers . . .' The message in both instances indicates that the meeting place is to be Galilee. We need not understand this as a contradiction of what the Gospels tell about meetings of the risen Jesus with disciples in Jerusalem. Rather it indicates (like the words of Jesus in 26.32) that as Galilee had been the place of the original call and training of the disciples, so it is to be the place of the renewal of that call (as verses 16–20 will show), and the place of their preparation for all that lies ahead of them in the service of their risen Lord.

# 28.11–15  The Report of the Guards

In 27.64 the chief priests and the Pharisees had expressed their fears that in time to come the disciples of Jesus might want to say of their Master, 'He has been raised from the dead'. Now as the guards report 'all that had taken place' that Sunday morning, there might have seemed no other reasonable explanation than that their fears had proved correct and the One they had crucified was risen. They therefore had to offer an alternative explanation. That explanation was that what they had tried to prevent (27.64) had taken place: the disciples had stolen the body. It was not to the credit of the guards that they had to say that they had slept, and that what they were there to prevent had actually happened. But any explanation of their powerlessness over what happened at the tomb would have been difficult.

Given 'a sum of money' and the assurance that the Jewish leaders would 'satisfy' Pilate (perhaps by a similar bribe) and 'keep (them) out of trouble' if the governor came to know of it, 'they took the money and did as they were directed'.

So that remained, and remains, as one alternative explanation of the empty tomb and the story that Jesus was alive again. The whole history of the Church, however, and, most of all, its early beginnings with the sacrificial, risk-taking witness of the first Christians, would indeed be hard to account for if the life of Jesus ended with the cross.

# 28.16–20 The Commissioning of the Disciples to Teach all Nations

This closing section of the Gospel is, in the first place, a record of the meeting in Galilee to which verses 7 and 10, as well as 26.32, have pointed. It was Galilee where Jesus had first called and trained the disciples, and it was to be the place of his final instructions for them. There has been no mention of the 'mountain' in the earlier references to the meeting in Galilee, but perhaps the 'mountain' of the great commission is intended to be linked with the mountain of the teaching about discipleship (5.1) and the mountain of the revelation of the glory of Jesus in the transfiguration (17.1).

The attitude of the disciples to the risen Jesus was one of worship, but initial hesitation on the part of some, who felt that the resurrection was too wonderful to believe, is understandable (compare Luke 24.41 and John 20.24–25).

Four things are involved in the words of Jesus that Matthew records here, each involving the word 'all' (the same word each time in the original Greek): God has given all authority to Jesus, his followers are to disciple all nations, they are to teach and obey all the commands of Jesus, and he will be with them all the days of the future.

## All authority

The Gospel has said a good deal about the authority of Jesus, in his teaching (7.29), in his power to forgive sins (9.6, 8), in the works that he did and the disciples he sends to do them in his name (10.1), and then in particular in the way that he acted in the climax of his ministry in Jerusalem (21.23–25). Now the disciples are to know that the One whom they are sent to serve has all authority in heaven and earth, the fulfilment of what Daniel 7.13–14 had said of the 'one like a son of man' coming 'with the clouds of heaven': 'to him was given dominion – that all peoples, nations, and languages should serve him . . .'

## The mission to all nations

The task was not just to spread the good news of Jesus but to 'make disciples'. This Gospel has said a great deal about discipleship and used the word 'disciple' more than 70 times. It involves commitment and learning what it means to follow Jesus.

Because of the way that the Acts of the Apostles speaks of the reluctance of the apostles to go out to the Gentile world, some have thought that such a commission to disciple people of all nations could not go back to the risen Jesus. There are factors, however, that may account for the reluctance, and we must say that there are many things in Matthew that foreshadow the mission to the Gentiles (see 2.1–12; 8.11; 12.21; 24.14 and 26.13).

The sign of discipleship is baptism and the Acts of the Apostles (2.38 and 41) indicates that Christians practised baptism from the earliest days of the Church. The Acts and the Epistles regularly speak of baptism as 'in' or 'into the name of Jesus'. Here 'baptizing . . . in the name of the Father and of the Son and of the Holy Spirit' does not necessarily mean a trinitarian formula for baptism such as the Church has come to use, but rather that the faith that is expressed in baptism sees God as Father, acknowledges Jesus as Saviour, and recognizes the presence and power of the Holy Spirit.

## Teaching

Teaching is important here as it has been in the whole Gospel. Matthew has constantly made us aware of Jesus' teaching work, and, as we have seen, the structure of the Gospel brings out what Jesus taught in the five great sections, all of which end in a similar way (see p. 3). Teaching, however, is not just informing the mind. It must lead disciples 'to observe all' that Jesus has commanded.

## Promise

The disciples' task was formidable, and in what Jesus said about their mission he made clear that they would face hatred and opposition, though they went with a message of love and peace (10.16–22). To the ends of the earth and to the end of the age were the terms, but his promise was to be with them always and thus to enable them to do what he had sent them to do.

---

### 📖 Study Suggestions

1 Compare what Matthew says about the resurrection of Jesus with the accounts in the other Gospels and in Acts 1. What do the others say that Matthew does not?

2 How does Paul in 1 Corinthians 15.1–11 agree with, and what does he add to, the things that the Gospels say about the resurrection of Jesus?

3 Follow the references in the comments on 28.16–20 and see the earlier indications in the Gospel that the mission of Jesus was to be a world-wide mission.

4 Compare the emphasis on obedience in 28.19 with what other parts of the Gospel say about the need to put the teaching into practice. For example, see 5.19; 7.24–27, 23.2–3 and 25.31–46.

5 Compare with these verses what Luke and John say about the ongoing task of the disciples of Jesus in Luke 24.43–49, Acts 1.8 and John 20.20–21. In what ways are these passages similar to, and in what ways are they different from, what we have at the end of Matthew?

# Essay 1: The Parables in Matthew's Gospel

## by David Huggett

The parables are among the best known features of the Synoptic Gospels. Although they are not always easy to interpret they deserve careful study. Matthew includes more than 20 parables, of which there are three distinct kinds.

## Extended metaphors or similes

First there are what we might describe as *extended metaphors or similes* in which one thing represents another. Some are no more than a single sentence in which Jesus uses a simple illustration to make his point. We find a good example of this kind of parable in Matthew 13.33, 'The kingdom of heaven is like leaven which a woman took and hid in three measures of meal, till it was all leavened.'

There are six similar parables in the latter part of chapter 13, five of them unique to Matthew. They all have to do with various aspects of the kingdom of heaven. Some are no more than simple comparisons. Others, though still brief, we could almost describe as mini short stories. They make no attempt to develop any plot, but are like a single scene from a longer story.

In this category we can also include extended similes like the lamp under a bowl (5.14–15), the wise and foolish builders (7.24–27), the new cloth on old (9.16), the new wine in old wineskins (9.17), and the fig tree (24.32–33). Although the Gospel writer does not describe them specifically as parables, they are clearly the same kind of extended simile as those in chapter 13.

Almost half (11) of Matthew's parables would come into this category. They are uncomplicated and relatively easy to interpret. This has led some scholars to suggest that they belong largely to the early part of Jesus' ministry when his popularity was high and his message open and straightforward. However, they suggest that, as Jesus' popularity waned and official opposition grew, he had to speak with greater care. He made his teaching more obscure. He told longer parables, and it became more difficult to interpret. This, these scholars claim, explains the difficult passage in chapter 13 when Jesus seems to imply that his parables can only be understood by those who have 'been given to know the secrets of the kingdom of heaven' (verse 11). Whether this is so or not, it is undoubtedly true that it is more difficult to interpret Jesus' longer parables.

## Longer narratives

The second category of parables in Matthew is that of these *longer narratives* – the famous stories we usually think of when we use the word 'parable'.

The Greek word for 'parable' literally means a 'placing of something alongside' and this element of comparison is an important part of understanding the meaning and purpose of the parables Jesus used in the Gospels. A popular definition of this kind of saying would be 'a short story which uses familiar events and pictures in order to illustrate some spiritual principle'.

Although Jesus lived in a land with striking scenery, bustling cities, vigorous commerce, and conflicting politics, the pictures Jesus used in his parables were ones that he clearly intended for the ordinary person. He took simple illustrations from nature – the weeds, the sower, the mustard seed, the sheep and goats. He referred to everyday customs – mixing dough, hiring labourers, patching clothes, working in a vineyard. He spoke about things familiar to most families – the wedding banquet, running out of lamp oil, building a house, dealing with servants.

Most of the narrative parables we find in Matthew are not in any of the other Gospels. One, the story of the tenants in the vineyard (21.33–44), is also in both Mark (12.1–11) and in Luke (20.9–18). Another, the lost sheep (18.12–14), is also in Luke (15.4–7). The interesting point about the latter is that Matthew and Luke use the same story but set it against a different background and draw different lessons from it. Luke says the story arose out of the complaints of the Pharisees and scribes that Jesus mixed with social outcasts. Matthew, on the other hand, gives the story as part of Jesus' warning against the dangers of despising children. This could imply that Jesus used the same story on more than one occasion to illustrate slightly different principles. Or it could be simply that each Gospel writer has used the material differently for his own teaching purposes.

## Allegories

The third kind of parable that Matthew uses, while still a narrative, we might better describe as an *allegory*. In an allegory, unlike an extended metaphor or simile, there is more than one connection between the story and the lesson it is trying to teach. There are just two allegories in Matthew – the sower and the soils (13.3–8; 18–23) which is common to all the Synoptic Gospels, and the weeds (13.24–30; 36–43) which is unique to Matthew. As with a number of the other narrative parables, these two include an interpretation. The difference, however, is that in these two each detail has a meaning of its own. For instance, in the case of the parable of the weeds Jesus does not simply suggest that the kingdom is like a field with a mixed crop. This would make it similar to the other parables of the kingdom which follow. Instead he explains the allegorical meaning of each item: the sower of the good seed is the Son of man, the field is the world, the good seed is the children of the kingdom, the weeds stand for the children of the devil who is the enemy sowing the weeds, the harvest is the end of the age, and the reapers are the angels. As well as being part of the overall picture, each item acts as a symbol of something deeper.

It is perhaps understandable that, on the basis of these allegories, early Christian interpreters assumed that they could handle many of the other parables of Jesus in the same way. In particular the parables of the good Samaritan and the prodigal son seem to have lent themselves to highly imaginative allegorical interpretations.

Although many of the more imaginative suggestions seem to us today to be no more than amusing curiosities, until the late nineteenth century allegory remained the most common way of interpreting most of the parables. On the other hand it is interesting to note that allegory has made something of a comeback among recent scholars, so that the British scholar Frances Young can say, 'Allegorical reading can set free the soul for creative engagement with transcendence.' The point is that a purely rational and logical approach to biblical interpretation – especially the parables – can impoverish our understanding and experience of the mystery and wonder of God's revelation.

Critical scholarship, in the person of the German scholar A. Jülicher, reacted in 1888 against what were often far-fetched interpretations of the parables. Instead he insisted that the purpose of each narrative was to teach or illustrate only one truth.

We can see the importance of this principle in the case of certain parables. Take, for example, the story of the hiring of labourers in the vineyard (20.1–16). Those who have tried to see here a pattern for relationships between employers and employees and issues concerning wages, or have seen it as a picture of the unfairness of life that simply has to be accepted, are reading too much into the story. Its simple lesson is to do with the grace of God who gives to each, however unworthy, in generous love.

However, Jülicher and the scholars who have followed him, valuable though their emphasis has been, cannot be entirely right. For one thing it is not always possible to decide which is supposed to be the one truth each parable is teaching, even in those cases where Jesus himself gives an interpretation. Also it is clear that on occasion Jesus himself intended his hearers to learn more than one lesson.

It seems that we need to strike some kind of balance between over-elaborate and over-simple interpretations. A modern approach must not only seek to understand what Jesus was saying to his original hearers, but also what these ancient stories, in whatever form they come, have to say to today's men and women. Many of the narrative parables come with their own interpretation, but that is not to say that we are excused from the effort to interpret them for our own age.

However we interpret the parables, we have to remember that they are stories. They may or may not have had a basis in real incidents, but the Gospel writers present them in fictional form. Recent studies in narrative criticism have alerted us to how stories work.

Stories have a power that the straightforward recording of facts, ideas, and beliefs lacks. For one thing they work at the level of our emotions as well as, or perhaps instead of, our intellect. All the elements of conflict, suspense, and surprise which are common to the story involve the listener or the reader in such a way that we absorb the 'message' almost without being aware of it, and sometimes in spite of ourselves.

The story gets under our skin and gets round our defences in ways that sheer statements of fact or belief do not. Sally McFague, a theologian from North America, makes the point like this: 'A parable is . . . an assault on the conventions, including the social, economic, and mythic structures that people build for their own comfort and security. A parable is a story meant to invert and subvert these structures and to suggest that the way of the kingdom is not the way of the world.'

The story is vivid and dramatic. It involves real people with whom we can identify. Because we see something of ourselves reflected there it is easier to apply the lesson that the story is teaching. But at the same time the story leaves us to make the application ourselves rather than rely on the sermonizing of someone else.

By no means least is the fact that the form of a story helps us to remember more easily what we have heard or read. Even when at first we do not understand its significance, or are unable to apply its lesson, we remember it. This is because the narrative stimulates our imagination and involves our emotions, so the nub of it remains with us awaiting some trigger that will bring it to life at a later date.

Albert Nolan, a theologian from South Africa, sums up how the parables work like this: 'Nothing could be more unauthoritative than the parables of Jesus. Their whole purpose is to enable the listener to discover something for himself. They are not illustrations of revealed doctrines; they are works of art which reveal or uncover the truth about life.'

## Parables in Matthew

| | Matthew | Mark | Luke |
|---|---|---|---|
| The lamp under a bowl | 5.14–15 | 4.21 | 8.16 & 11.33 |
| Wise and foolish builders | 7.24–27 | | 6.47–49 |
| New cloth on old | 9.16 | 2.21 | 5.36 |
| New wine | 9.17 | 2.22 | 5.37–38 |
| The sower | 13.3–8, 18–23 | 4.3–8, 13–20 | 8.5–8, 11–15 |
| The weeds | 13.24–30, 36–43 | | |
| The mustard seed | 13.31–32 | 4.30–32 | 13.18–19 |
| Yeast | 13.33 | | 13.20–21 |
| Hidden treasure | 13.44 | | |
| The pearl | 13.45–46 | | |
| The net | 13.47–50 | | |
| The house owner | 13.52 | | |
| The lost sheep | 18.12–14 | | 15.4–7 |
| The unmerciful servant | 18.23–34 | | |
| The vineyard workers | 20.1–16 | | |
| Two sons | 21.28–32 | | |
| The tenants | 21.33–44 | 12.1–11 | 20.9–18 |
| A wedding banquet | 22.2–14 | | |
| The fig tree | 24.32–33 | 13.28–29 | 21.29–31 |
| The faithful servant | 24.45–51 | | 12.42–46 |
| Ten bridesmaids | 25.1–13 | | |
| The talents | 25.14–30 | | 19.12–27 |
| Sheep and goats | 25.31–46 | | |

# Essay 2: Interpreting the Beatitudes in Latin America Today

by C. René Padilla

The traditional title – the Beatitudes – that even modern translations of the Bible (for instance the NIV and the NRSV) use to introduce Matthew 5.1–12 has a distinctly religious connotation. *Beatitude,* however, is derived from the Latin *beatus* ('happy' or 'blessed') and points to the Greek word *makárioi,* which stands at the very beginning of each of the eight sayings of Jesus in this first paragraph of the Sermon on the Mount. (The assumption here is that verses 10 and 11 do not contain two 'beatitudes' but only one, even though the word *blessed* appears at the beginning of each verse.)

That the term *blessed* occur nine times within the span of twelve verses should alert us with regard to the basic thrust of the whole passage. At first sight, what we have here is a description of people who may be considered happy or blessed, who stand in (implicit) contrast with others who would not be so described. The surprising thing, however, is that the people who are here called *blessed* are people who, according to normal standards in human society, have plenty of reason *not* to be thus regarded: those who are poor, those who mourn, those who are persecuted. What makes them blessed, since poverty, mourning, and persecution are not blessings in themselves? Let us see.

## The addressees

To begin with, it must be noticed that the so-called beatitudes are addressed to *the disciples* (or *learners*) of *Jesus Christ*. To be sure, according to verse 1 the Sermon on the Mount is given in the presence of many people – 'the crowds'. The text, however, leaves no doubt as to who it is that Jesus has more specifically in mind as his addressees: 'His *disciples* came to him, and he began to teach *them,* saying ...' (emphasis mine). What we have here, therefore, is a summary description of the sort of people that Jesus expects *his followers* to be, not only for their own sakes but also for the sake of the crowds to whom they will be sent.

The ethic implicit in these beatitudes is so high that many interpreters throughout the history of the Church, and especially in modern times, have seen it as totally unattainable and unrealistic for present-day life. The answer is that Jesus' teaching provides the absolute standard that his followers are to maintain constantly before their eyes as they seek to conform to the will of God for human life.

In the final analysis, as in the case of Galatians 5.22–23 (on 'the fruit of the Spirit'), what we have here is an ethical portrait of Jesus Christ himself. Jesus did not merely define ethical standards which his disciples were to try to live up to; he incarnated the ethics of the kingdom of God in his own life and action, thus becoming a model for a new humanity. His purpose was not to formulate abstract ethical principles that his disciples would have to keep as a new law, but to develop in all and each of his followers a *Christian character,* a character which would reflect his own and bring glory to God. Nor did he intend to give 'counsels of perfection' for a spiritual élite, but to emphasize the kind of attitudes that all the children of God were to exemplify in their daily lives. To the extent that they are transformed in the image of Jesus, all the citizens of the Kingdom of God bear the qualities to which the beatitudes refer.

## The Content of the Beatitudes

It is not accidental that the Sermon on the Mount begins with the Beatitudes. These sayings of Jesus throw into relief the importance of a Christian character as the very basis for Christian conduct. The Sermon describes a kingdom lifestyle, in which the will of God is fulfilled; the Beatitudes, at the beginning of the Sermon, show that the kingdom lifestyle is the expression of a character that has been – better yet, *is being* – moulded in the image of Jesus Christ. The Beatitudes are not instructions or directions on how to attain happiness, but a sort of spiritual portrait of those who, in communion with Jesus Christ, are being transformed according to God's purpose for humankind.

### *'Blessed are the poor in spirit, for theirs is the kingdom of heaven' (v. 3)*

The Lukan version of this beatitude reads: 'Blessed are you who are poor, for yours is the kingdom of God' (6.20) and the context there brings out the economic connotation of 'the poor', since it stands in contrast with 'the rich' (v. 24). There is no contradiction between the two versions of the beatitudes, however; the difference between the two simply shows that the quality that Jesus wants to emphasize about the poor is not their lack of money, but their attitude of freedom with regard to material wealth as such. To be sure, the disciples of Jesus were materially poor; for the sake of the gospel, they had lost 'homes, brothers, sisters, mothers, fathers, children and fields' (Mark 10.29–30). This kind of privation in all aspects of their lives, however, was simply the expression of their absolute allegiance to Jesus and their utter dependence on God. They were materially 'poor' and, as such, they did not have the kind of securities that money and power can provide. At the same time, they were 'poor in spirit' and, as such, in the midst of their poverty they could experience the reality of God's provision for every need. Who are best qualified to know the meaning of the request included in the Lord's prayer, 'Give us today our daily bread' (Matthew 6.41)? Certainly *not* those who have accumulated a reserve of bread, but the poor! *Theirs* is the Kingdom of God – they can see God at work giving them bread in the midst of hunger and hope in the midst of hopelessness.

## 'Blessed are those who mourn, for they will be comforted' (v. 4)

Mourning expresses affliction and there is nothing here to indicate the cause of the affliction of those who are called blessed. It could be that their affliction is a consequence of their faithfulness in living out the values of the kingdom. In that case, however, this beatitude would simply coincide with the last one, 'Blessed are those who are persecuted because of righteousness ...' (v. 10). It is more likely, however, that the affliction of those who mourn and yet are blessed is the kind of affliction with which Jesus Christ himself was afflicted as he bore upon himself all the sorrow of a fallen humanity. In fulfilling his role as the Servant of the Lord, Jesus 'took up our infirmities and carried our sorrows', yet 'by his wounds we are healed' (Isaiah 53.4, 5). For his sake, his followers are also called to bear the sorrow of the world. They do not stand in judgement over against the sinful world as if they did not belong to it; rather, they enter into the affliction that results from sin and mourn for the world, certainly not in their own strength but in the strength of their crucified Lord. Because of Jesus' resurrection, the promise was fulfilled, 'After the suffering of his soul, he will see the light of life and be satisfied' (Isaiah 53.11). Likewise, because of Jesus' resurrection, those who for the sake of the gospel now mourn for the world will be comforted.

## 'Blessed are the meek, for they will inherit the earth' (v. 5)

In Psalm 37.11, which is quoted here, 'the meek' stand in contrast with 'the wicked'. The wicked are characterized by pride, self-confidence, material ambition, violence, abuse of power. The meek, on the other hand, are those who trust God and do good. Their dependence on God is translated into humble service to others. The same Greek term that is here translated as 'meek' is used two other times in the Gospel of Matthew, and in both cases it is applied to Jesus. In 11.29 he is described as 'gentle [or *meek*] and humble in heart', who as such invites all who are weary and burdened to come to him and find rest. In 21.5 he is described in the words of the prophet as the king who comes into Jerusalem 'gentle [or *meek*] and riding on a donkey'. The disciples of Jesus Christ are called to reflect in daily life the same kind of attitude that characterized him, knowing that 'the earth' – the new creation that God has promised – will be given to them. The present world order is ruled by the wealthy and the oppressors. Against the logic of this order rooted in violence, however, the future does not belong to them but to the powerless, the marginalized, the 'nobodies'. *They* will inherit the earth.

### 'Blessed are those who hunger and thirst for righteousness, for they will be filled' (v. 6)

Both hunger and thirst point to basic needs – the need for food and the need for water, without which life is not possible. More basic than the need for food and water, however, is the need for righteousness, including our own rightness before God and God's justice on earth. A mark of the disciples of Jesus is a deep desire to lead a life that is truly pleasing to God and the recognition of their need for forgiveness of sins, since no human being is exempt from sin. That desire for personal righteousness, however, is accompanied by a great longing to see that God's will is done 'on earth as it is in heaven' – that God's glory becomes visible in society in terms of justice. The hunger and thirst for personal rightness and social justice will only be ultimately satisfied when the kingdom of God is fully established. Yet here and now, because in Jesus Christ the kingdom has already begun in anticipation of the end, a foretaste of the righteousness, the peace, and the joy of the kingdom is made available through the Holy Spirit (Romans 14.17). To those who have tasted the Bread of Life, the promise that they will be filled is not an empty promise but a sure hope.

### 'Blessed are the merciful, for they will be shown mercy' (v. 7)

No one who has truly experienced God's mercy can be anything but merciful toward those who are in need of mercy. The woman who anointed Jesus' feet in Pharisee Simon's house was described as one who loved much because, having lived a sinful life, she was forgiven much (see Luke 7.36–50). By contrast, said Jesus, 'he who has been forgiven little loves little' (v. 47). Mercy is shown in terms of forgiveness of sins but also in terms of action on behalf of those who suffer physical needs – the downtrodden, the outcasts, the victims of violence, the powerless. The disciples of Jesus may be identified as those who, like their Master, befriend the 'tax collectors and sinners', even though in doing so they run the risk of rejection and scorn on the part of those who think they have a claim on God because of their own righteousness. In his mercy Jesus took upon himself the shame of their sin; they are therefore willing to give up their own dignity for the sake of brothers and sisters who stand in need of mercy. And they can look forward to the day when God will bestow upon them the glory and honour that God reserves for those who have learned that sooner or later 'Mercy triumphs over judgement!' (James 2.13).

### 'Blessed are the pure in heart, for they will see God' (v. 8)

According to Psalm 24.4, the person who has 'clean hands and a pure heart' is able to stand in the Lord's holy place and to receive his blessing. To be 'pure in heart' is to be utterly honest, loyal and sincere before God and one's neighbours. This kind of purity is closely related to single-mindedness, but the single-mindedness that is commended in this beatitude and that makes God visible is the one which focuses on Jesus, in whose face the disciples are given 'the light of the knowledge of the glory of God' (2 Corinthians 4.6). When Jesus is in the limelight, everything else, including the concern to establish one's own righteousness through conformity to external religious forms, fades into nothingness. Integrity displaces every form of hypocrisy or concern for outer appearance. Confession of sin and sincere repentance are constituent elements of the disciples' pilgrimage toward the new creation, where God will be seen face to face. In the meanwhile, the pure in heart are blessed because they see God in the face of Jesus.

### 'Blessed are the peacemakers, for they will be called children of God' (v. 9)

To be peacemakers is not to be passive in the face of evil, indifferent with regard to the abuse of power, or silent in the midst of conflict. The peacemakers act on behalf of peace. Since peace is the fruit of justice (see Isaiah 32.17), they make every possible effort to see to it that God's justice is established among people all over the world. The peace they struggle for is not merely absence of armed conflict, but shalom – well-being, health, abundant life – which results from harmony with God, with one's neighbour, and with creation. They see themselves as agents of reconciliation through whom God continues to bring about his purpose of 'reconciling the world to himself in

Christ' (2 Corinthians 5.19) and, on the basis of Jesus' death on the cross, all forms of hostility are put to death and peace is made (see Ephesians 2.11–18). Through peacemaking the disciples of Jesus Christ show their family resemblance with God – by participating in God's peace mission, they demonstrate that they are 'children of God', in whom and through whom the God of peace manifests his purpose of reconciliation.

### 'Blessed are those who are persecuted because of righteousness, for theirs is the kingdom of heaven' (v. 10)

Jesus warned his disciples not to be surprised if they were persecuted. 'No servant is greater than his master,' he said. 'If they persecuted me, they will persecute you also' (John 15.20). A lifestyle characterized by the qualities to which the seven previous beatitudes make reference may provoke not only resistance but open hostility in a world that functions on the basis of values which are diametrically opposed to the values of the kingdom. The disciples' renunciation of wealth, self-centredness, self-assertiveness, and self-righteousness for the sake of commitment to Jesus Christ cannot be tolerated by those who call good what is evil, and evil what is good. Therefore, Jesus' followers must not expect to be rewarded, but rather insulted, persecuted and falsely accused. Yet in the midst of suffering for the sake of righteousness, they are to take comfort in knowing that in Jesus Christ they have been given nothing less than the kingdom of God. Furthermore, they are to rejoice and be glad, anticipating the 'reward in heaven', which will be granted to them as the successors of the prophets, who were also persecuted in the past (vv. 11–12).

The Beatitudes point to kingdom values that characterize the community of the crucified Messiah to the extent that community allows itself to be moulded by the Spirit of Christ. That community is truly blessed, not because it is widely accepted by people in the world, but because in Jesus Christ it has found the secret of abundant life. 'The fellowship of the beatitudes is the fellowship of the Crucified. With him it has lost all, and with him it has found all' (Dietrich Bonhoeffer).

# *Key to Study Suggestions*

Most of these 'answers' are only suggestions. Scripture is so rich that no one person can find everything that is in it; you may be able to find points that the writer of this Guide has missed. And many of the questions you will be able to work out for yourself.

**Page 16**

2 Galilee was an easier place for Jesus to have an undisturbed childhood and prepare himself for his ministry without opposition.

3 Both OT texts speak of God's love for his people and his care for them.

**Page 23**

2 God's blessing can come to human beings in a new way.

3 The other people needed to repent of their sins; baptism was a sign of God's forgiveness and a new beginning. Jesus' baptism was a new beginning for his ministry, not of a forgiven life.

**Page 25**

3 The first woman wanted the fruit of the tree for the pleasure and power it gave her; Jesus' temptations were to take power for himself, rather than use it for the glory of God.

4 He would have been aiming for the wrong things – power and glory for himself, not for God.

7 Jesus knows what temptation feels like, and knows that it is unavoidable in human life – but it must be dealt with immediately and firmly, in the strength of God and his word.

8 Remembering the words of Scripture reminds us of God's power and love – our real weapons in resisting temptation.

**Page 28**

2 In Jerusalem Jesus would inevitably have clashed with the Jewish authorities, before he had time to do his work; the people of Galilee may have been more open to new teaching and new ideas, because they were less rigidly traditional Jews.

**Page 32**

1 Following Jesus meant leaving other people and things behind – family, work, home – and going out with Jesus towards others.

2 They may have been prepared for the call of Jesus by being followers of John the Baptist.

5 Jesus himself says that they were to use their skills 'fishing' for men; they were down-to-earth men, used to working together in difficult conditions.

**Page 41**

2 Matthew's blessings are more general – speaking of all the poor, all the meek, etc., and very positive. Luke's are aimed more specifically at the disciples, and the 'woes' are more negative.

4 You will have your own ideas . . .
Luke 10: blessed are the merciful; Luke 18: blessed are the meek/those who hunger and thirst; Matthew 18: blessed are the merciful.

5 Light is not to be kept to ourselves; we shine in order to give light to others and glory to God, and we have to live as those who have the light.

**Page 47**

2 Trying to be 'perfect' means taking God's call and demands with mature seriousness, knowing that this is only attainable with God's help, so that we do not condemn those who fail but treat them with mercy.

3 The words of the law and the prophets were pointers to the reality of God; Jesus is the perfect revelation of God.

4 The basis of marriage is the close unity of the husband and wife. Only the deliberate destruction of that unity by one partner can be allowed to break the bond.

6 We are able to love others and resist hatred because God has first loved us.

**Page 52**

1 A hypocrite is literally someone who plays a part, who pretends to be different from what they really are.

2 See top of p. 51.

3 To have a debt is to take what other people give us without giving anything back to them. Sin is taking God's generous love and wasting it, so that we cannot give love back to him – we stay in debt to him.

4 Prayer helps us to rely on God, to think seriously about what we really need, and to express our trust in God's power to supply our needs.

5 It is encouraging when our efforts are noticed and appreciated – which is what God does when he rewards us.

6 In these Acts passages, fasting underlines the seriousness of prayer.

## Page 56

1 Looking for someone or something in a determined and persevering way.
2 Seeking the kingdom takes time and effort.
8 Treasures in heaven are our acts of love, kindness, forgiveness, healing, etc.

## Page 60

1 Wanting something very much and being determined to get it, however much it costs.
2 Israel's covenant with God was based on care for everyone else who was part of the covenant. The Law told people how to achieve this, and the prophets encouraged them to put it into action.
3 Luke makes more use of pictures and parables, which perhaps makes his version of Jesus' words a little gentler and less uncompromising than Matthew's.

## Page 64

2 What astonished people was the authority with which Jesus taught – the way he told people what they should do, and spoke on behalf of God.
3 Fools think they can manage without God and ignore him. The wise deliberately seek God and realize that only he can make sense of life.
4 Jesus deals with subjects which had been hotly debated in the OT and by the rabbis, and lays down clear guidelines. He deliberately contrasts his teaching ('but I say to you') with the teaching of the OT.

## Page 70

1 A witness is someone who provides evidence about something that has happened. We witness to what God has done in our lives by living as changed people.
2 As soon as Jesus spoke openly about who he was (the Messiah) he would be opposed by the Jewish authorities. He needed time for his ministry before he finally faced their opposition.
3 Matthew 8.2 shows faith in Jesus' ability to heal – he has the power, even though he may choose not to use it. Mark 9.22 questions whether Jesus does have the power to heal.

## Page 71

1 The centurion: care about his servant's suffering, and honesty about their relationship as master and servant. Jesus: appreciation of a Gentile's faith.

2 Right from the covenant with Abraham, God has intended Israel to be a source of blessing for *all* the peoples of the world.

## Page 74
1 Jesus set aside all the power he had as God. He really entered into our human experience.

## Page 78
2 You cannot force people to believe – they have to be willing to open the door to you.

## Page 81
2 Some illnesses are the physical result of mental and spiritual problems; when these problems are healed, the physical symptoms go. But this is not true of *all* illnesses, and sick people should not be made to feel guilty.
3 'Sinners' were those who broke the law. We use the word about other people in order to feel superior to them. Using it about ourselves is simply honesty!

## Page 84
2 New life needs to be expressed in new ways, which will make sense to each new generation. The Church needs to be constantly renewed.
4 Weddings as the joining of two people in a close union, and weddings as celebrations were both good pictures (used also in the OT) of our relationship with God in the kingdom.

## Page 88
3 Jesus continues and fulfils the life of God's Chosen People, and the covenant promises made to David.
4 The lostness and helplessness of people, their longing for God and for wholeness, and their pain.

## Page 92
1 They needed to be disciples before they were ready to be sent out as apostles. As disciples, they took in Jesus' teaching; as apostles, they gave it out to others.
3 Disciples serve in many different ways – some as leaders, others by quiet obedience.
4 Philip: brings other people to Jesus; approachable and friendly. Thomas: loyal, but takes things literally and needs to work things out for himself.
5 See notes on p. 92.
7 Hard work deserves a reward, even if it is only a word of appreciation, or decent working conditions.

**Page 97**
1 Being wise is very practical – not having your head in the clouds, but using common sense.
3 Those who are sent will meet all kinds of situations; they need to adapt and use different approaches in different situations.
4 See note on p. 97.
7 Human frailty can get in the way: can we be sure that we shall be fully concentrating on God as we go to preach, or is it better to set aside time for him beforehand?

**Page 104**
1 Sin gets in the way: pride makes people offended; carelessness makes them stumble; lack of courage and perseverance makes them fall away.
3 He was a prophet because he told people what God wanted them to do. He was more than a prophet because he played an active role in putting God's plan into action.

**Page 105**
1 Sodom, Tyre and Sidon sinned but knew no better; they were ignorant of God. The inhabitants of Galilee saw the works of Jesus and still refused to believe.

**Page 109**
1 People who have knowledge can think that they know everything and are not always open to new ideas or willing to change.
4 Jesus had compassion for people and brought them healing and release – but also demanded a response from them and changes in their lives, without burdening them with rules and guilt.

**Page 110**
Above all, ministers are servants.

**Page 112**
2 Jesus embodies the values of the kingdom; God's rule is present in him.
3 The battle with Satan demands positive, committed troops – anyone who is not wholly committed becomes a liability. But for those who are not yet committed followers, any good deed is a hopeful sign that in time they may become disciples.

**Page 116**
2 The Jews may have wanted a sign because their history had taught them that people are not always what they claim to be; they wanted proof of Jesus' identity. But they did not see the signs that were already there – the teaching and ministry of Jesus.

4 We will not stay emptied of sin and evil for very long: they will come back unless we deliberately seek the help of the Spirit to resist them.

## Page 124
1 These are all *positive* responses to the word of God, not passive (and shallow) acceptance, but active involvement with it.

## Page 129
1 Training ends when you are able to do a particular task. Discipling is the beginning of an open-ended journey of learning and discovery.

## Page 134
2 In many countries, being a Christian means losing your position in society, becoming unpopular, having to stand up for what is right. Herod was motivated by a need to please the daughter of Herodias and his guests, to be popular.

## Page 137
1 All meals are moments of communion with God, who provides the food for us.

## Page 141
2 Food is good in itself, but it needs to be kept in perspective – not allowed to dominate us through greed, or to be a cause of friction or condemnation.

## Page 143
1 People glorified God when they saw miracles of physical healing. But they will also glorify God when they see the miracle of changed lives leading to good works.
3 'Compassion' means literally 'suffering with' – being with people in their distress and sharing their pain, as well as working to help them through it.

## Page 145
1 See above, answer to question 2 on p. 116.

## Page 151
2 In earthly kingdoms, someone (usually the king, or a religious leader) takes responsibility for administering justice and leading the nation. The same will be true of the heavenly kingdom.

## Page 153
1 Here, Jesus is transfigured – his appearance changes to reveal his

glory. By the power of the Spirit, we too can be changed and reflect his glory.

2 They all look forward to an appearance of Elijah which will usher in the final days.

3 See notes above on p. 153.

4 Perhaps both: a sign for the disciples, a reassurance for Jesus.

5 The earlier voice marked a new phase in Jesus' ministry, as this voice marks another phase as he moves towards his death.

## Page 157
1 Both passages record a moment of glory and achievement, followed by the let-down of lack of faith.

## Page 162
1 Humility is closely connected with love and service.

## Page 168
1 Forgiveness is not a matter of rules ('seven times' or settling accounts); it needs to be surrounded by kindness, love, warmth, peace and holiness.

## Page 173
1 See notes on p. 171.

2 How can you become 'one flesh' with more than one other person?

## Page 178
3 Look at, for example, Romans 5 and 1 John 4.

## Page 181
4 Slaves do what their masters tell them; they get no reward for their service; but ours is a willing slavery, done with love.

## Page 186
1 See notes above on p. 186.

2 The anger of Jesus was the anger of authority in action, declaring the will of God. The anger of the chief priests and scribes was the product of fear and resentment because their authority was challenged.

3 The common threat to their power.

## Page 193
4 See, for example, 11.22, 24 and 22.13.

6 The gift of leadership (1 Timothy); the gift of salvation (Hebrews 2).

**Page 198**

1 God appoints rulers, who need taxes to run the country; so Christians should pay lawful taxes – and at the same time not neglect to give God what is due to him.

3 See note on p. 195.

4 'The living' now – and most importantly – include Jesus himself, who guarantees our resurrection.

**Page 207**

4 Tithing garden plants is a very unimportant part of religion, but keeping such rules can lead to pride and self-satisfaction. Justice, love, kindness etc. are far more important.

5 The Pharisees are so busy concentrating on minor external rules that they miss the important inner transformation.

**Page 213**

5 'Witness' is witness to what we know about God, our evidence for who and what he is. These characteristics and values *are* the good news, the rule of God *is* the kingdom. Him we proclaim.

**Page 224**

11 An inheritance is something given to us by our parents, a precious possession (such as a house) which is handed down from parents to children over generations. This is what God will give us; we are not simply citizens of the kingdom – in the future we shall share the ownership of it with God.

**Page 239**

5 Given the teaching and work of Jesus, and the opposition of the Jewish leaders, something like the crucifixion was bound to happen, and had been foreseen in Scripture. The only way Jesus could avoid death was to refuse to obey his Father – the temptation he faced in Gethsemane.

**Page 244**

1 They were prepared to accept false evidence, and the chief priest tried to get Jesus to condemn himself with his own words – which was forbidden by Jewish law. And what Jesus said was not strictly blasphemy.

2 Daniel's Son of man is victorious, receiving power from God and judging the earth.

4 Just as our good deeds encourage others to give glory to God, so our bad deeds encourage people to reject God and think less of the followers of Jesus.

**Page 255**

1 The Jewish leaders felt threatened; Pilate did not want to stir up political trouble; and the soldiers enjoyed some cruel and thoughtless amusement.

# Index

Since the Contents list is very detailed, this Index contains only subjects or names which are mentioned in several different places, or whose appearance in a section is not obvious from the Contents.